LOUISIANA CREOLE PEOPLEHOOD

LOUISIANA CREOLE PEOPLEHOOD

Afro-Indigeneity and Community

EDITED BY

RAIN PRUD'HOMME-CRANFORD, DARRYL BARTHÉ,
AND ANDREW J. JOLIVÉTTE

UNIVERSITY OF WASHINGTON PRESS
Seattle

Copyright © 2022 by the University of Washington Press

Composed in Charis SIL, typeface designed by SIL International

This corrected version includes notes that were missing from chapter 7 in the first printing.

All rights reserved. No part of this publication may be reproduced or transmitted in any form or by any means, electronic or mechanical, including photocopy, recording, or any information storage or retrieval system, without permission in writing from the publisher.

UNIVERSITY OF WASHINGTON PRESS
uwapress.uw.edu

LIBRARY OF CONGRESS CATALOGING-IN-PUBLICATION DATA
Names: Goméz, Rain C., editor. | Barthé, Darryl, Jr., editor. | Jolivétte, Andrew, 1975– editor.
Title: Louisiana Creole peoplehood : Afro-indigeneity and community / edited by Rain Prud'homme-Cranford, Darryl Barthé, and Andrew J. Jolivétte.
Description: Seattle : University of Washington Press, [2022] | Includes bibliographical references and index.
Identifiers: LCCN 2021012066 (print) | LCCN 2021012067 (ebook) | ISBN 9780295749488 (hardcover) | ISBN 9780295749495 (paperback) | ISBN 9780295749501 (ebook)
Subjects: LCSH: Creoles—Louisiana—Ethnic identity. | Indians of North America—Louisiana—Ethnic identity. | Indians of North America—Mixed descent—Louisiana. | African Americans—Race identity—Louisiana. | Louisiana—Ethnic relations. | Louisiana—Race relations.
Classification: LCC F380.C87 L68 2021 (print) | LCC F380.C87 (ebook) | DDC 305.8009763—dc23
LC record available at https://lccn.loc.gov/2021012066
LC ebook record available at https://lccn.loc.gov/2021012067

♾ This paper meets the requirements of ANSI/NISO Z39.48-1992 (Permanence of Paper).

In memoriam

Janet Ravare Colson, mother of the Creole Preservation Revitalization Movement and founding director of the Creole Heritage Center

Terrel Alphonse Delphin Jr., father of the Creole Renaissance and mayor of Cane River

To Creole culture bearers: Gilbert Martin, John Oswald Colson, zydeco queen Ida Guillory, zydeco musician Willis Prudhomme, and all our relations

And to our great-grandparents, grandparents, parents, and communities mési/yakoke/hiweyú/tikahch

Thank you

We are descendants of the French, the Spanish, the Africans, the Indian . . . Gombo People.

> *—Sybil Kein, "La chaudiére pélé la gregue," from* Gombo People: Poésie Créole de la Nouvelle-Orléans

CONTENTS

INTRODUCTION. Ayou Komensé: Louisiana Creole Land, Community, and Recognition
RAIN PRUD'HOMME-CRANFORD, DARRYL BARTHÉ, AND ANDREW J. JOLIVÉTTE 3

PART 1: SACRED HISTORIES: FROM KINSHIP TO CULTURAL RESURGENCES

CHAPTER 1 Post-Contact Peoplehood: History, Kinship, and Redefining Louisiana Creole Indigeneity
RAIN PRUD'HOMME-CRANFORD 21

COMMUNITY RESPONSE. So, Have You Heard the One about the Louisiana Creoles Who Fight the System of Indigenous Erasure?
CAROLYN M. DUNN 44

CHAPTER 2 Speak White, Speak Black, Speak American: Assimilation in Creole New Orleans
DARRYL BARTHÉ 50

COMMUNITY RESPONSE. The Racialization of Creole Identity and Heritage Language Loss
JOSEPH DUNN 66

CHAPTER 3 Acadian/African/Indigenous Trinity: An Identity Mosaic from Nova Scotia to New Orleans
ANNALYSSA GYPSY MURPHY 74

COMMUNITY RESPONSE. It's Not the Weight, but How You Carry It: A Prose Poem
KELLY CLAYTON 83

CHAPTER 4 Bulbancha Is Still a Place: Decolonizing
the Tricentennial of New Orleans
JEFFERY U. DARENSBOURG 86

COMMUNITY RESPONSE. Bulbancha Is Still a Place:
Decolonizing the History of the Present
LEILA K. BLACKBIRD 93

PART 2: LANDBASE: FROM HOMELANDS TO FOOD AND HEALTH

CHAPTER 5 Filé Man: Creole Food Harvesting and Sovereignty
TRACEY COLSON ANTEE 103

COMMUNITY RESPONSE. Colson's Creole-Indigenous
Cultural Continuity: Filé Man
ROBERT B. CALDWELL JR. 111

CHAPTER 6 Telling It Right: In Search of the Ishak
JEFFERY U. DARENSBOURG 115

COMMUNITY RESPONSE. Comments on "Telling It Right:
In Search of the Ishak"
JOHN DEPRIEST 121

CHAPTER 7 A Perfect Circle Bound in Chains: Creole-NDN Health,
Historical Trauma, and Settler Colonialism
T. SHAWNEE 124

COMMUNITY RESPONSE. Caught in the Cycle
SUMMER WESLEY 138

PART 3: LANGUAGES: LITERACIES AND BODIES

CHAPTER 8 Language Revitalization, Race, and Resistance in
Creole Louisiana
OLIVER MAYEUX 143

COMMUNITY RESPONSE. NOTHING TO MANIFESTO
TANNER MENARD 159

CHAPTER 9 No Body Sings the Blues Like a FAT Body:
Gender, Race, and Eco-Colonialism
RAIN PRUD'HOMME-CRANFORD   172

COMMUNITY RESPONSE. Thunder Thighs: A Storm's Brewing /
Sorte cette laville avant l'ouragan commence
FRANCES E. HOPSON-CUEVAS   192

COMMUNITY RESPONSE. "Fatten Up, You're Too Skinny":
Body, Color, and Trauma
ANDREW J. JOLIVÉTTE AND JOELLE JOLIVÉTTE-
GONZALEZ (IN MEMORIAM)   197

CHAPTER 10 Don't Scratch My Washboard, but You Can Pull My
Fiddle: Negotiating Queerness in the Creole Diaspora
ANDREW J. JOLIVÉTTE   201

COMMUNITY RESPONSE. Bending the Story
M. CARMEN LANE   215

PART 4: CEREMONIALS AND CULTURAL PRACTICE: FROM
TESTIMONIALS TO ACTIVISM

CHAPTER 11 On Passing and Survival: Memories of
a Choctaw-Apache
THOMAS PARRIE   221

CHAPTER 12 LA to L.A.: Growing Up Louisiana Creole in
the Los Angeles Diaspora
CAROLYN M. DUNN   224

TESTIMONIAL 1. Louisiana Creole Peoplehood:
Mixed Race Foodways
JOHN LAFLEUR II   240

TESTIMONIAL 2. A Reflection
DANNY LEE LANDRENEAU-PETRELLA   245

TESTIMONIAL 3. Interview with Kenneth L. Jolivétte
ANDREW J. JOLIVÉTTE   247

TESTIMONIAL 4: Reflection
PIERRE BROOKS METOYER 251

CONCLUSION. Nouzot Kréyol: Louisiana Creole Peoplehood or all our Relations Resisting Settler Violence and Indigenous Erasure
RAIN PRUD'HOMME-CRANFORD, DARRYL BARTHÉ, AND ANDREW J. JOLIVÉTTE 253

IN MEMORIAM. Reflections on Janet Ravare Colson, Cane River Creole Matriarch
ANDREW J. JOLIVÉTTE, RAIN PRUD'HOMME-CRANFORD, AND CAROLYN M. DUNN 263

APPENDIX. Louisiana State Legislature Resolution and Certificate of Special Recognition from the Governor of the State of Louisiana in honor of Janet Ravare-Colson 269

List of Contributors 271

Index 281

LOUISIANA CREOLE PEOPLEHOOD

INTRODUCTION

AYOU KOMENSÉ

Louisiana Creole Land, Community, and Recognition

RAIN PRUD'HOMME-CRANFORD, DARRYL BARTHÉ, AND ANDREW J. JOLIVÉTTE

CALL: DARRYL

This is a story of conscious self-determination, reclamation, and decolonization. Conceptually, this book was brought into being at a lunch table in New York City in the summer of 2016. Four cousins, dislocated in diaspora, came together to eat: two from San Francisco, one from Oklahoma, and one from Amsterdam by way of New Orleans. It was a Dominican restaurant because we all eat beans and rice. We cousins, we Creole people, we Latinidad-Caribbean people, we Indigenous people, products of French and Spanish colonization: we all eat beans and rice. After eating, we went to Lehman College, in the Bronx. Three of us were to speak on a panel, as academics, and as representatives of Louisiana's Indigenous communities. The title of the panel was "Indigenous Blues: The Eroded Land of the Gulf" and the event was billed as a "discussion and a concert presentation depicting the current conditions of the Indigenous people of the Gulf shores of Louisiana." In the green room, before the presentation, we all met with Donald Harrison, "The King of Nouveau Swing." Donald Harrison is a New Orleans native and a "Mardi Gras Indian." This is to say, he was born in New Orleans, he is of African heritage, and he is of Native Amerindian heritage. Our cousin, Alex Trapps-Chabala, had brought a family tree, as a gift for Harrison, showing him exactly

FIGURE I.1. The editors (*left to right*): Darryl Barthé, Rain Prud'homme-Cranford, Andrew J. Jolivétte. Photograph courtesy of Alex Trapps-Chabala.

where his Native ancestors were from. Harrison scoffed. "Those people don't claim me," he said, referring to his Native ancestors. "Why should I claim them? I'm descended from Africans."

"Of course you are descended from Africans," I replied. "I am, too. In fact, everyone in this room is descended from Africans. So what? We just gave you documentation showing that you're Native and our people don't come in parts. Am I supposed to say, 'I'm one-eighth this and one-fourth that?' White people do that; our people don't do that. We're Indigenous people. We're Creole people. That's it."

There was a tense standoff for a moment. In that instant, decades upon decades of anti-Blackness and Indigenous erasure, Jim Crow, and hypo-descent laws all came to a head. Both Harrison and I knew that the poison of anti-Black prejudice runs deeply in Louisiana, even in Creole communities and Native tribal communities. In that moment, however, we'd created a space outside of that history. In that moment, we'd called into being a different interpretive and relational framework. In that moment, we made a conscious decision to assert our unity, our solidarity, our kinship.

"Every Native in this room claims you," I said.

RESPONSE: RAIN

This story is one of relation. We are all related. This sentiment or expression is expressed in many ways across tribal nations on Turtle Island: Nouzot tous ki gen rapó (Louisiana Creole); Wi hokišak kuš (Atakapa Ishak); Itinkanomi hupia (Choctaw); Wahkohtowin (Cree); Mitákuye Oyásin (Dakota/Lakota). This concept has many meanings. At the most basic level, it is the act of being related to one another. From an Indigenous epistemological perspective, it is the act of being in "good relation" to all life, the universe, and by extension to have responsibility and accountability to one another, community, land, animals, plants, and the cosmos. I often teach my students that if we find the ways we connect (family, people we have in common, experiences, interests, places we have lived, etc.)—if we do the work to make that relationship—then we change how we engage with one another. We move from being in a binary relation of student/professor to being in community or communal relation. If we consider one another as relatives, to be connected or kinshipped on a shared history, experience, or people, then we change how we relate to one another. We become related, and with relatedness should come responsibility and accountability.

On this note, it might not surprise many folks to know that the editors of this collection are related. We are related through cultural, experiential, and familial bloodlines—literally related. Moreover, many of the contributors to this collection share kinship in a multitude of ways, sometimes closely, sometimes distantly. Indian country is a small place. Creole-NDN country is equally small.[1] Darryl Barthé often says "we Creoles are a study in gene puddles." See, our French and Spanish progenitors, our African and Indian grandparents and great-grandparents, found ways to keep our bloodlines and culture alive by marrying across Louisiana Creole communities as well as continuing to keep an inflow of Indigenous blood. A Creole ancestor having children with a Native ancestor, their child having children with another Creole, and their children with another Native, or other such constructs, weaving us though community and blood across Louisiana. As editors and contributors we share family and land-bases from Opelousas to Cane River, Point Coupee to Marksville, New Orleans to Zwolle, Louisiana to Oklahoma and Texas. We even reach out to the diaspora in California, Illinois, New York, and beyond. We call ourselves into being through our relational constellations. In recognizing the ways in which different family lines split, converge, and split again we honor our ancestors while acknowledging our multiple ancestries and relationships: first and fifth cousins from Cane River on one line, third and fourth from Opelousas on another, and second and fifth from Point Coupee, and other variations across ancestors and landscapes. *We call who we are into who we were*—a mosaic in blood and land creating our Creole culture. There is a Choctaw phrase that relates to this issue:

> We are tied to our land. Our land, like our blood, keeps memory. It is in Choctaw *yakni isht ikhana*: land memories, land record keeper. . . . These events inhabit the land and keep memories . . . memories that rise up from land, as does culture. Culture rises up from land into people. Louisiana's history of racial mixing has given rise to specific Indigenous descended communities.[2]

This reinforces that we are all related both through our ancestors and the landbases they called home.

While we as editors and contributors share relation (cultural, experiential, familial etc.), we do not always identify the exact same way. Some of us in this collection identify as Creole-NDN, Choctaw-Creole, Creole métis, Ishak-Creole, Black-Creole, Creole-Freedmen, multi-tribal specifics, and simply as Louisiana Creole—or a multiplicity of these identifiers and others not named. We are also marked by our positions in life, educations, and acknowledgment that we all exist on a cultural spectrum. Just like no two Native people, even cousins, have the same cultural experiences and knowledges, neither do all the Creole (nor the Native or Black) contributors to this collection. I would argue this makes the collective voices gathered here only stronger by recognizing and representing the diversity of Creole (Indigenous) experience in our ancestral homelands of Louisiana to our families and communities in the diaspora.

There are many expert scholars on Louisiana Creole culture, language, and society, an Indigeneity included in this edited collection: Andrew J. Jolivétte, Darryl Barthé, Jeffery U. Darensbourg, Tracey Colson Antee, Carolyn M. Dunn, Oliver Mayeux, myself, and others. For us as editors and many of our contributors, our Creole activism begins with the late Janet Ravare Colson. However, there are other important voices within conversations of Louisiana Créolité we should mention: Mona Lisa Saloy, Christophe Landry, John Laudun, and Sybil Kein, to name a few. While the academic chapters are mostly written by professors and top experts in the field who claim and are claimed by Louisiana Creole communities, the community responders, like chapter authors, range from members of Louisiana Creole communities to federal and state recognized tribes, to Freedmen and other Red-Black communities. The responders in this collection vary in both their age and education, including PhDs, master's, high school graduates, and GEDs. They are members of community who hold positions as teachers, librarians, artists, writers, office and factory workers, parents and/or grandparents, lawyers, and activists. Yet collectively we raise our voices to weave a chorus across Louisiana Creole experience reflecting our shared Peoplehood: language, history, religion, and land.

RESPONSE: ANDREW

We are a story of a people. We come from the bayous, the Gulf, and the prairies of Louisiana. We come from our ancestors. We specifically chose to produce a work that is collaborative in theoretical framework, methodology, and voice. Too often in under-researched and marginalized communities we tend to over assert the knowledge of academic "experts" without acknowledging that cultural keepers and everyday citizens provide the basis for what expertise we may call on to conduct our research. We invited community members to respond to each chapter and to offer testimonials, and to participate in a national survey to balance academic and nonacademic voices on the topic of Louisiana Creole Peoplehood.

Since first contact with Europeans and subsequent intermarriage and cultural blending with Africans, Louisiana Creoles have been studied at the margins of academic inquiry. This marginalization has limited attention to the Indigenous presence in Louisiana both past and present. As with other mixed-blood Indigenous groups anti-Blackness has been central to settler-colonial projects that attempt to erase and disenfranchise Creoles as an Afro-Indigenous people—all of this is the result of what I call "North American racial exceptionalism." Our tables, churches, ceremonial grounds, and sacred sites all served a specific purpose, a determined purpose. *Rem arbitrium* (determined purpose/decision) in this book is a reassertion of our purpose on this land to leave it better than we found it. Determined purpose and decision means, at this juncture in our history as a people, asserting our rights under the United Nations Declaration on the Rights of Indigenous Peoples (UNDRIP) to define our own genealogies and epistemologies as an Indigenous people. We believe and argue that there is no greater measure of sovereignty than the ability and right to self-definition and self-determination regardless of state or federal recognition by outside governments.

Toward this purpose we do not draw lines of community and cultural autonomy based on color, faith, blood quantum, or location within the diaspora. Instead we seek to highlight the complexities of these different aspects of Afro-Indigeneity among Louisiana Creoles. We take seriously our responsibility as community members to speak to the lived realities and contemporary social issues facing Louisiana Creoles in Louisiana and across its vast diaspora as post-contact Indigenous peoples. In order to speak to the most pressing issues among Louisiana Creoles, we have organized the book into four sections that seek to address gaps in the current research literature on Louisiana Creoles, Native American and Indigenous peoples, as well as Latinx and Afro-Indigenous/Afro-Latin communities across the Americas.

SITUATING LOUISIANA CREOLE CULTURE AND COMMUNITIES

In chapter 1 we offer a definition of Louisiana Creole community and culture not predicated on notions of blood quantum, Indian, African, or European, but as a culture dependent on recognizing "the totality of" our "ethnic/cultural matrices" including various Southeast and Gulf "American Indian tribes, African American, Caribbean, French-Indian, and European" heritage. To this end in chapter 1 we situate our overarching definition of Louisiana Creoles "as a post-contact Indigenous group connected to *specific* Louisiana Creole communities" with "historic ties to specific tribal communities/histories, narratives, landbases, and practices within Louisiana terrains." The chapters in this collection focus on a number of communities, including (but not limited to) Natchitoches/Cane River, Opelousas, Point Coupee, Marksville, New Orleans, Lake Charles, Calcasieu, and diasporas in Houston, Chicago, San Francisco, and Los Angeles. Louisiana Creole post-contact Afro-Indigenous communities are best understood within a Peoplehood matrix of landbase, language, religion, and sacred history.³

The editors of and contributors to this collection hope the conversational call and response nature of the text models a process by which we can further understandings of kinship between sovereign tribes and nations, state recognized tribes, non-recognized tribes and communities, and post-contact Indigenous and Afro-Indigenous communities and culture. It is through the inclusion of various Creole thinkers and community members alongside federal- and state-enrolled community thinkers and noncitizen descendants, that this text practices dialogues and ongoing conversations around situating Louisiana Creole culture. We take seriously the self-determination and legal status of American Indian and Indigenous peoples. We also take seriously the Indigeneity of our African ancestors as well as our Native American ancestors.

While this is a book about Afro-Indigeneity in Louisiana, and we hope the conversations herein add to ongoing discussions about mixed-race and mixed cultural identities and Black-Native peoples and cultures, the content included is specific only to Louisiana Creole peoples and the tribes represented by the individual authors themselves. The editors, and by extent contributors, do not make claims about the legal standing of federal- and state-recognized tribes. However, we do discuss the politics of racial representation in the BIA recognition processes in Louisiana and across the Americas. We respect the rights and self-determination of the federal- and state-recognized tribes of Louisiana, as well as the rights and self-determination of those unrecognized and seeking recognition in Louisiana. We also acknowledge the politics and legal stakes involved in recognition while also accepting the inherent rights of Indigenous peoples to assert their identities without the recognition of the United States government. Our first commitment and responsibility is to the people and communities we write about in this book, so our primary consultation has been with people who identify as Louisiana Creole, and so by extension, people who identify as Indigenous peoples from both North America and West Africa. We ask that our rights as Creole peoples also be respected and that our right to discuss our histories be done so through the kinship ties that are most appropriate to our region. Recognizing and tracing Louisiana Creoles as our own specific post-contact Afro-Indigenous communities also means identifying and upholding the rights of sovereign nationhood within Indian country, while asserting Louisiana Creole rights toward defining our own cultural belonging and sustainability.

HISTORIOGRAPHY, INTERDISCIPLINARY FRAMEWORKS, AND EPISTEMOLOGIES

The work in this edited collection certainly follows the work of Jack D. Forbes (Powhatan-Renapé and Lenape descent) on Red-Black peoples, wherein "study of interethnic contact and racial classifying" leads "to progress in the field of human rights by highlighting and clarifying a major area of abuse: the arbitrary and often racist practice of defining the identities of other human beings by powerful outsiders as well as by governments and institutions."[4] Owing to the initial work of Forbes, recent years have seen new and current scholarship centering Red-Black peoples. Of particular note within the last fifteen years are texts exploring Black Indigeneity and Red-Black histories such as Tiffany Lethabo King's *The Black Shoals: Offshore Formations of Black and Native Studies* (2019); Mark Rifkin's *Fictions of Land and Flesh Blackness, Indigeneity, Speculation* (2019); Shane Lief's *Jockomo: The Native Roots of Mardi Gras Indians* (2019); Nathalie Dajko and Shana Walton's *Language in Louisiana: Community and Culture* (2019); Robert Keith Collins's *African and Native American Contact in the United States: Anthropological and Historical Perspectives* (2017); Keith Cartwright's *Sacral Grooves, Limbo Gateways: Travels in Deep Southern Time, Circum-Caribbean Space, Afro-creole Authority* (2013); Shona N. Jackson's *Creole Indigeneity: Between Myth and Nation in the Caribbean* (2012); David A. Chang's *The Color of the Land: Race, Nation, and the Politics of Landownership in Oklahoma, 1832–1929* (2010); and Tiya Miles's *Crossing Waters, Crossing Worlds: The African Diaspora in Indian Country* (2007). While this collection certainly is in conversation with the texts listed above, we would offer that at its heart it seeks to take up and take back space. In this political time where paracolonial occupied nations, such as the United States and Canada, seek to address hundreds of years of anti-Blackness, Indigenous erasure, and violence against BIPOC peoples, we ask what about those of us whose histories occupy Black and Native, colonizer and colonized, slave and slave holder?[5] What about the cultures and bodies of Afro-Indigenous people whose phenotypes span the opus of human composition, and yet have been silenced, negated, and written out of settler governmental policy and forced into binary constructions leaving Louisiana Creoles without agency as post-contact Afro-Indigenous peoples of Turtle Island?

For the editors, this book not only enters into the current conversations around Red-Black and Black and Indigenous community and academics, but certainly owns its responsibility to Andrew J. Jolivétte, who intervened in the White/Black binary of Louisiana Creole ethnicity and Indigenous erasure espoused by settler-colonial discourse with his 2007 monograph *Louisiana Creoles: Cultural Recovery and Mixed-Race Native American Identity*. As Jolivétte insists, a "specific threat of a multiracial majority in Louisiana posed serious problems. . . . To successfully expel both Creoles and Indians as well as to erase any connections between the groups, a new racial categorization system had to be implemented. . . . This new classificatory system depended on . . . whiteness and blackness as monolithic descriptors."[6] Therefore, Louisiana Creoles, who historically spoke Kouri Vini (a Louisiana Creole language with French, Native American, and African influences) and defined themselves as "mixed . . . an offspring of the Old world [Native] and the New [African, European]," were thrown into a system where they were not a part of either White or Black society, but rather forced into one descriptor or the other.[7] Creoles, like other post-contact Indigenous communities who are méstiz@/métis peoples have kin ties to tribal communities, peoples, and the southscape of Louisiana predating US statehood. Land grants from the French and Spanish, long-standing Native land claims, and rights as *gens de couleur libres* (free peoples of color) have often been discounted through White/Black binary structures designating race based on White/Black phenotype structures.[8]

Moreover, this collection owes its framework to *Reasoning Together: The Native Critics Collective* (2008), voted one of the ten most influential books in the first decade of the twenty-first century by the Native American and Indigenous Studies Association in 2011. Similar to *Reasoning Together*, we seek to make this edited collection an "anthology of stories . . . that are a part of the larger whole," which kinships theory and history with activism and community cultural practice and memory.[9] Like *Reasoning Together*, wherein authors engage in dialogue with one another's thoughts, stories, criticism, and activism; *Louisiana Creole Peoplehood* creates chapters engaging in conversation with each other, while offering a decidedly communal element of call and response between academic articles and community responses to academics.

Addressing previous and current literature reducing Louisiana Creole experience to racially reductionist frameworks, the editors and contributors build up, extend, and analyze previous scholarship. This means we do not seek to rehash reductionist, dated, binary discussions of colonial Louisiana. Nor is this collection a treatise on the process of creolization (méstizaje/métissage) or other post-contact "Creole" communities globally. We offer an understanding of Creole community identity formation and practice deeply tied to Indigeneity, globalization, diaspora, and law within the culture/landbase of Louisiana Creoles specifically. *Louisiana Creole Peoplehood* proposes a new analysis of the Creole population within the fields of public health, gender and sexuality studies, arts and literature, language, history, and cultural ecology that have yet to be addressed in previous Louisiana Creole studies—making this collection an original and much needed intervention into current Indigenous, Black/Africana, southern, and critical ethnic studies. Much of the inspiration for this work stems from ongoing conversations between the editors, other Louisiana Creole scholars, and community members about the shifting terrain of Louisiana Creole studies within the context of Native American and Indigenous studies, as well as Latinx studies, as sites for unpacking the ways that culture and land speak more directly to ethnic identity than simple geographically constructed boundaries. Each of the contributors comes from a different landscape in Louisiana, and yet, we are able to trace the intersections because we articulate land as a central component to identity, based on the sacred and not on nationalism alone.

We begin by engaging settler-colonial discourse alongside critical mixed-race studies and cultural autonomy, following the traces and continuances of a sovereign Creole Peoplehood. In defining Creole Peoplehood, we articulate new imaginings of geopolitical organization that are not based on arbitrary borders, heteropatriarchy, or a necropolitics of division, while incorporating voices from Louisiana Creole peoples and communities through both surveys/interviews and direct response dialogues. Together these contributors invite new directions in the fields of critical mixed race studies, Native American and Indigenous studies, ethnic studies, arts, and history, among other fields. As an interdisciplinary and dialectical project, *Louisiana Creole Peoplehood* calls on readers, community leaders, and scholars alike to rethink how multiracial Afro-Indigenous communities are redefining place through determined purpose in the United States and across the Americas in the face of settler colonialism and anti-Blackness. We offer both this introduction and the edited collection as an exercise in theory and practice, wherein we come together as Louisiana Creole relations creating a dialectic of experience around Louisiana Creole Peoplehood.

STRUCTURE AND CONTENT

As *Louisiana Creole Peoplehood* intervenes in the erasure of Creole Indigeneity and histories of Black/Indian cultural sustainability, contributors consider Louisiana Creole culture at the intersections of both the African and Indigenous diasporas. Utilizing the concept of the Peoplehood matrix, we illustrate how Indigenous communities are culturally and historically grounded in lived realities and traditional homespaces. Peoplehood transcends "notions of statehood, nationalism, gender, ethnicity," and recognizes that "language, sacred history, religion (ceremonial cycle), and land" are "interwoven and dependent on one another."[10] Organized around the Peoplehood matrix this book is divided into the following sections:

1. "Sacred Histories: From Kinship to Cultural Resurgences"
2. "Landbase: From Homelands to Food and Health"
3. "Language: Literacies of Language and Body"
4. "Ceremonials and Cultural Practice: Testimonials to Activism"

Like *Reasoning Together*, *Louisiana Creole Peoplehood* creates chapters engaging in conversation with one another, but also creates a call and response between academic articles and community responses. Throughout the first three sections, community members "respond" to each chapter. These responses take a multiplicity of forms. Some engage in direct response/conversation with the academic claims and discourse, some reflect on feelings, emotions, memory, or concepts in essays, poetry, or personal reflections. These community responses are ultimately a way for community voices to "speak back" to academics without the confines of academic genre, discourse, or discipline.

Therefore, the text displays how our communities rejoin, think, feel, react (artistically/emotionally), and challenge the work on Creole scholarship, while ensuring the work we create is beholden to the communities we call home.

The fourth and final section includes personal memoirs/testimonials, reflections, and interviews from community members offering an additional lived experience or practice in conversation with the theory and history found in the academic chapters. As editors we have sought to preserve the voices of the community responders and testimonies. This means allowing for variations in language, rhetorical practice, and structure to best preserve and reflect community voices. *Louisiana Creole Peoplehood* is the first collection of its kind addressing its Creole culture as connected to land, sustainability, history, language, and religion through the processes of métissage/méstizaje cultural formation while promoting communal dialogue and active community reciprocity.

Part 1, "Sacred Histories: From Kinship to Cultural Resurgences" articulates a counter-narrative to existing literature that reduces Creole identity to a Black-White framework. Rain Prud'homme-Cranford sets the tone of the collection in chapter 1, "Post-Contact Peoplehood: History, Kinship, and Redefining Louisiana Creole Indigeneity," asking readers to consider how Louisiana Creoles articulate their Afro-Indigenous identities through both the Peoplehood matrix and the United Nations Working Group on Indigenous Populations, addressing issues of land, language, spirituality, and kinship. By asserting a definition based on *rem arbitrium*, Prud'homme-Cranford and the authors in this section force us to reconcile the seemingly divergent and discordant parameters of identity that traditionally isolate African and Latin-European ancestry from Indigenous roots in Louisiana and across its Creole diaspora. Similarly, works by Darryl Barthé, Jeffery Darensbourg, and Annalyssa Gypsy Murphy address New Orleans specifically, tackling issues of Americanization, Indigenous erasure, and colonial transnational miscegenation. In chapter two, "Speak White, Speak Black, Speak American: Assimilation in Creole New Orleans," Darryl Barthé builds on the notion of *rem arbitrium*, highlighting the ways that Creoles in New Orleans were specifically forced into White and Black segments of society and how Americanization led to a "Whitening and Blackening" of Creoles that is also responsible for the lack of contemporary attention to Bulbancha (New

Orleans) as a site of Indigenous place-making and cultural production. Chapter 3, "Acadian/African/Indigenous Trinity: An Identity Mosaic from Nova Scotia to New Orleans," documents early Creole and Métis relationships as well as Acadian (Cajun) cultural confluences in the making of Afro-Indigenous histories from Canada to Louisiana, producing a third root or tri-racial ethnic/cultural formation unique to Louisiana. In chapter 4, "Bulbancha Is Still a Place: Decolonizing the Tricentennial of New Orleans," Jeffery Darensbourg astutely points to the erasure of an Indigenous landbase in New Orleans in the celebration of the three-hundred-year anniversary of the city's "founding," even though it already existed and was known as Bulbancha by local Native communities. Taken together, these chapters and community responses call out the overt racism, Jim Crow segregationist tactics, and anti-Black and anti-Indian racism in Louisiana that attempt to erase the existence of Indigenous, Afro-Indigenous, and thus Creole peoples. In calling attention to counter-historical narratives the authors demonstrate how Louisiana Creoles as a people throughout history and into the present moment have refused to be erased and denied social, cultural, legal, and political rights.

Part 2, "Landbase: From Homelands to Food and Health," explores the connectivity between health and wellness, landbase, and cultural food practices. Tracey Colson Antee explores the Afro-Indigenous roots of Creole cuisine and food harvesting, reminding us that "food is political" and thereby "the stories, practices, and production of traditional foodways for Louisiana Creole people are tied to land and cultural sustainability." Jeffery Darensbourg connects Atakapa-Ishak history and erasure with "an understanding of Ishak People on the current population, which is overwhelmingly comprised of people who can also, accurately, consider themselves Louisiana Creoles, Acadians, or combinations thereof." Lastly, T. Shawnee in her chapter "A Perfect Circle Bound in Chains: Creole-NDN Health, Historical Trauma, and Settler Colonialism," offers a much-needed intervention into the practice of Creole and Freedmen Afro-Indigenous erasure within the fields of medicine and counseling. Shawnee astutely argues that "Creole-NDN and Freedmen communities have been underrepresented in research and programming in the most typical ways—by focus and by definition. Genetically and culturally complex communities, such as our own, have been 'defined out' of studies by not clearly fitting into racial or ethnic assignments that are typically required."

Shawnee addresses for the first time serious public health challenges facing Louisiana Creoles and other Afro-Indigenous communities, and in doing so, demonstrates the ways that anti-Black and anti-Indian racism intersects with settler colonialism, producing historical and intergenerational trauma that has become embedded in the DNA of Afro-Indigenous / Red-Black peoples in Louisiana and Oklahoma.

In part 3, "Languages: Literacies of Language and Body," we explore the many stories, narratives, and literacies that are both spoken and embodied by Louisiana Creole people. Language is a central component of any community and its ability to survive and pass on culture to future generations has been a subject of study in Louisiana for decades; however, there are new movements and efforts toward language revitalization, especially those that also center Indigenous impacts on language and identity in Louisiana. Oliver Mayeux takes a linguistically historical look at the construction of the Louisiana Creole language, illustrating how "Creole-identified activists have established a form of Louisiana Creole *languagehood*. . . . Reifying Louisiana Creole as a language in its own right and emphasizing its distinctiveness from Louisiana French, activists seek to reclaim and rearticulate Louisiana Creole peoplehood on their own terms." In addition to interrogating spoken languages, there are chapters in this section that address how we communicate and embody queerness and body politics. In chapter 9, "No Body Sings the Blues Like a FAT Body: Gender, Race, and Eco-Colonialism," Rain Prud'homme-Cranford addresses issues of body aesthetic, sexuality/gender, land desecration, and violence against women. Chapter 10, "Don't Scratch My Washboard but You Can Pull My Fiddle: Negotiating Queerness in the Creole Diaspora," follows Andrew Jolivétte on a nearly twenty-year journey into queer Creole both public and private, documenting the ways that Creole men navigate queerness in relationship to racial, religious, and gendered identity. Examining the sores and silences of queerness and body image as well as language and shame, the authors in this section challenge readers to think about the modes of cultural production by Indigenous and Afro-Indigenous peoples in the face of settler colonial violence.

Lastly, the final section, "Ceremonials and Cultural Practice: From Testimonials to Activism," showcases personal reflections from various community members across the Louisiana Creole, Native American, and Latinidad diaspora. These responses include essays, memoirs, and interviews. This section builds off the community writings throughout the first three sections of the book, where community members respond to the academic essays. Some of these responses are critical, while others are personal, and still others are creative. In both part 4 and in the responses to the academic chapters, in an effort to help preserve and maintain the authentic voices of respondents, the editors have chosen to let their words stand on their own. This means the editors have chosen not to explain, organize, or shape the response essays in an effort to showcase the diversity, emotion, and cultural responses of the community respondents.

Collectively these essays are a first in Native American and Indigenous studies as well as Louisiana Creole studies. Drawing from critical mixed-race studies and critical ethnic studies we argue that Louisiana Creoles as a post-contact Afro-Indigenous community represent a seldom understood or studied dynamic across the Americas and especially in the United States. In calling for a sort of "call and response" process with the community, we seek to restore a balance that was interrupted by first contact and that continues to be pervasive within the US settler state. *Louisiana Creole Peoplehood* is a call out to other Afro-Indigenous peoples and nations across the Americas to document, organize, and tell their own stories, too. As the arc of history is beginning to turn once more with population demographic shifts, it becomes all the more important and relevant that Afro-Indigenous peoples are asserting our right to exist, to document and create our own policies, and finally to find our own form of *rem arbitrium*. We are a story that deserves to be heard.

NOTES

1. In Red English, NDN is a shortening of "Indian" (i.e., Native American).
2. Rain P. Cranford Goméz, "Hachotakni Zydeco's Round'a Loop Current: Indigenous, African, and Caribbean Mestizaje in Louisiana Literatures," *Southern Literary Journal* 46, no. 2 (2014): 91–92, www.doi.org/10.1353/slj.2014.0001.
3. For more on this definition and the Peoplehood matrix, please see chapter 1.
4. Jack D. Forbes, *Africans and Native Americans: The Language of Race and the Evolution of Red-Black Peoples* (Urbana: University of Illinois Press, 1993), 5.
5. BIPOC: Black, Indigenous peoples of color.

6 Andrew J. Jolivétte, *In Louisiana Creoles: Cultural Recovery and Mixed-Race Native American Identity* (New York: Lexington Books, 2006), 96.
7 Janet Ravare Colson, *THE Creole Book* (Natchitoches, LA: Creole Heritage Foundation, 2012), 7.
8 Virginia R. Domínguez, *White by Definition: Social Classification in Creole Louisiana* (New Brunswick, NJ: Rutgers University Press, 1997), 46, 207.
9 Janice Acoose et al., *Reasoning Together: The Native Critics Collective* (Norman: University of Oklahoma Press, 2008), 8.
10 Tom Holm, J. Diane Pearson, and Ben Chavis, "Peoplehood: A Model for the Extension of Sovereignty in American Indian Studies," *Wicazo Sa Review* 18, no. 1 (2003): 11–12, www.doi.org/10.1353/wic.2003.0004.

PART 1

SACRED HISTORIES

From Kinship to Cultural Resurgences

CHAPTER 1

POST-CONTACT PEOPLEHOOD

History, Kinship, and Redefining Louisiana Creole Indigeneity

RAIN PRUD'HOMME-CRANFORD

> Les cenelles. Ye repousse Ferme et beau, comme notre fidele, amour Creole.
> ARMAND LANUSSE, "Pour Ulysse Richard"

T'AS ENTENDU LE CONTE POUR . . .

Anumpa nan anoli sv'bʊnna. This is a story of a People. People I call ancestors, family, and my community. People I love. Our Creole[1] identity and culture has been defined, redefined, and historically written about. It has been mythologized, exoticized, eroticized, and the victim of binary southern structures and hypodescent (Jim Crow).[2] Moreover, there has been an overwhelming focus on New Orleans[3] and often an overlooking of other Louisiana Creole communities and their connections to tribal populations in the state of Louisiana. It is certainly a complex and evolving culture. But what is key is it is a *culture*, one that is a product of métissage/méstizaje tied to the landbase of Louisiana. According to Janet Ravare Colson, a founder and former director of the Creole Heritage Center in Natchitoches, the denial of acknowledging the rich multiracial history and perseverance of Louisiana Creoles and their formation of communities that foster family and culture in the face of binary oppression is the result of "being misunderstood, misrepresented, and misinterpreted."[4] Therefore, defining Louisiana Creole culture and identity, with respect to our Indigeneity, grounded in our landbase, culture, and political presence as a post-contact Afro-Indigenous people, is an ever more vital discussion within Creole discourse. It is, as Andrew Jolivétte attests, a way by which we as community, family, and multigenerational méstiz@ peoples assert *rem arbitrium* (determined purpose/decision). These conversations encourage us toward more productive methods for cultural sustainability, political and ecological rights, and larger dialogues on Indigenous and African studies, as well as African/Indigenous diasporas.

In this chapter, I seek to invoke *rem arbitrium* by redefining Louisiana Creoles' relationship to our Indigeneity. I offer a definition of Louisiana Creole Indigeneity by resituating our relationships/kinships, histories, and cultural practices within the concept of the Peoplehood matrix. Additionally, I dialogue with prominent definitions of Indigenous Peoples (including the United Nations Working Group on Indigenous Populations), exploring political experiences/actions, and offering a sample of these practices in a short literary explication. This definition is grounded in communities/kinship, politics, landbase, and practice (culture), rather than myth-story (mythic history) and absence (dated southern binary opposition). How *we define* ourselves as Louisiana Creoles, rather than how we have been defined, is ever more pertinent to our communities and political solidarity—particularly if we seek to retain, grow, and protect our ecological homelands toward broader constructs of cultural sustainability. So, have you heard the one about the Louisiana Creoles who fight the system of Indigenous erasure? *T'as entendu le conte pour* . . .[5]

POU NOUZÒT LAMOU KRÉYOL: LOUISIANA CREOLES AND PEOPLEHOOD

Ça fé inavé.[6] This is a story for our Creole love. Resituating our relationships/kinships, histories, and cultural practices within the concept of the Peoplehood matrix and the United Nations Definition of Indigenous Peoples creates a narrative of Louisiana Creole identity that accounts for its transnational/transcontinental and transracial heritage, while simultaneously asserting its Indigenous ties both culturally and genetically to Louisiana landbases. Blackness has been the dividing line not only between whiteness in the US South but also

"Indianness." As Andrew Jolivétte (Louisiana Creole / Atakapa-Ishak / Choctaw / Opelousas) asserts in consultation with Janet Ravare Colson (Cane River Creole / Tunica-Choctaw-Biloxi descent), Louisiana Creoles comprise "American Indian, African, French, and Spanish ancestry" and are tied by familial, landbase, and residence ties to Louisiana.[7] In other words, Creole identity is an Afro-Indigenous culture produced through méstizaje. Further, following Ana María Manzanas Calvo and Jesús Benito Sánchez's work, we can situate Louisiana Creole culture within the Caribbean Latinidad and Latinx peoples as productions formed out of colonial contact and borderlands from processes of méstizaje—Indigenous, African, European—creating new Indigenous-Afro peoples in the border spaces.[8] Therefore, the processes of méstizaje and history of colonialism that created the peoples of Latin America and the Caribbean "is the same social, political, economic, linguistic, and cultural process that produced the Creole culture in the state of Louisiana."[9]

However, due to conceptions of race via hypodescent and Jim Crow, "anyone with visible or known African ancestry . . . was considered Black or colored for most purposes. An Indian community with even a small degree of Black ancestry is much less likely historically to have been acknowledged as an Indian community by governments, social scientists, and surrounding populations than a community with greater degrees of white ancestry."[10] In his research with the state-recognized Clifton-Choctaw community in Rapides, (whose family communities coalesced from Rapides, Natchitoches, and Sabine), Brian Klopotek (Louisiana Choctaw) notes the ways that "we need to recognize the source of Indian antiblack racism within a broader colonial project and acknowledge its hidden impact not only on Indian resources, but also on Indian senses of self."[11] This rupture between "Indian," "Creole," "Blindian," and Blackness is most apparent in the notion of Black ancestry verses Creole ancestry in the identity of the Clifton Choctaw. In his work with the Clifton-Choctaw on issues of African/Black ancestry, Klopotek met great resistance. However, the reaction to Cane River Creole ancestry received a markedly different response:

> I told her I thought it was commonly acknowledged that some members of the Clifton-Choctaw community had black ancestry, in particular through its ties to the Cane River Creoles of Color.

Her eyes brightened in recognition and what appeared to be relief, and she said, "Oh, well, yes, the Cane River Creoles, we do share ancestry with them." In local terms, the Cane River Creoles, who have African, French, and Native ancestry, were distinguished from blacks by their large percentage of European ancestry, their history as free people of color and slaveholders themselves (which carries connotations about both race and class), their francophone traditions, and their celebrity as bearers of a unique tradition that sets Louisiana apart from the rest of the United States. In central Louisiana, they were "a race apart from blacks," certainly in their own minds and to a significant degree in local custom as well.[12]

Louisiana Creoles' status as "a race apart from black," due to their Native American and European ancestry, Indigenous and Latinidad cultural (religious) practices, and history with slaveholding (similar to that of the Five Civilized Tribes), exemplifies how Louisiana Creoles (while part of the African and Indigenous diaspora) politically and culturally occupy a separate space when viewed from internal Louisiana community structures of race and identity. It also highlights insular community practices between certain Creole communities and between Creole communities and tribal communities. However, despite this, as tribes have sought recognition in the state of Louisiana, the reality of anti-Black racism and Indian isolation has increased. As Vice Chief Brenda Brooks of the recently state recognized Natchitoches Tribe of Louisiana writes, "There is nothing wrong with being Creole. I, myself, have the mixed blood of Creoles. I consider myself Native American . . . You mentioned Creole. Our people took on that name. We were also called Black, Mexican, French, Spanish, White, German."[13] This historiography of connotations around "Creoleness" owes its inheritance to both anti-Black racism and Indigenous erasure. Hence, Creole is tainted by bifurcations of "Blackness" versus "whiteness," wherein asserting "Native American" devoid of African ancestry is tied to the anti-Black racism in processes in the politics of recognition. This stems from the implementations of strict racial divisions under US racial codes like Jim Crow. These structures led to scenarios wherein "sometimes, Creoles identified themselves as Creoles, but sometimes they didn't. . . . Sometimes, Creoles were Americans and sometimes they were not; sometimes they were Acadian or French or Spanish or German. Sometimes, Creoles identified themselves as Amerindians."¹⁴ According to Darryl Barthé Jr. (Louisiana Creole métis), this "phenomenon amounted to a culture of 'situational passing' in which people of color who appeared to be white would assume a white identity for convenience *without* forsaking their non-white identity"¹⁵—practice quite different from *passe blanc* (passing white).¹⁶ Moreover, when it comes to census records due to both racial/cultural admixtures of Louisiana Creoles, issues of situational passing, cases of *passe blanc*, and assumptions of phenotype over familial and cultural affiliations show that "designation(s) as mulatto [were] not in [themselves] confirmation of African ancestry and certainly [are] not confirmation of a lack of Indian ancestry."¹⁷

This conundrum or gray space occupied by Louisiana Creoles can be explained as one of the results of being a post-contact Indigenous people (or specifically post-contact Afro-Indigenous people). As members of the Indigenous and African diasporas Louisiana Creoles, depending on community, often hold various kinships to multiple tribes in Louisiana and extending through Louisiana Territory into Canada (Ontario, Manitoba, Québec, Nova Scotia, and New Brunswick). Moreover, the "disruptive impact Europeans had through disease, trade goods and the importation of their perpetual internecine warfare, inevitably and fundamentally influenced the cultures of Indigenous peoples,"¹⁸ wherein tribal peoples found new ways to coalesce and regroup: "Sometimes these disruptions were so severe, they nearly decimated existing communities, and survivors were integrated into other groups, or new cultural practices arose to cope with changing conditions. . . . For groups to become distinct, post-contact Indigenous peoples, a distinct culture had to arise."¹⁹ In Louisiana, examples of post-contact Indigenous peoples include both state and federally sovereign nations. Some of these legally recognized tribes and nations in current incarnations arose from the violence, disruption, and repercussions of settler-colonial structures wherein disparate individuals and fractured communities integrated into new definitive tribal nations including the Choctaw-Apache, Tunica-Biloxi (Tunica, Biloxi, Choctaw, Ofo, Avoyel), the Natchitoches Tribe of Louisiana, the United Houma Nation (UHN), Biloxi-Chitimacha-Choctaw (formerly part of the UHN), and the petitioning for state recognition Atakapa-Ishak Nation of Southwest Louisiana and Southeast Texas. There are of course other post-contact Indigenous tribes and communities outside of Louisiana, as well as distinct individual post-contact cultures and communities such as the Freedmen (descendants of Natives and slaves within the Five Civilized tribes), Xican@s, and others.

As distinct post-contact Afro-Indigenous peoples with a distinct culture, Creole peoples still must meet the criteria of what it means to be a product of both Indigenous Peoplehood and working legal or political definitions of Indigeneity. The Peoplehood model, developed by Tom Holm (Mvskoke [Creek] / Cherokee), J. Diane Pearson, and Ben Chavis (Lumbee) draws from the work of Cherokee scholar Robert K. Thomas. Peoplehood is culturally and historically grounded in lived realities and traditional homespaces of Indigenous peoples. Peoplehood transcends "notions of statehood, nationalism, gender, ethnicity," and recognizes that "language, sacred history, religion (ceremonial cycle), and land" are "interwoven and dependent on one another."[20] This concept illustrates how land influences language, language reflects ceremony/religion, and how in turn, events that take place on land are tied to the people who inhabit their homescapes and constantly re-remember (access history/identity) through land, and thereby language, in turn tying land, kinship, and language to community ways of knowing (epistemologies). Additionally, Peoplehood addresses "disenfranchised or colonized Native American groups," which is key for post-contact Indigenous peoples:

> The concept goes beyond the notion of race and even nationality. Historically, Native American peoples adopted captives of several races. Adoption meant that the captive, regardless of race, became a member of a kin group. . . . Race, to Native Americans, was not a factor of group identity or Peoplehood. Nations—which are primarily viewed as the territorial limits of states that encompass a number of communities—do not necessarily constitute a people nor do they have the permanency of peoplehood.[21]

The concept of Peoplehood is therefore grounded in concepts free of settler-colonial notions of blood quantum and the nation-state. It is linked to culture, community, and landbase, and makes allowances for the impacts toward the formation of post-contact Indigenous communities.

"Between 2004 and 2007, the United Nations set about the task of setting out individual and collective rights of Indigenous peoples, as regards culture, identity, language, education, health, and other collective issues."[22] The finalized 2007 document, the United Nations Declaration on the Rights of Indigenous Peoples (UNDRIP), "also 'emphasizes the rights of Indigenous peoples to maintain and strengthen their own institutions, cultures, and traditions, and to pursue their development in keeping with their own needs and aspirations.'"[23] Moreover, the 1986 UN Working Group on Indigenous Populations (WGIP) definition of Indigenous peoples is the most thorough and widely used, even though the United Nations "never officially adopted this definition as a prerequisite for participation in the WGIP."[24] The WGIP definitions on Indigenous communities include: "Self-identification as indigenous peoples at the individual level and accepted by the community; Historical continuity with pre-colonial and/or pre-settler societies; Strong link to territories and surrounding natural resources; Distinct social, economic or political systems; Distinct language, culture and beliefs; Form non-dominant groups of society; Resolve to maintain and reproduce their ancestral environments and systems as distinctive peoples and communities."[25] For familial groups, state tribes, and certainly Louisiana Creole communities, the concept of Indigeneity is certainly clarified when viewed through UNDRIP and WGIP definitions. Most Creole communities and Louisiana state tribes, while not federally enrolled, are tied to multiple pre-settler tribal communities, amounting to an ability to establish histories of pre-colonial contact, landbase continuity, distinct language and culture, as well as both historical/familial and ecological (including food culture and harvesting) ancestral environments. The marginalized community(ies) with distinct culture(s) and language(s) are tied to Indigenous peoples still inhabiting the same landbase.

As a post-contact Afro-Indigenous people, Louisiana Creoles recognize the totality of their ethnic/cultural matrices. These matrices encompass American Indians of the Gulf South (Choctaw, Houma, Caddo, Chitimacha, Tunica, Biloxi, Creek, Atakapa Ishak, Natchez, and others); African Americans; Caribbeans (Afro-Spanish-French-Indigenous-Caribbean);[26] French-Indian (including métissage with the Wabanaki Confederacy, Sac and Fox, Ojibwé, and Miami), and multi-generationally kinshipped tribal groups and landbases in what is now the state of Louisiana. It should be mentioned that this is a stark difference from communities that claim métissage/méstizaje based often on a singular identified Indian ancestor, such as the current Métis claims by recent groups in Ontario, Nova Scotia, and New Brunswick or the Mikinak Nation of Ontario. According to Lise Brisebois, a self-proclaimed "descendant of an Algonquin grandmother," she always "felt Indian."[27] Chief of the so-called Mikinak Nation, Brisebois asserts that the recent *Daniels* decision[28] means "that anyone with Aboriginal ancestry, whether 10th or 2nd generation, it says you are Indians."[29] Brisebois and other groups like hers assume an ethnic identity based on a genealogical ancestor and misunderstandings of métissage and post-contact Indigenous communities, rather than the realities of intergenerational First Nations / Indigenous / American Indian inter-relationships/intermarriages, cultural practices, and political identification. In his work with the Indigenous claims of Québécois and other eastern "métis" claims, Darryl Leroux notes that these assertions and history are based not on "recent" intergenerational racial and cultural métissage but rather on claims of Indigenous genealogy from 300–350 years prior to current claims.[30] These claims of distant Indigenous ancestry not grounded in intergenerational Indigenous biological, cultural, political histories, and survivance (survival plus resistance) wash "away Quebec's history of colonialism while reinforcing Quebec's own experiences as a colonized people" and in doing so usurp Métis Nationhood in Canada.[31] Hence, there is a marked claim between the continuous intergenerational kinshipped and cultural communities of Louisiana Creoles and their relationships to métissage/méstizaje.

Louisiana Creoles are composed of *specific* communities, each with their own contemporary and historic ties to tribal communities/histories, narratives, landbases, and practices within Louisiana terrains. In a recent survey and questionnaire of over one hundred Louisiana Creoles, conducted by Andrew Jolivétte and myself, 75 percent agreed or strongly agreed that the political term post-contact Afro-Indigenous be used to describe Creoles, and 100 percent stated that "Native American, African, and European" was a key part of their "cultural (and/or ancestral) makeup."[32] Moreover, roughly 87 percent[33] identified their specific Indigenous ancestry within Louisiana and/or Neutral Ground[34] specific tribes: Atakapa-Ishak, Choctaw (including Choctaw-Biloxi), Tunica-Biloxi (including Choctaw, Biloxi, Avoyell, and Ofo), Opelousas, Caddo (Natchitoches, Hasinai, and Kadohadacho), Quapaw, Houma, Chitimacha, Coushatta (Koasati), Apache, and

Wichita.³⁵ Cane River Creoles intermarried/procreated among other Creoles, traded, and hold ancestries/ties to particular Indigenous groups, including Caddo, Choctaw, Wichita, Chitimacha, Tunica, Choctaw-Biloxi, Apache, Talimali (Apalachees), and Quapaw.³⁶ Opelousas Creoles intermarried/procreated among other Creoles, traded, and hold ancestries/ties to particular Indigenous groups, including Atakapa-Ishak, Bayougoula, Cherokee, Opelousas, Natchez, Koasati, and Mvskoke. Point Coupee Creoles intermarried/procreated among other Creoles, traded, and consist of particular Indigenous groups including Choctaw, Houma, Chitimacha, Atakapa-Ishak, Biloxi, and Apalachees.³⁷ Therefore, Louisiana Creoles are linked to their Louisiana landbase communities with a post-contact specific culture (of Indigenous, African, European) through a continuous history of at least three hundred years—this is just as long as the Canadian Métis, and as long as many Louisiana state and federally recognized tribes.

Borrowing from Chelsea Vowel (Lac Ste. Anne Métis) and Chris Anderson's (Saskatchewan Métis) definition of Métis,³⁸ we can further our understanding of Louisiana Creole people as a post-contact Afro-Indigenous group connected to specific Louisiana Creole communities. Creoles *are not* Métis, as in the Métis Nation (Métis National Council) of Canada. They *are* a métis, méstiz@ ethnic-cultural group who form their own distinct Indigenous-Afro / Afro-Indigenous (Red/Black Latinidad) post-contact Louisiana communities grounded in a Peoplehood matrix—landbase (territory), language (Kouri-Vini), religion (ceremonial cycles), and sacred history (community narrative, religious and cultural narratives, "racial" oppressions, and opposition to Americanization). Moreover, Christophe Landry (Louisiana Creole), who has worked tirelessly on Louisiana Creole language revitalization and retention, also worked to have Kouri-Vini (a Louisiana Creole language) recognized as an endangered language Indigenous to Louisiana. Kouri-Vini has been documented as being spoken as early as 1740. "Lexical, syntactical and phonemic influences in Louisiana Creole language include a heavy dose of vocabulary from present-day France, distinctive provincial Louisiana intonation, and significant Caddo, Ishák (Atákapa) and Louisiana Choctaw lexicon," including "words from Louisiana Spanish, Wolof, Mandinga, Igbo, and Ewe, the latter four most visible in Louisiana folklore."³⁹ Further, Louisiana Creole is a "stable language" that is not interchangeable with French, "no more so than Danes can understand English, and Italians can understand Brazilians."[40]

Taking the WGIP definition into conversation with the Peoplehood matrix, Jeff Corntassel argues the following: "By utilizing Holm et al.'s version of the peoplehood model, my proposed indigenous definition includes all four, interlocking concepts of sacred history, ceremonial cycles, language, and ancestral homelands, while elaborating somewhat on their complex interrelationships."[41] Corntassel braids together Peoplehood with former WGIP and various academic/political definitions of Indigenous. These points include:

> Peoples who believe they are ancestrally related and identify themselves, based on oral and/or written histories, as descendants of the original inhabitants of their ancestral homelands; Peoples who may, not necessarily, have their own informal and/or formal political, economic, and social institutions, which tend to be community-based and reflect their distinct ceremonial cycles, kinship networks, and continuously evolving cultural traditions; Peoples who speak (or once spoke) an indigenous language, often different from the dominant society's language—even where the indigenous language is not "spoken," distinct dialects and/or uniquely indigenous expressions may persist as a form of indigenous identity; Peoples who distinguish themselves from the dominant society and/or other cultural groups while maintaining a close relationship with their ancestral homelands/sacred sites, which may be threatened by ongoing military, economic, or political encroachment or may be places where indigenous peoples have been previously expelled, while seeking to enhance their cultural, political, and economic autonomy.[42]

Therefore, Corntassel's points of Indigenous community identity certainly apply to Louisiana Creole communities. However, due to settler-colonial stagnant hierarchical constructs of race and ethnicity, "Americans could not accept racial cohabitation . . . demanding Creoles to deny their French, Spanish, and Native American lineage and use the 'one drop rule' to define their identity."[43] As addressed in the introduction, Louisiana Creole community and culture are not predicated on notions of blood quantum, Indian, African, or European, but as a culture dependent on recognizing "the totality of" our "ethnic/

cultural matrices." In other words, if we remove the Indigenous elements (or African, etc.) from Louisiana Creole culture, community, and/or kinship, then Louisiana Creole culture ceases to exist. We are the sum of all our relations umbilically tied to the landbase called Louisiana.[44]

It is important when having conversations about métis/méstiz@ peoples arising from processes of métissage/méstizaje not to conflate or infringe on the rights and processes of sovereign Native nations of Turtle Island. The same can be said when speaking broadly about post-contact Indigenous peoples including the Métis of Canada who have very specific communities and rights through law and policy, and other post-contact communities in the United States and Canada who are recognized as First Nations bands or sovereign nations. Because post-contact communities include broadly both sovereign nations, state tribes, and métis/méstiz@ communities, specificity is paramount.

Hence having conversations around Louisiana Creoles peoples as Afro-Indigenous peoples, as specific products of post-contact Indigenous ethnogenesis arising through the violence of the colonial project and settler-colonial structures, also means recognizing the ways that Creole communities, while kinshipped to First Nations, Métis, and Inuit / Native peoples, are not sovereign nations. However, I offer that Louisiana Creoles should support the rights of sovereign Native peoples, and I hope sovereign nations will support the issues faced by unrecognized post-contact Afro-Indigenous communities and peoples such as Louisiana Creoles (Freedmen, Chicanos, etc.). Recognizing and tracing Louisiana Creoles as their own specific post-contact Afro-Indigenous communities means doing this while recognizing and upholding the rights of sovereign nationhood within Indian country, while also challenging our rights to what cultural belonging and sustainability means as disenfranchised Afro-Indigenous peoples under UNDRIP.

"CREOLE INDIANS": MAPPING BLINDIAN LITERARY MÉSTIZAJE

> Our names return three or
> Four centuries to ancestors
> Shipped here like sardines,
> Saltwater Africans coupled
> to Euro English, Irish,

> French . . . Natives Choctaw,
> Houma, Natchez, and
> Alabama . . . Families with
> roots like the Live oaks
> firmly planted
>
> MONA LISA SALOY, "Sankofa NOLA"

In 1833, William Apess's "An Indian's Looking-Glass to the White Man" sought to decry racial inequality through evoking Christian rhetorical sensibilities of goodness and humility.[45] Apess, of Pequot, African, and European ancestry, is one of the first Blindian (Black and Indian) orators, activists, and authors to publish in the United States. Apess writes:

> If Black or red skins or any other skin of color is disgraceful to God, it appears that he has disgraced himself a great deal—for has made fifteen colored people to one white and placed them here upon this earth. . . . Now let me ask you, white men . . . have you the folly to think that the white man, being one in fifteen or sixteen, are the only beloved images of God?[46]

Contrasting perceptions of phenotypic appearance in the eyes of God, Apess addresses a flawed humanity playing with notions of color and race as a rhetorical tactic, thus showcasing Christian hypocrisy, subjugation, and degradation of Indians and Blacks during the nineteenth century. Apess was committed to "sovereignty"[47] for Mashpee Pequot and other Indian communities, but also to Black abolitionist rights and freedom from oppression for all people of color. While Apess has often emerged as the most notable image within early Red/Black dialogues on Indigeneity in the Americas, unique post-contact Indigenous communities, rather than individuals, have to, and continue to, struggle for recognition in our settler colonial state constrained by binary constructs and hypodescent.[48]

Twelve years after Apess's "An Indian's Looking-Glass to the White Man," in 1845, enters *Les Cenelles: Choix de poésies Indigènes* (*The Hawthorn Berries: Selected Indigenous Poems*), the first collection of poetry by Louisiana Creoles and *gens de couleur libres*—and therefore the first compilation by people of African American *and* Native American descent published in the Americas. In defiance to the ban on publication of works by people of color, Armand Lanusse (New Orleans Creole poet, educator, and editor) gathered eighty-five poems composed by seventeen gens de couleur libres—including prominent Louisiana Creole authors—creating the only collection of its kind. Written in French and later translated to English, the collection remains largely ignored as either African American or Native American literature, most often finding its way into the realm of francophone studies. The poetry is written with regard for its time and circumstance, in the wake of Haitian liberation and the *cordon bleu*— elite gens de couleur libres who studied in France and some who lived in Haiti—reflecting French and Haitian romanticism as well as veiled odes to inequality found wanting in Louisiana when compared to Haiti.[49] This text is a fitting example of the erasure and absence Louisiana Creole identity and production has historically occupied.

Some, such as Catherine Savage Brosman, dismiss the volume's use of *indigenes* in its subtitle, saying that "indigenous indicates simply that the contributors were of native stock," meaning from Louisiana.[50] In her *Louisiana Creole Literature: A Historical Study*, while Indians make appearances in regard to early Louisiana history as subjects in literature written by Creoles (both white Creoles and Creoles of color), Brosman never connects Indians with the Louisiana Creoles (of color) writing about them. Rather Brosman, primarily drawn to Louisiana Creole literature (by her own admission) for its French language, focuses on linguistics, then plot, and finally the concept of New Orleans Creoles of color in binary opposition—romanticized peoples caught between Black and white. This unfortunately is the same tired trope of the tragic mulatto exoticized within Louisiana's Gulf Caribbean and francophone setting. For the most part, this 2013 collection is the only "definitive study" we have on Louisiana Creole literature. Yet it neglects Creoles as an African *and* Indigenous méstiz@ people while also neglecting the majority of Creole peoples *outside* of New Orleans. When it comes to understanding the rich cultural history of Red/Black experience in the Americas, Louisiana Creole productions have often been left untouched despite the complexities of collections like *Les Cenelles: Choix de poésies Indigènes*, written in French by writers who are products of African, French, Native American, Haitian-Taíno, and Spanish bloodlines within Louisiana. In fact, my insistence on the translation of *Les Cenelles* as "The Hawthorn Berries" is in opposition to its standard translation as "The Holly Berries or

Hawthorn Berries."[51] A majority of scholars persist on translating the phrase *Les Cenelles* as "The Holly Berries" when the title—*Les Cenelles: Choix de poésies Indigènes*—seeks to highlight Indigenous plants and cultures (i.e., "Indigenes"). This implies the authors are talking about Hawthorn berries (i.e., mayhaws), a plant indigenous to the US southern wetlands. This further solidifies the connection of *Les Cenelles* and its authors to a sense of place and culture, as Indigenous to Louisiana: "Distinctive people's connections and prolonged existences within their unique territory in turn yield a history—a shared memory and an organic peoplehood."[52] To be Native, to claim the land and a place means something: *les cenelles* (hawthorn berries—mayhaws) and *Indigènes* (Natives/Indigenous persons).

In 1916 Alice Dunbar-Nelson, a New Orleans Creole, would attempt to define what would be, at the time of her writing, 217 years of negotiating nations through méstizaje—creating a new, unique Louisiana Creole identity. Dunbar-Nelson alternately self-identified as both Creole and African American. Her ancestry, like many Louisiana Creoles, comprised "a combination of white, African American, and Native American roots. This background influenced her upbringing and experiences. As a middle-class woman with the privilege of initially passing as white, Southern prejudice still worked against her."[53] In *People of Color in Louisiana* Dunbar-Nelson writes, "A Creole is a native of Louisiana, in whose blood runs mixed strains of everything un-American, with the African strain slightly apparent. The true Creole is like the famous gumbo of the state, a little bit of everything, making a whole, delightfully flavored, quite distinctive, and wholly unique."[54] Dunbar-Nelson's reference to gumbo not only highlights the well-known Creole dish, but is the metaphor for creolization/métissage, wherein elements of African (rice, okra), Native American (filé, aka sassafras, *kafi* in Choctaw; *Litsea glaucescens*, aka Mexican bay leaf; local fish and game; peppers; wild onion), and European (roux) meld to form a unique culinary dish tied to place encompassing racial/ethnic cultural foodways.

Dunbar Nelson also confronts racism and the miscegenation laws that came with Louisiana statehood; as evidenced with her language, "a Creole is a native of Louisiana, in whose blood runs mixed strains of everything un-American."[55] Her language acknowledges that for Europeans / white Louisianans, racial mixing was seen as tainting whiteness, addressing African and Native American blood as "un-American." This exposes the irony of racial caste systems that consider Native bodies as removed from place and status. As a Louisiana Creole of color, Dunbar-Nelson recognizes the problem of colorism and racism, "in which skin color determined social class."[56] Dunbar-Nelson's literary attempts to articulate Creole cultural, political, and historical space are not new. Like *Les Cenelles: Choix de poésies Indigènes*, her work is part of an ongoing process negotiating and articulating how Creole identity is understood through processes of colonialism, slavery, assimilation, and resistance to Americanization.

Almost one hundred years after Dunbar-Nelson's *People of Color in Louisiana* comes Mona Lisa Saloy's 2014 collection of poetry *Second Line Home: New Orleans Poems*, which radiates from the Crescent City reality of lived experience during and in the aftermath of hurricanes Katrina and Rita. Saloy also simultaneously embodies the storied bones of Creole culture from foodways, language, kinship, worship, diaspora, second line sashays for lives well lived—Creole—*la joie de vivre*. From within the text Saloy gives acknowledgment and acceptance of our totality—images of Creoles whose mixed genealogy is spread about the page in a spiraling dance of words:

> Our names return three or
> Four centuries to ancestors
> Shipped here like sardines,
> Saltwater Africans coupled
> to Euro English, Irish,
> French . . . Natives Choctaw,
> Houma, Natchez, and
> Alabama . . . Families with
> roots like the Live oaks
> firmly planted their arms
> Embracing & arching over like an
> umbrella[57]

Calling forth the ever-present Middle Passage, the thread of African diaspora unites Creole blood as exiled from Africa. However, as an admixture, Creoles are home in the Americas (as both African *and* Native American), and therefore within the "family," sheltering arms of the protection of the live oaks. The same oaks whose shelter and fed their Native peoples, from Choctaw to Natchez, who mixed with African blood, growing Creole peoples—sewn from Louisiana soil. The Creole people are transracial, transnational, yet intrinsically connected to the land of Africa and Louisiana as products of diaspora, a culture met at intersections of "Euro," African, and "Native" yet called by the West African process of sankofa—looking back and remembering to go forward.[58] By calling intersecting events, sankofa, into being, there is no past, just events connected to the people, which in turn exhibit the reality of inherited experience and genealogy of Creoles. This specifically addresses Creole diaspora in the US South, highlighting southern Indigenous-descended survivance in today's world. It is a process that is an extension of what LeAnn Howe (Choctaw Nation) calls tribalography, pulling all elements of a storyteller's tribe, land, and culture, and holding within them materials of the people themselves, of the geographic place and setting of their origin.[59]

The poem continues: "Cultures together celebrating each one's crafts / Teaching each one's generations grounded in this / Crescent City landscape of camellias, bougainvillea, hydrangea, iris, in / 'Sippi & Pontchartrain clay, with swamp, 'squitoes & sunshine."[60] Saloy's insistence on exhibiting Creole connections to land (swamps, Mississippi River, Lake Pontchartrain) emphasize Indigeneity as found in the weaving of cultural practices rising from the land into the people—Louisiana Creoles, who are in turn the products of transnational diasporas. Creoles are tied inherently to the land of Louisiana, and for Saloy, particularly New Orleans. Cultures are shared, "celebrated," "taught," and tended, growing from the land and people as naturally as the flora and fauna. Creole identity, indigenously tied to landbase, is insisted on within this southern space, while fully acknowledging the transracial, trans-Indigenous, and transnational histories that impact Creoles as members of Afro-Indigenous diasporas birthed within Louisiana.

Lanusse (and *Les Cenelles* more broadly), Dunbar-Nelson's *People of Color in Louisiana*, and Saloy's use of Creole language, articulations of métissage/méstizaje, alongside specific Louisiana and Gulf land imagery, grounds their work within Peoplehood via cultural homespace and shared or sacred history (including kinship to peoples and land and resistance to Americanization), not just as replications of culture, but from the land into the people, and from the peoples into language. This reinforces the concept that as Indigenous-descended peoples we are tied to land:

> The power of homescapes and the relational, therapeutic politics they generate are animated by stories, songs, and signs radiating outward from their many known and tended places as well as from the ceremonies human beings perform within their boundaries. A distinctive people's connections and prolonged existences within their unique territory in turn yield a history—a shared memory and an organic peoplehood.[61]

Creole authors, artists, and communities, like any Indigenous author, artist, and community, draw on land and communal memory. According to Howe, Indigenous stories/narratives "pull all the elements together of a storyteller's tribe, meaning their people, the land, and multiple characteristics and all their manifestations and revelations and connect these in past, present, and future milieus."[62] Using this interconnected sense of memory and place, tribalography, Creole storytellers / theorists / culture bearers put into practice calling past into the present within singular geographic space(s). The culture of home, of space, rises from a landbase wherein Louisiana Creoles, who are Indigenously connected to Choctaw, Chitimacha, Opelousas, Ishak, Biloxi, Caddoan, Tunica, and other Louisiana Gulf tribal peoples, since before 1714, the official founding of Fort St. Jean Baptiste des Natchitoches. This reinforces Indigenous histories as connected to the lands Creole peoples, families, and communities inhabit in Louisiana, despite the assumption of Indian absence and either-or—Black or white—notions of hypodescent. Hence, the colonizing project intersects with the land and the totality of family and familial land memory. In the end, what is reaffirmed is Creole Afro-Indigenous Peoplehood as connection to shared history, kinship, language, and landbase.

SHORT DEFINITION OF LOUISIANA CREOLE IDENTITY

Louisiana Creoles are made of *specific* communities, each with their own historic ties to specific tribal communities/histories, narratives, landbases, and practices *within* Louisiana terrains. Louisiana Creoles are part of Louisiana Latinidad. We can understand Louisiana Creole people as a post-contact Indigenous group connected to *specific* Louisiana Creole communities. As a post-contact people, Louisiana Creoles recognize the totality of their ethnic/cultural matrices, encompassing *specific* yet multiple American Indian tribes, African American, Caribbean, French-Indian, and European (usually French and Spanish) inheritance. They are a métis, méstiz@ ethnic group defined by culture who form their own distinct Indigenous-Afro (Red/Black Latinidad) Louisiana communities *grounded in a Peoplehood matrix*—landbase (territory), language (Kouri-Vini), religion (ceremonial cycles), and sacred history. Moreover, Louisiana Creole is an Indigenous language to Louisiana, having its roots in French and Native American languages (pidgin) and is listed on the international list of endangered languages.

NO ÇÉ KRÉYOL: WHERE WE GO FROM HERE

Placing and contextualizing Louisiana Creole Indigeneity within larger conversations of Indigenous peoples, studies, community, and Peoplehood is simultaneously complicated, rewarding, and requires us to ask historical and hard questions: particularly about community, cultural sustainability, and community continuity (taking into account internal community continuity versus external perceptions of community in a bifurcated South). As we address Louisiana Creole's Afro-Indigenous Indigeneity and its relationship to other post-contact Indigenous peoples—addressing ways in which community, political, and cultural identity manifest themselves is important. If we as Louisiana Creoles accept the premise, as many of us do, that we identify ourselves through the Creole community(ies) that we belong to / hail from—family names, kinship, space/place (i.e., who your people be and where your people from). Therefore, placing ourselves within broader conversations of post-contact Indigenous / Afro-Indigenous communities and Louisiana Peoplehood is a natural step to retain political, cultural, and ecological autonomy and sustainability. Anumpa nan anoli hupia. We are (all) story.

NOTES

Armand Lanusse, "Pour Ulysse Richard" (1845)," lines 12–15. Translation: "The hawthorn berries (mayhaws). They grow / Once again, strong and beautiful / Like your faithful Creole love." Armand Lanusse, ed. *Les Cenelles:*

Choix de poésies Indigènes, trans. Mia D. Reamer (Shreveport, LA: Tintamarre, 2003).

1. Throughout this chapter I use both Louisiana Creole and Creole interchangeably. It should be noted when using Creole, I am only referring to Louisiana Creoles.
2. The practice of determining racial classifications/stereotypes of mixed-race peoples by assigning a definition of racial subordination based in eugenics on the least "desirable" social racial admixture. Hence a person of African, French, and Chitimacha, unless able to pass visually as Caucasian, would often be classified as Black. This became most commonly applied as the One Drop Rule during Jim Crow and led to both Louisiana Creoles and Louisiana Indians *passe blanc* (passing white) and engaging in paying for changes of racial designation from parish to parish.
3. Focus on New Orleans Creoles has historically veered toward Black/white binary structures, romanticism, and exploitation of racial tropes. Because of this, Darryl Barthé's work in both this book and the dissertation-to-monograph project, "Becoming American in Creole New Orleans: Family, Community, Labor and Schooling, 1896–1949" (PhD diss., University of Sussex, 2016; Baton Rouge: Louisiana State University Press, 2021), is an integral and needed intervention in studies/conversations around New Orleans Creoles.
4. Janet Ravare Colson, *THE Creole Book* (Natchitoches, LA: Creole Heritage Foundation, 2012), 7.
5. Translation: "Have you heard the one about . . ." See Barry Jean Ancelet, *Cajun and Creole Folktales: The French Oral Tradition of South Louisiana* (New York: Garland, 1993), xxvii.
6. The phrase in the subhead title translates to "For our Creole love." Thanks to Christophe Landry for the translation.
7. Andrew J. Jolivétte, *Louisiana Creoles: Cultural Recovery and Mixed-Race Native American Identity* (New York: Lexington Books, 2006), 6–11.
8. See María Manzanas Calvo Ana and Sánchez Jesús Benito, *Narratives of Resistance: Literature and Ethnicity in the United States and the Caribbean* (Cuenca : Ediciones de la Universidad de Castilla–La Mancha, 1999).
9. Andrew J. Jolivétte and Haruki Eda, "Louisiana Creoles and Latinidad: Locating Culture and Community," in *Converging Identities: Blackness in the Modern African Diaspora*, ed. Julius Adekunle and Hettie V. Williams (Durham, NC: Carolina Academic Press, 2013), 275.
10. Brian Klopotek, "Dangerous Decolonizing: Indians and Blacks and the Legacy of Jim Crow," in *Decolonizing Native Histories: Collaboration, Knowledge, and Language in the Americas*, ed. Florencia E. Mallon (Durham, NC: Duke University Press, 2012), Kindle.

11 Klopotek.
12 Klopotek.
13 This is particularly evident in the newly organized and state-recognized Natchitoches Tribe of Louisiana. Based in Black Lake, the community is historically tied to the Cane River community, and many of the Indian progenitors provided in recognition documents are also Indigenous progenitors of the Cane River Creole community. For more see the introduction to this volume, "Ayou Komensé: Louisiana Creole Land, Community, and Recognition"; "Nine Thoughts on 'The Natchitoches Tribe of Louisiana Gains State Recognition,'" *Natchitoches Parish Journal*, February 12, 2018, https://natchitochesparishjournal.com; as well as the author's upcoming monograph, Rain Prud'homme-Cranford, *Gumbo Stories: Quantum Relation-Making and Decolonizing the Creole South*.
14 Barthé, "Becoming American in Creole New Orleans," 87
15 Barthé, 88; emphasis mine.
16 Barthé's work, while primarily focused on New Orleans, as sociopolitical and cultural repercussions toward situational passing, Anglo-American indoctrination, and education, is equally valuable to Louisiana Creoles outside of New Orleans.
17 Forbes quoted in Klopotek, "Dangerous Decolonizing."
18 Chelsea Vowel, "Who Are the Métis?," âpihtawikosisân, April 1, 2019, https://apihtawikosisan.com.
19 Vowel.
20 Tom Holm, J. Diane Pearson, and Ben Chavis, "Peoplehood: A Model for the Extension of Sovereignty in American Indian Studies," *Wicazo Sa Review* 18, no. 1 (2003), 11–12, www.doi.org/10.1353/wic.2003.0004.
21 Holm, Pearson, and Chavis, 16–17.
22 From the author's upcoming monograph, Rain Prud'homme-Cranford, *Gumbo Stories: Quantum Relation-Making and Decolonizing the Creole South*.
23 UNDRIP quoted in Prud'homme-Cranford. The Declaration was adopted by the UN General Assembly in 2007. See the full Declaration at www.un.org/esa/socdev/unpfii/documents/DRIPS_en.pdf.
24 Jeff Corntassel, "Who Is Indigenous? 'Peoplehood' and Ethnonationalist Approaches to Rearticulating Indigenous Identity," *Nationalism and Ethnic Politics* 9, no. 1 (2003): 88, www.doi.org/10.1080/13537110412331301365. Corntassel writes that the UN failed to adopt this definition "mainly due to an adamant insistence by indigenous participants on an unrestricted self-identification policy."
25 WGIP, "Indigenous Peoples, Indigenous Fact Sheet," United Nations, 2006, www.un.org/esa/socdev/unpfii/documents/5session_factsheet1.pdf. WGIP is now defunct, having been replaced by the Expert Mechanism on the Rights of Indigenous Peoples in 2008.

26 In my use of Caribbean, I am acknowledging various Caribbean peoples (Haitian, Dominican, Puerto Rican, etc.) who themselves are products of méstizaje, wherein Taíno, African, Spanish, and/or French inheritance make up both the genealogy and culture of the people. Moreover, I seek to include the Natchez, who were enslaved and exiled to Haiti by Bienville after revolts against the French in 1731, leaving them to finish out their days as slaves on the "sugar plantations of Santo Domingo" (Barnett, xvi). For more information, see James F. Barnett, *The Natchez Indians: A History to 1735* (Jackson: University Press of Mississippi, 2007); and Robert M. Pool, "What Became of the Taíno?," *Smithsonian Magazine*, October 2011, www.smithsonianmag.com.

27 Noël Brigitte, "This Unrecognized Aboriginal Community Is Pissing Off Quebec Mohawks," Vice, August 22, 2016, www.vice.com.

28 In 2016, the Canadian Supreme Court of Canada decided in *Daniels v. Canada*, classifying non-status Indians and Métis as "Indians" under section 91(24) of the Constitution. This clarifies that both groups are a constitutional responsibility of the federal government and not the provinces. However, contrary to several early misunderstandings, the *Daniels* decision does not make métis and non-status Indians status Indians under the Indian Act.

29 Brigitte, "This Unrecognized Aboriginal Community."

30 Darryl Leroux, "Native Studies Speakers Series: Darryl Leroux, 'Now I Am Metis: How White People Become Indigenous,'" SoundCloud, recorded March 12, 2015, https://soundcloud.com/indigenousstudiesusask/native-studies-speakers-series-darryl-leroux-now-i-am-metis-how-white-people-become-indigenous.

31 Chelsea Vowel, "Settlers Claiming Métis Heritage Because They Just Feel More Indigenous," Rabble Canada, March 11, 2015, https://rabble.ca/blogs/bloggers/apihtawikosisan/2015/03/settlers-claiming-m%C3%A9tis-heritage-because-they-just-feel-more/.

32 Rain Prud'homme-Cranford and Andrew J. Jolivétte, "Louisiana Creole Culture and Identity: Part 1 and Part 2, 2018," survey, May 4–July 31, 2018.

33 I state "roughly 87 percent" as there was one survey response that listed Latinx / Mexican Native tribal inheritance in their tribal culture/ancestral makeup.

34 Land between Louisiana and Texas in the eighteenth and nineteenth century was not definitively divided, nor was it between Oklahoma and Texas in the nineteenth century. These strips of land were often referred to as "Neutral Ground." Historically this space became a haven for Indians, Creoles, mixed-race communities, runaway slaves, and outlaws.

35 Prud'homme-Cranford and Jolivétte, "Louisiana Creole Culture and Identity."

36 Prud'homme-Cranford and Jolivétte. See also Juliana Barr, *Peace Came in the Form of a Woman: Indians and Spaniards in the Texas Borderlands* (Durham: University of North Carolina Press, 2009); Kathleen Balthazar Heitzmann, *Cane River Genealogy* (Climax, NY: Cane River Trading Co., 2003); Andrew J. Jolivétte, *Louisiana Creoles: Cultural Recovery and Mixed-Race Native American Identity* (Lanham, MD: Lexington Books, 2007); Brian Klopotek, *Recognition Odysseys: Indigeneity, Race, and Federal Tribal Recognition Policy in Three Louisiana Indian Communities* (Durham: Duke University Press, 2011); Gary B. Mills, *The Forgotten People: Cane River's Creoles of Color* (Baton Rouge: Louisiana State University Press, 2013); Helen Sophie and Smith F. Todd Burton, *Colonial Natchitoches: A Creole Community on the Louisiana-Texas Frontier* (College Station: Texas A&M University Press, 2014).

37 Prud'homme-Cranford and Jolivétte, "Louisiana Creole Culture and Identity." See also Barr, *Peace Came in the Form of a Woman*; Burton and Smith, *Colonial Natchitoches*; Mills, *Forgotten People*; Heitzmann, *Cane River Genealogy*; Brian Klopotek "Dangerous Decolonizing" and *Recognition Odysseys*; Jolivétte, *Louisiana Creoles*; and Christophe Landry, "Louisiana Creole Families with Some Indian Ancestors," Louisiana Historic and Cultural Vistas, accessed April 19, 2021, www.mylhcv.com.

38 Anderson's work *"Métis": Race, Recognition, and the Struggle for Indigenous Peoplehood* (Vancouver: UBC Press, 2015) additionally claims the importance of understanding post-contact Métis Indigeneity "while recognizing that it is also a constitutive fact of the indigeneity of numerous Indigenous peoples around the world whose origins are post-contact" (16).

39 Christophe Landry, "Louisiana Creole Language," WordPress, April 20, 2007, www.wordpress.com.

40 Landry.

41 Corntassel, "Who Is Indigenous?," 91.

42 Corntassel, 91.

43 Ravare Colson, THE *Creole Book*, 7.

44 I am reminded of a conversation with a young Métis Nation scholar who relayed the frustration in people asking them "What tribe are you?," and when they respond, "I am Métis," continued to be met with "Yeah but what tribe are you?" The dismissal of Métis Nationhood and Red River Métis cultural identity as its own specific post-contact Indigenous identity is a frustration not lost on many Louisiana Creoles with whom I have spent time. It is not a matter of "what tribe are you," but rather accepting Louisiana Creole as its own clear post-contact Indigenous / Afro-Indigenous community, with its own politics, histories, resistances, and perseverance in the face of settler colonialism. This has impacted the ways in which Louisiana Creoles have sought understanding of naming, claiming, and evolving articulations their identity (in the face of nationhood, segregation, paper genocide, Jim Crow, etc.).

45 Portions of the discussions in this section are taken from or included in the author's forthcoming monograph *Gumbo Stories: Quantum Relation-Making and Decolonizing the Creole South*.
46 William Apess, *On Our Own Ground: The Complete Writings of William Apess, a Pequot*, ed. Barry O'Connell (Amherst: University of Massachusetts Press, 1992), 156–58.
47 Bernd Peyer, *The Tutor'd Mind: Indian Missionary-Writers in Antebellum America* (Amherst: University of Massachusetts Press, 1997), 164.
48 My referencing of Apess as one, if not the, most notable Blindian of the nineteenth century in no way detracts from crucial voices and bodies of text (written and material) by such Red/Black authors/storytellers as Paul Cuffee, Mary Edmonia Lewis, Okah Tubbee, Olivia Ward Bush-Banks, and others.
49 Armand Lanusse, *Les Cenelles: A Collection of Poems by Creole Writers of the Early Nineteenth Century*, trans. and ed. Regine Latortue, and Gleason R. W. Adams (Boston: G. K. Hall, 1979), xi–xii.
50 Catharine Savage Brosman, *Louisiana Creole Literature: A Historical Study* (Jackson: University Press of Mississippi, 2013), 80.
51 See Thomas Haddox, "The 'Nous' of Southern Catholic Quadroons: Racial, Ethnic, and Religious Identity in Les Cenelles," *American Literature* 73, no. 4 (2001): 757–78; and Floyd D. Cheung, "'Les Cenelles' and Quadroon Balls: 'Hidden Transcripts' of Resistance and Domination in New Orleans, 1803–1845," *Southern Literary Journal* 29, no. 2 (1997): 5–16.
52 D. Anthony Tyeeme Clark and Malea Powell, "Resisting Exile in the 'Land of the Free': Indigenous Groundwork at Colonial Intersections," *American Indian Quarterly* 32, no. 1 (2008): 6, www.doi.org/10.1353/aiq.2008.0009.
53 "Southern Lit Presents Alice Dunbar-Nelson," Southern Fried Karma, June 22, 2018, https://southernfriedkarma.com.
54 Alice Dunbar-Nelson, "People of Color in Louisiana: Part II," *Journal of Negro History* 2, no. 1 (1917): 367, www.doi.org/10.2307/2713476.
55 Dunbar-Nelson, 367.
56 Thadious M. Davis, *Southscapes Geographies of Race, Region, and Literature* (Chapel Hill: University of North Carolina Press, 2014), 227.
57 Mona Lisa Saloy, "Sankofa NOLA," in *Second Line Home: New Orleans Poems* (Kirksville, MO: Truman State University Press, 2014), lines 1–19.
58 Saloy.
59 See LeAnne Howe's definitions and discussion of "tribalography" in "The Story of America: A Tribalography," in *Clearing a Path: Theorizing the Past in Native American Studies*, ed. Nancy Shoemaker (New York: Routledge, 2001), 42.
60 Saloy, "Sankofa NOLA."
61 Clark and Powell, "Resisting Exile in the 'Land of the Free,'" 6.
62 Howe, "Story of America," 42.

COMMUNITY RESPONSE

SO, HAVE YOU HEARD THE ONE ABOUT THE LOUISIANA CREOLES WHO FIGHT THE SYSTEM OF INDIGENOUS ERASURE?

CAROLYN M. DUNN

In her chapter "Post-Contact Peoplehood: History, Kinship, and Redefining Louisiana Creole Indigeneity," Rain Prud'homme-Cranford seeks to rectify years of misinformation, stolen cultural practices, misidentification, and the theft of identity that contemporary and historical Louisiana Creole communities face. It is very fitting that Prud'homme-Cranford's essay is the first chapter in this book, as she seeks to situate Creole identities as experienced in both Louisiana as well as in the diaspora, as a tri-racial, tri-culturally competent identity that is Indigenous to the Americas. Our culture, language, lifeways, traditions, and even our culinary practices have been colonized by white America, through Jim Crow–era practices bent upon identifying us racially as one ("White") or the other ("Black"). Also fitting into this narrative of "otherness" is the erasure of American Indian peoples in Louisiana (e.g., Louisiana's first inhabitants), where a narrative of erasure insists our tribes ceased to exist long ago. Prud'homme-Cranford's essay unpacks the racial binaries assigned to Creoles by others outside of our culture, and those who sought to differentiate between white and black, following southern narratives of race and place that fall strictly along color lines.

"Therefore, defining Louisiana Creole culture and identity, with respect to our Indigeneity," Prud'homme-Cranford posits, "grounded in our landbase, culture, and political presence as a post-contact Afro-Indigenous people, is an ever more vital discussion within Creole discourse." So many essays, blog posts, and historical articles discussing various aspects of Creole identity have been published over the years. Particular evidence of these narratives lies within the travel industry. Post-contact Indigeneity, Prud'homme-Cranford argues, results from the survival of disparate Indigenous peoples out of the violence of the colonial project; in the case of Louisiana Creoles it is the blending of three distinct cultures to become one across the state. However, racial designation in the South and Jim Crow-era erasure of our identity as defined by racial phenotype continues to complicate how we are viewed by the outside world.

Travel writer Megan Romer's article on TripSavvy, titled "What's the Difference between Creole and Cajun?,"[1] breaks down the differences in the typical racial and regional classification. According to Romer, Creoles can be either mixed with white and European or black and European; however, in the modern era the term Creole refers to people of mixed European and African ancestry. "Creole is also a term of identification for people of color of mixed African and European descent," Romer writes, "again largely from families who have been in Louisiana since colonial days."[2] Romer further argues that Cajuns are primarily of white French and French Canadian descent, who did not necessarily procreate with Native populations in Canada and Louisiana, but nonetheless there was cultural mixing where the Native influence in "Cajun" food is present in lifeways such as fishing, food, and music. "Cajuns" "regrouped and formed communities," Romer continues, "and over the years incorporated cultural influences from their new Native American neighbors, and fellow settlers of German, Irish, Spanish, and English descent, as well as African-descended people, both enslaved and free, and French-from-France folks."[3] The illustration that accompanies Romer's article shows Cajun identity as white, male, and blond; Creole identity is accompanied by a photo of a curly haired woman of color that seems to signify that these groups are distinguished along racial lines. The implication then, in many travel writers' minds, is that "Cajun" means "White" and Creole means "Black."

Travel and culinary writers, in general, seem fond on discussing these "differences" between Creole and Cajun peoples. The Cajun and

Creole culinary popularity of the 1980s, which has continued well into the twenty-first century, seems to be the impetus for these many discussions of who Louisiana Creole people are. Kevin Farrell writes in his article "This Is the Difference Between Cajun and Creole" that the difference is racial as well as regional: "French Creole is sometimes used to identify people that trace their roots primarily back to European ancestors in the city, while Louisiana Creole is used at times to describe mixed-race or black descendants today."[4] Farrell's assertion insinuates that color lines are mutually exclusive and reside along the black/white binary that does not include the third strand of our identity, the Indigenous, or the tribal. Specifically, our tribal identities have been erased from this equation, and White Creoles become Cajuns and mixed-race Blacks with French or Spanish ancestry become Creole.

Additionally, Farrell states that the difference between the Cajuns and Creoles are actually regional: think Creole as being exclusively New Orleans with its metropolitan, global, and urban vibe; Cajun is more rural and traces its identity and lifeways back to maritime cultures in France and Canada before settling via waterway in rural southwestern Louisiana.[5] Cajuns, the "White" Louisianians, are the country folk, living among waterways whose subsistence is basically hunting and fishing; while the Creoles, "Black" Louisianians, are urban, whose French provincial connections are evidenced in culinary practices.[6] In opposition of this Cajun/Creole, White/Black, urban/country binary, Prud'homme-Cranford situates our identity as Creole people as land-based, referencing three of our ancestral communities specifically (Point Coupee, Cane River, and Opelousas) as anchor points of identity as seen through the lens of the Peoplehood matrix. As Prud'homme-Cranford articulates, "Louisiana Creoles are composed of *specific* communities, each with their own contemporary and historic ties to tribal communities/histories, narratives, landbases, and practices within Louisiana terrains." The Peoplehood matrix describes a relationship between people, land, language, and culture.[7]

I think specifically of my mother's family, whose diasporic cultural experience in Los Angeles I write about later in this book, through this lens. Opelousas is one of our communities; this is the place from which we emerged as a post-contact Indigenous community. If we assign these classifications posited by the travel writers Romer and Farrell, then my family should not exist. The assertions of nonracial or cultural mixing between these post-contact peoples negates the existence of generations of my Ancestors. This erasure is not uncommon, as evidenced by racialized legislative practices in Louisiana that sought to classify our communities as White (Cajun) and Black (Creole), completely negating the Native by asserting our tribes had disappeared early in post-contact Louisiana.

The issue then, for Creoles of Louisiana within the homeland and in the diaspora, is that others have identified us without any real knowledge or understanding of the difference between race and ethnicity. Michael Omi and Howard Winant's sociological definition of race as a social construct, where racial categories are determined by political, social, and economic forces, places race as socialized identity.[8] Ethnicity, on the other hand, relates to communities who share a "behavioral map" or "matrix," including kinship, linguistic, religious, territorial, and blood relational ties.[9] Given these, we can certainly argue, as Prud'homme-Cranford does, that Louisiana Creoles are indeed a cultural group, as is her argument for post-contact Indigeneity: we are indeed "culturally and historically grounded in lived realities and traditional homespaces of Indigenous peoples." Given Clifford Geertz's definitive study of culture and Prud'homme-Cranford's carefully detailed and constructed argument, we can see that Creole people meet the definitions of a cultural, ethnic, historical, linguistic, and land-based people. Moreover, Prud'homme-Cranford's own positionality, like my own inheritance, is one of not only "Black" Creole, and "White" Cajun, but southeastern Native American, and specific Freedmen descent. It positions her with a unique understanding of Black-Native relations as well as sovereignty: "Recognizing and tracing Louisiana Creoles as their own specific post-contact Afro-Indigenous communities means doing this while recognizing and upholding the rights of sovereign nationhood within Indian country, while also challenging our rights to what cultural belonging and sustainability means as disenfranchised Afro-Indigenous peoples under UNDRIP."

When I was in fourth grade, we were asked to self-identify our ethnic and cultural groups for an annual school demographic survey. I grew up in a predominantly white, upper-middle-class community. There were only four families of color: my family of origin was one, my cousins were one of the other, and our neighbors two streets over were the last. Of those four families, three (including mine and my cousins') were racially mixed: our two Creole families, including my aunt's

Japanese American identity (meaning my cousins are half Japanese American, and half an admixture of Louisiana French, Tunica-Choctaw-Biloxi, Attakapas-Ishak, and Black), and the other family's one Japanese from Japan parent and the other Cherokee/Creek Freedman (Cherokee/Creek and Black). The teacher asked, in class, what we identified with. Calling out the categories, most of the students raised their hands for white when she called out the white, or Caucasian, category. Next she called out the Black category. Several of my peers turned and looked at me, and I looked back at them. When I did not raise my hand, they insisted, rather quietly and under their breaths, that I raise do so. Culturally, I was not Black. Ethnically, I was not black, nor was I white. When the teacher called out American Indian, I raised my hand. I of course was the only self-identified American Indian in the class. My Indigeneity has always been called into question by others because of my Creole identity, and how we Creoles are perceived on that Black/White paradigm; nor are we seen as wholly American Indian (we really aren't wholly one thing or the other), but a mixed-race Indigenous people whose American Indian Ancestors emerged from the mounds in Mississippi to greet the Sun, and continued moving, evolving, and mixing culturally for the survival of our peoples.

This is one of the first books, maybe the only one, that discusses Creole identity along the Peoplehood matrix of the twenty-first century. Because we are a culture, language, kin, landed communities, and religion that has resulted in a mixed-race status that is not recognized by almost any state, nor the federal government, as what Prud'homme-Cranford calls a post-contact Afro-Indigenous people and community (tied to specific histories and lands) we lack the status afforded to other such communities. The argument that we reside in a type of limbo is completely accurate: we are not recognized as Indigenous peoples; we are not wholly black and do not ascribe ourselves culturally as Black Americans; nor do we identify as wholly White Americans either. The difference between "White passing," or *passe blanc*, and Darryl Barthé's term "situational passing," is that some Creoles across the diaspora may be identified by others as White, yet these Creoles do not deny their "otherness"—that is, their Native and African identities. While trying to fit into a paradigm of "Otherness," that is the classification of race as one or the other to fit who we are, we are a people who do not fit into one or the other. We are a people whose language, culture, lifeways (including our often co-opted culinary traditions), and landbase have been dictated to us. The racial classifications do not fit us, and they never will, and the time for us to assert our Franco/Latinx Afro-Indigeneity is not just now, but it always has been, since both pre- and post-contact.

NOTES

1. Megan Romer, "What's the Difference between Creole and Cajun," TripSavvy, updated May 28, 2019, www.tripsavvy.com.
2. Romer.
3. Romer.
4. Kevin Farrell, "This Is the Difference between Cajun and Creole," USA Today 10Best, March 19, 2018, www.10best.com.
5. Farrell.
6. Farrell.
7. See Prud'homme-Cranford's extensive discussion of the Peoplehood matrix, a theory of relational, land-based identity formation first introduced by Cherokee scholar Robert Thomas, and a further developed concept introduced later by Indigenous scholars Tom Holm (Mvskoke Creek / Cherokee) and Ben Davis (Lumbee) with their colleague J. Diane Pearson. I also have argued elsewhere in my scholarly work that the concept of tribalography, Choctaw playwright/novelist and scholar LeAnne Howe's theory of cultural performativity specifically attributed to American Indian nations, is a theoretical praxis that Creole identities fall under. See Carolyn M. Dunn, "First People's First," Pangea World Theatre, 2009, www.pangeaworldtheater.org.
8. Michael Omi and Howard Winant, *Racial Formation in the United States* (New York: Routledge, 1986), 66.
9. Clifford Geertz, *The Interpretation of Cultures* (New York: Basic Books, 1973), 5–6.

CHAPTER 2

SPEAK WHITE, SPEAK BLACK, SPEAK AMERICAN

Assimilation in Creole New Orleans

DARRYL BARTHÉ

From the earliest colonial encounters, through the Civil War and Reconstruction, Creole spaces and American spaces in the city of New Orleans have been constructed in opposition to one another. The process through which Louisiana Creole people in New Orleans were compelled to imagine themselves, and their community, as "American," involved the establishing of an Anglo-American ethno-linguistic, and racial, social order. This was accomplished in the early twentieth century through mandatory English-language education and Jim Crow, but also through the promise of upward mobility and material prosperity, for those Creoles willing (and able) to "Americanize."

It is telling that this place, known by the Choctaw as "the place of foreign tongues," would only become "American" through the imposition of English.[1] For New Orleans's Creole community, however, "becoming American" involved not only the adaptation of a new linguistic identity, but also the adaptation of a new language based around settler-colonial constructs of race and ethnicity. Creoles navigated this language of race in protean modes: morphing from "Frenchmen" to "Indians" to "Free People of Color" to "Colored" to "Negro" or to "Whites" (and, sometimes either, or, or any of the above, situationally). For Creoles, who could pass for white, and who were willing to accept white caste propriety, becoming "American" brought with it the promise of opportunity to pursue the American Dream, and therefore economic and social prosperity.

ENCOUNTERS BETWEEN CREOLES AND KAINTOCKS

In 1832, Washington Irving produced an account of his journey into the western frontier of the United States, land that had been acquired through the Louisiana Purchase. Irving's companions in *A Tour on the Prairies* included a number of memorable characters. Two were Europeans, one from England and the other from Switzerland. In St. Louis, these three intrepid tourists were joined by the Creole Tonish:

> a personage of inferior rank, but of all-pervading and prevalent importance: the squire, the groom, the cook, the tent man, in a word, the factotum, and, I may add, the universal meddler and marplot of our party. This was a little, swarthy, meagre, French Creole, named Antoine, but familiarly dubbed Tonish: a kind of Gil Bias of the frontiers, who had passed a scrambling life, sometimes among white men, sometimes among Indians; sometimes in the employ of traders, missionaries, and Indian agents; sometimes mingling with the Osage hunters. We picked him up at St. Louis, near which he has a small farm, an Indian wife, and a brood of half-blood children. According to his own account, however, he had a wife in every tribe; in fact, if all this little vagabond said of himself were to be believed, he was without morals, without caste, without creed, without country, and even without language; for he spoke a jargon of mingled French, English, and Osage. He was, withal, a notorious braggart, and a liar of the first water.[2]

Irving's commentary reveals much about the way Anglo-Americans perceived the people created in the colonial encounters of Latin America: "swarthy," "without morals, without caste, without creed, without country, and even without language." These were the traditional arguments offered in justification for the dispossession and enslavement of Indigenous people in the Western Hemisphere, and of Africans, echoing the sixteenth-century Spanish jurist Sepulveda, who demanded that "persons of inborn rudeness and of inhuman and barbarous customs" were "natural slaves" and that civilized people were, by contrast, the "natural lords" of such people.[3]

In Chouteau, Oklahoma, Irving introduced two more Creoles. The first, also named Antoine, Irving described as having "a vehement propensity to do nothing, being one of the worthless brood engendered and brought up among the (Catholic) missions . . . a little spoiled by being really a handsome young fellow, an Adonis of the frontier, and still worse by fancying himself highly connected, his sister being concubine to an opulent white trader!"[4] The second Creole to join Irving's company in Chouteau is a hunter, Pierre Beatte, who is offered to readers as an archetypical "noble savage," imbued with both menace and wonder, in equal parts:

> I confess I did not like his looks when he was first presented to me. . . . His features were not bad, being shaped not unlike those of Napoleon, but sharpened up, with high Indian cheek-bones. Perhaps the dusky greenish hue of his complexion aided his resemblance to an old bronze bust I had seen of the Emperor. He had, however, a sullen, saturnine expression, set off by a slouched woolen hat, and elf locks that hung about his ears. Such was the appearance of the man, and his manners were equally unprepossessing. He was cold and laconic. . . . He had altogether more of the red than the white man in his composition; and as I had been taught to look upon all half-breeds with distrust, as an uncertain and faithless race, I would gladly have dispensed with the services of Pierre Beatte.[5]

This "uncertain and faithless" race that left Irving (and his readers) so full of dread and wariness were the people of the "Creole Crescent." The Creole Crescent includes the territory encompassing Acadia, Quebec, the "Creole Corridor" (including what was once the northern Louisiana Territory) extending down through present-day Louisiana and western Mississippi, and then south and east into the Gulf, and the Caribbean beyond.

Jean-Baptiste Colbert, the comptroller general of finance and minister to New France under Louis XIV from 1665 to 1683, demanded that French colonists, in cooperation with the Roman Catholic Church, "civilize the . . . savages who have embraced Christianity, and dispose them to come and settle them in the community with the French, live with them, and bring up their children in their manner and customs . . . in order that, having one law and one master, they may form only one people and one blood."⁶ This colonial imperative resulted in the emergence of Indigenous communities of people of mixed heritage everywhere the French extended their influence in the Western Hemisphere. The people of these communities identify themselves in many ways and include French Canadians, Métis (and métis), Acadians (and "Cajuns"), Creoles (and Kréyols), and Haitians.

This policy, embodied and exemplified by the French *coureurs des bois* and *voyageurs*, ultimately found their pinnacle expression in both the Métis people of Canada and the Creole people of Louisiana. Roman Catholic vicar-general Henri Rouleaux de La Vente, in promoting the policy of "one blood," went as far as to proclaim that "the blood of the savages does no harm to the blood of the French," and defended those "Euro-Louisianians" who wished to intermarry with women of color (provided, of course, that those women were Catholic).⁷

In 1992, anthropologist Ulf Hannerz observed "Creole cultures—like creole languages—are intrinsically of mixed origin, the confluence of two or more widely separated historical currents . . . [that] come out of multi-dimensional cultural encounters." The French's "one blood" policies that so encouraged métissage (that is, "interracial marriage" or "miscegenation") were also accompanied by processes of creolization resulting in the emergence of French-lexicon based Creole languages throughout the Creole Crescent including Michif, Haitian Kréyol, and Louisiana Creole, or Kouri-Vini.⁸

FRANCÉ NÉG

Kouri-Vini, the Louisiana Creole language, had always been known by different names. It was often referred to simply as "Creole," but was also known as "broken French," and by outsiders particularly as "gumbo French" or "patois." Louisiana Creole was also called "Francé Nég," vulgarly translated as "nigger French."

I would argue it is the last moniker, "nigger French," that promises the clearest vantage on this most curious intersection of race, nation, and linguistic identity. Kouri-Vini was, and is still, spoken by people from every walk of life. However, the association of Kouri-Vini, and French more generally, with nonwhite people, spelled doom for the people of Louisiana's Francophone and Creolophone communities after 1803.

LOUISIANA, USA

The operational ideology of British colonization in North America differed significantly from the French. Far from promoting métissage, Anglo-American colonial contexts were more often actively opposed to it. The Anglo-Americans were not Creoles; Anglo-Americans, if anything, were anti-Creoles. As historian Adam Rothman makes clear, the Anglo-American settlers who pushed into the Lower Mississippi River Valley after the Louisiana Purchase were intent on turning Louisiana into "slave country," as they'd known it in Virginia, and Carolina, where Africans were often regarded as a separate species of beings, designed specifically for enslavement by Europeans.

For Louisiana's Creoles, the arrival of thousands of white settlers and African American slaves from the United States represented unwelcomed challenges to the social order that had prevailed under both the French and the Spanish. The rigidity and characteristic severity associated with the racist American slave regime in Louisiana proved particularly troubling for those free Creoles of color who had historically navigated between (and sometimes across) racial boundaries.[9] After emancipation, when all people of color became, nominally, "free," Creoles of color who did not present themselves, and pass, as white people, found themselves relegated to the same racialized caste position (in relation to full citizenship, which was reserved only for "whites") as those who had been enslaved.

The explicit articulation of the United States' post-emancipation white supremacist legal regime was accomplished in 1896 through the US Supreme Court's verdict in *Plessy v. Ferguson*, in direct contention to *passe blanc* New Orleans Creole Homer Plessy. While the US Supreme Court agreed that racial separation was constitutional, provided that separation entailed equality, the majority decision was issued with the caveat that the Justices were not convinced that the phenotypically white Homer Plessy was, in fact, a person of color given his appearance. Though the Supreme Court suggested that Plessy challenge his blackness in court, Plessy never bothered.[10]

AMERICANISM AND AMERICANIZATION

The United States entered the twentieth century as a Jim Crow nation, and at the helm was Theodore Roosevelt, president of the United

States from 1901 until 1909. Roosevelt, in the words of historian Robert Wiebe, was "a man of unlovely traits" who "nursed harsh personal prejudices," "relished killing human beings," and was an ardent proponent of an aggressive "New Nationalism."[11] Just three days before his death in January 1919, Roosevelt articulated the position of the American hegemon in a letter to his acquaintance Richard Hurd:

> There must be no sagging back in the fight for Americanism . . . There are plenty of persons who have already made the assertion that they believe the American people have a short memory and that they intend to revive all the foreign associations which most directly interfere with the complete Americanization of our people. . . . There can be no divided allegiance here. . . . We have but room for one flag, the American flag . . . We have but room for one language here and that is the English language, for we intend to see that the crucible turns our people out as Americans, of American nationality, and not as a polyglot boarding house.[12]

Roosevelt's comments were directed at European immigrants who, if willing to assimilate and become "American," could expect to be "treated on an exact equality with every one else, for it is an outrage to discriminate against any such man because of creed, or birthplace or origin."[13] However, understood in light of the *Plessy* verdict, perhaps some qualification of Roosevelt's comments are in order. After all, what European immigrant braved the Atlantic crossing in hopes of being escorted to jail by law enforcement for having a seat in a train car reserved for Whites only?

New Orleans Creoles *were not* immigrants, but they still had no legal claim to the "exact equality with every one" available to foreign-born (white European) immigrants that Roosevelt mentioned in his missive. When Roosevelt decried the "hyphenated American" in 1915, he had demanded that

> the one absolutely certain way of bringing this nation to ruin, of preventing all possibility of it continuing to be a nation at all, would be to permit it to become a tangle of squabbling nationalities, an intricate knot of German-Americans, Irish-Americans, English-Americans, French-Americans, Scandinavian-Americans, or Italian-Americans each preserving its saperet [sic] nationality,

each at heart feeling more sympathy with Europeans of that nationality than with the other citizens of the American Republic.[14]

Roosevelt's inclusion of "English-Americans" among the list of unacceptable hyphenated identities must have seemed like a magnanimous courtesy to the predominately Irish Catholic crowd of Knights of Columbus gathered at Carnegie Hall that evening. Yet, for all his magnanimity, it is doubtful that anyone in the crowd took those flattering words at face value. It was the privilege of Anglo-American elites, like Roosevelt (himself of Dutch heritage), to imagine their own context and perspective as "the norm" to which other prospective Americans ought to conform.

As Robert Wiebe observed:

> Few found it possible to deny that somehow the United States was caught up with Britain in a common destiny, a vague yet compelling belief that the American Negro soldier captured with grim unintentional humor when he spoke proudly about "us angry Saxons." Even the citizens accused of being "German-American" or "Irish-American" never thought to retaliate with "British-American," for fundamentally "British-American" was the norm by which one calculated deviations. "Anglophile," the closest counterpart, carried none of the hyphen's divisive, disloyal connotations.[15]

It is telling that Roosevelt's musing on prospective citizens included no "Japanese-Americans" or "Chinese-Americans." Nowhere in Roosevelt's nationalist diatribe was there any mention of "Native/Indigenous-Americans" much less "African-Americans," and certainly there was no mention of Creoles. Creoles in New Orleans at the beginning of the twentieth century were foreigners in their own country, a country that many of their ancestors had occupied since antiquity. As Carolyn Dunn has stated, Louisiana Creoles became "a dispossessed people, a people not recognized by government entities as white, Indian, or black."[16] Rendered politically powerless as a community, Creoles were disenfranchised and at the mercy of white men who, for the most part, regarded them as racially inferior, who did not speak their language, and who referred to the Creole population in racially derogatory terms.

As the nineteenth century rolled into the twentieth, Creoles were forced to accept not only Anglo-American notions of racial propriety but also the language of the Americans after white Anglo-American legislators in Louisiana made it illegal for Creoles to educate their children in their own language in 1916. The transition to English-only education in Louisiana reflected a new national, political, and economic order that might have inspired more resistance if it did not bring with it the promise of an abundance of economic opportunities for English speakers in faraway places like Chicago and Los Angeles and New York, especially if those English speakers looked white.

AMERICAN OPPORTUNITIES

Legendary New Orleans Creole Civil Rights attorney A. P. Tureaud recalled moving to Chicago as a young man in search of job opportunities.

> They were advertising for whites. They wouldn't take Negroes, even in a job like elevator attendant.... In every case where there was an opportunity for [*passe blanc* Creoles] to do so, they would take these jobs. Normally some of those people were too dark to be white in New Orleans; they would be easily identifiable as colored. But in Chicago they wouldn't know that much difference between them. In cases where the hair was the determinant, they'd cut their hair short. Or sometimes, they would use an accent.[17]

When the work day was done, these *passe blanc* Creoles in Chicago would go home to their families in their transplanted communities and resume their lives as people of color, enjoying "dinner and gumbos" with other Creoles who had also made the journey to the Windy City.[18] This history of Creole con artists pilfering the privileges of whiteness, by its nature, does not lend itself to an abundance of case studies. Again, because the order of the day was "don't ask, don't tell," many chose not to ever speak of such things. Still, there are certainly a few high-profile stories demonstrating this dynamic that A. P. Tureaud describes. Perhaps the most compelling of them is that of the creator of the syndicated comic strip *Krazy Kat*, George Joseph Herriman.

George Joseph Herriman's paternal family origins in North America extend to the early seventeenth century and a man named John Harriman from Uldale, Cumberland, England, who settled in Massachusetts. His great grandfather, Stephen Herriman, was born in Jamaica, Queens, in New York, but moved to New Orleans in the 1850s with his wife, Jeannette Spencer, also from New York.[19] His grandfather, George Herriman Sr., married a Creole woman named Justine Olivier, who appears in the 1850 census as a "mulatto" born in Louisiana in 1797.[20] Both George Herriman Sr. and his son, George Herriman Jr., were members of the seminal New Orleans Creole fraternal society, the Fraternité #20 Masonic Lodge.[21] George Herriman Jr. married Clara Morel, both of whom appear in the 1880 US census as "mulatto" and both of whom reported having been born in Louisiana.[22]

According to the most comprehensive biography of George Joseph Herriman's life, *Krazy Kat: The Comic Art of George Herriman*, Herriman identified himself to his friends as a Creole and ascribed his "kinky hair" to what he suspected was his "Negro blood."[23] It is unlikely that he shared these suspicions with his colleagues, however, which led some of his contemporaries to invent ethnic biographies for him. Comics journalist Jeet Heer said it best in a 2011 article, noting that "Herriman . . . didn't just pass for white, rather he became an ethnic chameleon. His colleagues and friends at various times referred to him as Greek, French, Irish, and Turkish, and he himself dreamed of returning to life as a Navajo: he was of all races and of no race."[24] George Joseph Herriman never claimed his African heritage publicly and thus forged a career for himself in a profession where people of color had no representation at all. Like Tureaud's job at the bakery, Herriman's livelihood rested on the *assumption* that he was white. Unlike Tureaud's bosses, Herriman's employer, William Randolph Hearst, was never apprised of his nonwhite ancestry. Because he was willing to remain silent as to the details of his ancestry, Herriman kept his job.

At the time of the 1900 census, George Herriman Jr.'s family lived in Los Angeles, where they were listed as "white."[25] While it is possible that the Herrimans identified themselves as white, the responsibility of recording the race of respondents fell to census workers who were directed to record respondents' race as they perceived it, not necessarily as respondents identified themselves. In the 1900 census, George Herriman Jr.'s parents' birthplace is listed as "France," but if he were asked "Where were your parents from?" it is not unlikely that he would respond "Ye français" or, in English, "They (are/were) French," which is how many Creoles referred to themselves.

Equally compelling is the story of Anatole Broyard, the original hipster, whose great-grandfather Henry Broyard allegedly passed as a *gen de colour* in order to marry Marie Pauline Bonée, the daughter of free colored refugees from the Haitian Revolution who had settled in Louisiana. His grandfather, Paul Broyard, served in the Louisiana Native Guard in its initial incarnation as a Confederate unit and in its reincarnation as a Union regiment. In fact, Paul Broyard fought at the battle of Port Hudson with the legendary Creole André Cailloux, who claimed to be of "pure African" ancestry.[26] Broyard's parents moved from New Orleans to New York City during the Depression. During World War II, Broyard enlisted for service in the army.

Remembering A. P. Tureaud's observations about Creoles relocating to Chicago, it seems that the recruiting agents in New York did not see a black man, or even a Creole, when they saw the young Anatole. They saw a white man, which is how they listed his race. As a white man, Broyard was able to apply for the Officer Corps, for which he was accepted and, as Brent Staples observed in an editorial about Broyard from 2003, like 150,000 other men classified as "colored" prior to the war, "sailed permanently into whiteness during the 1940's."[27]

Released from the constraints of black caste identification, Broyard became a bohemian bookstore owner in Greenwich Village, New York City. Eventually, his talent for writing would bring him to positions of instruction at the city's major universities, NYU and Columbia, as well as the position of reviewer at the *New York Times*, for which he is best known. Removed from the context of the Creole community in New Orleans, there was no barrier for the phenotypically (Mediterranean) European Broyard to embrace whiteness—beyond the pressures of his own conscience. With a native command of the English language, there was no barrier for the "white" Broyard to full participation in the American Dream.

CONCLUSIONS: CREOLE AMERICANS

The late Gilbert E. Martin Sr., a Louisiana Creole activist, recalled being a "young Creole growing up during the Great Depression and the Jitterbug era" not knowing why his elders hated the Americans so much.²⁸ For Martin, the American community and the Creole community were self-evidently distinct from one another, with a "natural" resentment for the former embraced by the latter. This resentment, at times, was racialized, but not always: sometimes the "Americans" were white, but sometimes they were not. For Martin, the beginning of the true abatement of Creole hostility for their American neighbors, and a sign of the waning of a self-conscious Creole identity separate from American identity, was World War II. Wartime propaganda made it impossible to equivocate: Creoles in New Orleans were, nominally, citizens of the state of Louisiana and, thus, of the United States of America. And as such the government of the United States of America needed every man it could muster in the fight against the Axis Powers. Service in World War II cultivated a truly "American" sensibility among many Creoles that had never existed before.

Henry Oubre was a cook in the US Navy during World War II. Before his time in the service, he had never ventured far from Vacherie, Louisiana, except to go to New Orleans. In a July 2013 interview, Oubre recalled a sense of camaraderie with his American crewmates, both on the ship and at port, that had a powerful influence on him. His quarters were not segregated, for example, and every night he slept between two white crewmates. Together, he and his fellow sailors went on the town in northern cities in places like New York, Massachusetts, and Quebec.²⁹ This is not to say, however, that his experience was free of the stain of ethno-racial marginalization. He recalled that the "white boys" on ship treated him differently from his African American crewmates, who hailed from Memphis, Tennessee, and Cambridge, Massachusetts. Though Oubre would go drinking with his white crewmates, they did not associate with the African Americans sailors, in part because the African American sailors were more antagonistic toward them. According to Oubre, his African American crewmates also viewed him with a sense of otherness as his self-identification as a Louisiana Creole aroused their suspicions that he might practice voodoo. Still, none of these stories, anecdotal as they are, address the larger issues of racial discrimination that Oubre experienced serving in the US military as a black man.³⁰

Oubre described his struggle during World War II as a conflict against "two enemies . . . because they had the Germans that was the enemy and they had [American] Whites that was the enemy, too . . . white supremacists." Oubre was a cook because black men in the navy could only be cooks or stewards. Oubre's voice took on a mournful tone when he recounted seeing black men with "two years of college" serving white officers as valets aboard ship. He also recalled the humiliation of arriving in the train station in Atlanta en route home to Louisiana and, though dressed in full uniform, being refused service in a restaurant where he saw German POWs eating and enjoying themselves. Oubre had served under the American flag in the North Atlantic and the South Pacific, but Atlanta was a more welcoming place for Nazis than it was for a person of color like himself.[31]

Henry Oubre was a sailor in the US Navy who had proudly served his country, but back home in New Orleans, dressed in his uniform, he pretended to be from India in order to avoid racist victimization by a white man who, rather than serve in the military, had stayed home where he "made big money all during the war." Oubre recalled visiting his sister after coming home from the war and taking his nieces to a movie theater in Jim Crow New Orleans:

> Let me tell you something about how stupid segregation is . . . I stayed in the South Pacific, on my ship, for over a year, you know . . . I came back home . . . [My nieces and I] walked to that little theater and I failed to realize where I was . . . They had a bar and restaurant across the street [from the theater]. We got our tickets to go in the theater but we had to wait a while. I was out of cigarettes so I fooled around and walked across the street and went in [the segregated bar and restaurant] on the white side and asked for change for a dollar because cigarettes were maybe something like forty cents . . . The door happened to open and I saw all these black people because the kitchen was between the two—the white side and the black side. Well, when they opened the door, I must have shown some kind of expression because this white boy came to me and asked me, "Are you a nigger? What are you?" I said, "No, I was born in India and raised in New York." This damn fool bought me two double whiskeys. He kept apologizing to me . . . Believe it or not, you know, I was a candidate for an ass-whipping even in my uniform.[32]

By the end of World War II, Creoles in New Orleans had been thoroughly Americanized. As highlighted in this chapter, the transformation of ethnic identity from Creole to American that began in 1803 was accelerated in the twentieth century through the imposition of Jim Crow segregation and English-only schooling, but by no means was Americanization always accomplished through coercive influences. Creoles participated in the Great Migration and started new lives, like millions of other immigrants in American cities like Chicago, New York, and Los Angeles where they reinvented themselves as Americans. Sometimes, in reinventing themselves as Americans, Creoles reinvented themselves as Whites. In post–World War II New Orleans, many Creoles still maneuvered between racialized color lines, situationally, just like their frontier ancestors, those twilight people who hovered "about the confines of light and darkness," like bats.[33] Yet, racial lines in Louisiana had hardened considerably by the end of WWII. Creoles in postwar New Orleans were sometimes regarded as white, but more often they were not. The persistence of racist marginalization and Indigenous multiethnic erasure, directed at the Creole community, compelled Creoles in New Orleans to embrace the struggle for black civil rights and to stand with other people of color in the United States in a solidarity based on an explicitly American language of racial identity.

NOTES

1 See Jeffery U. Darensbourg, *Bulbancha Is Still a Place: Indigenous Culture from New Orleans #1* (Bulbancha: POC Zine Project, 2018). An alternate translation is also "where many languages are spoken."
2 Washington Irving, *A Tour on the Prairies* (London: John Murray Albemarle Street, 1835), 6–7.
3 Lewis Hanke, *Aristotle and the American Indians: A Study of Race Prejudice in the Modern World* (London: Hollis and Carter, 1959), 44–45.
4 Irving, *Tour on the Prairies*, 12.
5 Irving, 19–20.
6 From 1666 and 1667 dispatches quoted in Samuel Mack Eastman, *Church and State in Early Canada* (Edinburgh: T. & A. Comstable, 1915), quoted in Jerah Johnson, "Colonial New Orleans: A Fragment of the Eighteenth-Century French Ethos," in *Creole New Orleans: Race and Americanization*, ed. Arnold R. Hirsch and Joseph Logsdon (Baton Rouge: Louisiana State University Press, 1992), 22–35; emphasis mine.
7 See Jennifer M. Spear, *Race, Sex, and Social Order in Early New Orleans* (Baltimore: Johns Hopkins University Press, 2008), 33–34.
8 See Prud'homme-Cranford's contribution to this volume for commentary on both the connection between linguistic identity and "peoplehood,"

and to Mayeux's on the significance of "Kouri-Vini" as a distinct identifier of the language of Louisiana Creoles.
9   Adam Rothman, *Slave Country: American Expansion and the Origins of the Deep South* (Cambridge, MA: Harvard University Press, 2007), 37–40. See also Joseph G. Tregle Jr., "Early New Orleans Society: A Reappraisal," *Journal of Southern History* 18, no. 1 (February 1952): 20–36; Joseph G. Tregle Jr., *Louisiana in the Age of Jackson: A Clash of Cultures and Personalities* (Baton Rouge: Louisiana State University Press, 1999).
10 Plessy v. Ferguson, 163 US 537 (1896), available online at www.law.cornell.edu/supct/html/historics/USSC_CR_0163_0537_ZO.html.
11 See Theodore Roosevelt, *The New Nationalism* (New York: Outlook Publishing, 1910); and Robert Wiebe, *The Search for Order, 1877–1920* (New York: Farrar, Straus and Giroux, 1967), 189.
12 Theodore Roosevelt, letter to Richard Hurd, January 3, 1919, digital reproduction of copy from Transcript Division, Library of Congress, available online at www.theodorerooseveltcenter.org/Research/Digital-Library/Record?libID=o265602.
13 Roosevelt.
14 "Roosevelt Bars the Hyphenated," *New York Times*, October 13, 1915.
15 Wiebe, *Search for Order*, 257–58.
16 Carolyn M. Dunn, "How I Gots My Gumbo Ghosts," in *Smoked Mullet Cornbread Crawdad Memory*, by Rain C. Goméz (Norman, OK: Mongrel Empire Press, 2012), iv.
17 Photocopy of typescript of interview of A. P. Tureaud by Dr. Joseph Logsdon, box 164-1, pp. 72–73, A. P. Tureaud Collection, Earl K. Long Special Collections, University of New Orleans.
18 Tureaud-Logsdon.
19 Biographical information on John Harriman derived from "Lhota Family Tree: John Harriman" accessible online with source citations at http://trees.ancestry.com/tree/26105659/person/2038058367 (accessed August 8, 2014).
20 US Federal Census 1850, New Orleans Municipality 3, Ward 1, Orleans, Louisiana, roll M432_238, page 46B, image 97.
21 Minutes books for meetings of Fraternité #20 show George Herriman and George Herriman Jr. George Longe Collection, Amistad Research Center, Tulane University. See also Caryn Cossé Bell, *Revolution, Romanticism, and the Afro-Creole Protest Tradition in Louisiana, 1718–1868* (Baton Rouge: Louisiana State University Press, 1995), 290.
22 US Federal Census 1880, New Orleans, Orleans, Louisiana, roll 462; family history film 1254462, page 596B, enumeration district, 051, image 0174. Also, it is worth pointing out that the term "mulatto" and "mulâtre" were terms that had historically been applied to mixed-Indigenous people as well. See the letter from Jean-Baptiste Duclos to Antoine de Cadillac, governor of Detroit, dated December 25, 1715, Archives de colonies, Archives nationales de France, series C13a, 3:819–24,

for conflation of the terms "métis" and "mulâtre." Jennifer Spears speaks to this discrepancy in usage between the Spanish and the French in *Race, Sex, and Social Order* (236). See also Gwendolyn Midlo-Hall, "African Women in French and Spanish Louisiana: Origins, Roles, Family, Work, Treatment," in *The Devil's Lane: Sex and Race in the Early South*, ed. Catherine Clinton and Michael Gillespie (New York: Oxford University Press, 1997), 249; Andrew J. Jolivétte, *Louisiana Creoles: Cultural Recovery and Mixed-Race Native American Identity* (New York: Lexington Books, 2007), 7; and Joan Martin, "*Plaçage* and the Louisiana *Gens de Couleur Libre*: How Race and Sex Defined the Lifestyle of Free Women of Color," in *Creole: The History and Legacy of Louisiana's Free People of Color*, ed. Sybil Kein (Baton Rouge: Louisiana State University Press, 2000), 59.

23 Patrick McDonnell, Karen O'Connell, and Georgia Riley de Havenon, *Krazy Kat: The Comic Art of George Herriman* (New York: Abrams, 1986), 30.

24 Jeet Heer, "Racism as a Stylistic Choice and Other Notes," *The Comics Journal*, March 14, 2011, www.tcj.com.

25 US Federal Census 1900, Los Angeles Ward 6, Los Angeles, California, roll 90, page 14B, enumeration district 0052, FHL microfilm 1240090.

26 "Who Are the Creoles?," ACC 11, Literary and Historical Manuscripts, box 12, Historical C–F, Marcus Christian Collection, Earl K. Long Special Collections, University of New Orleans. See also Bell, *Revolution, Romanticism, and the Afro-Creole Protest Tradition*, 240; Ochs, *A Black Patriot and a White Priest: Andre Cailloux and Claude Paschal Maistre in Civil War New Orleans* (Baton Rouge: Louisiana State University Press, 2006), 68–87; and Rodolphe Desdunes's recollections of André Cailloux from *Our People and Our History* (n.p.: Pelican Publishing Co., 2015), 124–25. The definitive account of the 54th Regiment Massachusetts Volunteer Infantry regiment, the subject of a popular 1989 Hollywood film, is the first-person account written by Captain Luis F. Emilio, *A Brave Black Regiment: The History of the Fifty-Fourth Regiment of Massachusetts Volunteer Infantry, 1863–1865* (Cambridge, MA: Da Capo Press, 1995). See also Bliss Broyard, *One Drop: My Father's Hidden Life—A Story of Race and Family Secrets* (New York: Little, Brown and Company, 2007); the Native Guard roster from James G. Hollandsworth, *The Louisiana Native Guards: The Black Military Experience during the Civil War* (Baton Rouge: Louisiana State University Press, 1995), appendix; and National Park Service of the US Department of the Interior, "Soldiers and Sailors Database," searchable database at www.nps.gov/civilwar/soldiers-and-sailors-database.htm.

27 Brent Staples, "Editorial Observer; Back When Skin Color Was Destiny, Unless You Passed for White," *New York Times*, September 7, 2003.

28 See Gilbert E. Martin Sr., "The Creoles Promised Treaty Rights," French-Creoles.com, accessed Mary 18, 2013, www.frenchcreoles.com. See also

Gilbert E. Martin Sr., *French Creoles: A Shattered Nation* (Montgomery, AL: E-Booktime LLC, 2006).

29 Henry Oubre, interview by the author, July 28, 2013, recording in the author's possession.
30 Oubre.
31 Oubre.
32 Oubre.
33 Irving, *Tour on the Prairies*, 20–21.

COMMUNITY RESPONSE

THE RACIALIZATION OF CREOLE IDENTITY AND HERITAGE LANGUAGE LOSS

JOSEPH DUNN

Modern perceptions of identity, especially in the United States, are mostly informed by skin color, racial designations, and genealogy. Rarely do monolingual English-speaking Americans consider the question of language as a main characteristic of identity. In this chapter, I will explore the links between the institutionalized segregation of Louisiana's French and Creole language heritage speakers in the early twentieth century and the resultant rapid decline in these languages following World War II.

In 1699, French explorers declared sovereignty over land that they would call "Louisiana." Throughout the succeeding century and until the transfer of the territory to the United States in 1803, the Lower Mississippi River Valley, and westward areas that roughly resemble the modern state of Louisiana, would be populated not only by thousands of Indigenous people, but also by European colonists of mostly French, German, and Spanish extraction, enslaved Africans, and Acadian refugees from Atlantic Canada. The French language and its Louisiana Creole counterpart (also now known vernacularly as "Kouri-Vini") became the principal languages spoken by this diverse population.

Three years later, following the military defeat of French troops by revolutionaries in Haiti, Bonaparte sold Louisiana to the United

States, an act that precipitated a flood of Americans that poured into the territory seeking land and economic opportunity. It was, at least partially, in reaction to that American immigration that a stalwart Louisiana Creole identity emerged.

This new Louisiana Creole identity was defined by native birth; the French, Creole, and/or Spanish languages; and the Roman Catholic faith. Transcending race, "Creole" was claimed by people of White, Black, and mixed-race heritage. It also included the descendants of Acadian exiles (known today in English as "Cajuns") as evidenced in countless French-language historical documents, ecclesiastical records, francophone literature, and transactions and inventories involving enslaved people.[1] As Rien Fertel writes in his 2014 work *Imagining the Creole City: The Rise of Literary Culture in Nineteenth-Century New Orleans*, in "nineteenth century New Orleans the designation Creole operated as a birthright, a symbol of exceptionality, and an identity marker."[2] There was power embedded in the word "Creole."

For this diverse population of Creoles, their identity was anchored in and defined by their heritage languages. To illustrate this intrinsic and personal relationship to the French language, the prominent (White) Creole physician and novelist Alfred Mercier wrote in 1883, "Le jour où on ne parle plus français en Louisiane ... il n'y aura plus de Créoles" ("The day when French is no longer spoken in Louisiana ... there will be no more Creoles").[3] Later, in the short story "Ma tante Louise," published in *Comptes-rendus de L'athénée louisianais* in July 1901 detailing Creole cemetery traditions on La Toussaint (All Saints' Day), Ulysse Marinoni describes the visit of the Uptown cousin to the family tomb: "Elle amenait ses boys, et tante Louise dut faire l'aimable en anglais (chose qu'elle détestait)" ("She brought her boys, and Aunt Louise had to make nice in English [a thing she hated]).[4] In short, for Mercier, Marinoni, and their contemporaries, "Creole" was synonymous with Francophone and set apart from "les Américains."

PUBLIC EDUCATION AND FORCED ASSIMILATION

Though education in the French language had regained some stability in Louisiana following the Civil War in the late nineteenth century, the first decades of the twentieth century would be turning points for Louisiana Creoles as Americanization brought further institutionalized racial segregation and forced assimilation into the English language.

As Shane Bernard notes in his *The Cajuns: Americanization of a People*, "the concept of Americanization has traditionally borne an undertone of Anglo-Saxonism. This ethnic bias has existed in America since colonial times and persisted into the twentieth century. It expressed itself in numerous ways, but it commonly centered on the issue of language."[5]

In 1916, the General Assembly of the Legislature of the State of Louisiana adopted Act 27, providing "for the compulsory school attendance of children between the ages of seven and fourteen."[6] Attendance could be in a public or private institution. However, these schools were racially segregated, first for White and "colored" children, and later for Native Americans.

Divided into three separate school systems, these French- and Creole-speaking children were separated from their Francophone/Creolophone peers. Five years later, in 1921, the State of Louisiana adopted a new constitution. Article XII, Section 12 reads, "The general exercises in the public schools shall be in the English language."[7]

The adoption of these English-language policies in Louisiana public education would have far-reaching implications on the identity of Louisiana Creoles and their descendants. Initially, this reconstruction was not voluntary, but forcibly imposed. Contrary to popular belief, the English-only education mandate did not make it illegal to speak French in public, nor did it target Creoles of Acadian descent (today's "Cajuns"). It applied to all heritage language groups in Louisiana, namely Francophones and Creolophones, Hispanophones, Germanophones, and of course speakers of Native American languages.

Application of the English-only rules seems to have varied from school to school, with some principals and teachers easing the schoolchildren into the new language, while others notoriously resorted to corporal punishment. There are innumerable firsthand accounts from older Louisiana Francophones and Creolophones describing these tactics to enforce English, from writing the lines "I will not speak French on the school grounds" to being forced to kneel on grains of rice. Among the accounts are stories of hands that were paddled for deviating from English. There are stories of children soiling themselves because they were incapable of asking in English to go to the toilet. Beyond the specter of corporal punishment, students were often subjected to psychological abuse and denigration by teachers who impressed on them the idea that their language was "bad," "broken," or "not real" French and that it was incomprehensible to Francophones beyond Louisiana. Despite being the mother tongue of tens of thousands of Louisiana schoolchildren, from every race and walk of life, until the Second World War, the French language, spoken in Louisiana since the founding of the colony in 1699, would henceforth be labeled and taught as a "foreign language" in the state's public schools. This remains the case as of this writing.

CONTEXTUAL EROSION OF LOUISIANA FRENCH AND CREOLE LINGUISTIC ECOSYSTEMS

Ahead of the public school system, Catholic schools in Louisiana had begun shifting instruction into English as early as 1906.[8] Nearly concurrent with the 1921 Constitution, historically Francophone Catholic churches in New Orleans began to transition from French into English in the 1920s, with some outlying, rural church parishes resisting the change until 1955.[9] Removed first from the educational sphere and then by the omnipresent and influential Catholic Church, the rapid decline of French as a lingua franca in Louisiana would achieve a critical velocity by the middle of the twentieth century.

Those children who began school as monolingual heritage language speakers would experience a targeted indoctrination in "American" values through immersion in the English language. At the same time, their intellectual and social development in French was abruptly interrupted. If one considers the language capacity of a French- or Creole-speaking child beginning first grade being forcibly assimilated/immersed into English in a public school classroom, it is easy to imagine the child's language capacity being restricted to what they were able to contextually absorb *before starting school*. In essence, their language development in French or Creole was greatly stunted or altogether ceased when they were six or seven years old. They never studied subject matter in French nor were they offered French language arts in school. As a result, Louisiana schoolchildren would be reprogrammed in English to believe that their own spoken language(s) were a substandard dialect far removed from the "Parisian French" taught in classrooms as a "foreign language," creating a relational disconnect to their heritage languages.

WORLD WAR II AND AMERICANIZATION

While the work of historian Shane Bernard focuses on Creoles of Acadian descent who now ethno-racially and genealogically self-describe as "Cajuns," one could easily substitute the word "Creole" for "Cajun," drawing parallel conclusions about assimilation and language loss. Bernard states, "It would take a historical event of unprecedented scale to trigger the rapid, widespread Americanization of the Cajun people, and that event was World War II," but this was as true for Creoles without Acadian heritage as it was for those with it.[10]

Following the war, service members who had been far away from the linguistic and social cocoons of their families and communities, fully immersed for the first time in English as a result of the US war effort, returned to Louisiana. These veterans, imbued with a newfound sense of national pride and belonging, embraced Americanism. Generational transmission of French in Cajun-identified households plummeted from 83 percent at the turn of the twentieth century to 21 percent for children born between 1956 and 1960.[11] Though research to date has almost exclusively focused on the French language in "Cajun" communities, it is not unlikely that heritage language transmission among Creole-identified households mirrored that of their Cajun relatives and neighbors. In this new postwar era, the English language became synonymous with economic prosperity. English was at the foundation of state educational requirements and, with the advent of (English) television programming, "American" identity itself. In light of these circumstances, the further decline of the French language in Louisiana commenced unabated.

Within one generation, a majority of adult Louisiana Creoles (including Cajuns) would make the conscious decision not to transmit their non-English heritage language(s) to their children. In part, this was a decision made to spare their children the social shame and physical punishment they had experienced in school themselves. It was also a decision made to offer their children greater social and economic mobility in a broader English-speaking America. English proficiency among Louisiana Creoles provided for greater opportunities particular with widespread American expansionism. As Barthé mentions in his chapter, many Creoles of color escaped Jim Crow during this time, relocating to places like New York, Chicago, and Los Angeles, where English proficiency was often a key to economic success.

ETHNIC PRIDE

The concept of language as a minority criterion is mostly unknown in the United States, since minority status in this country is generally claimed or conferred based on skin color, ethnic identity, and country of origin. Furthermore, because there is no de jure or official language of the United States, the idea that the dominant, majority language group controls historical and contemporary narratives, along with social, political, and economic spaces, is foreign to its citizenry.

The ethnic pride movements in the United States of the 1960s are clear illustrations of a shift away from language to race, especially among Creoles of color who migrated toward inclusion in the African American community. White Creoles often embraced a generic "American White ethnic" identity or, more generally, "French." For those who preferred to retain some connection to their heritage, there was a reclamation and embrace of the "Cajun" identity, which allowed some to proclaim their pre-American (i.e., Creole) heritage, while simultaneously distancing themselves from the perceived "Blackness" that came to be associated with the term "Creole."

CODOFIL AND THE FRENCH LANGUAGE RENAISSANCE

The Council for the Development of French in Louisiana (CODOFIL) was formed in 1968. The new agency was legislatively mandated to "do any and all things necessary to accomplish the development, utilization, and preservation of the French language as found in Louisiana for the cultural, economic and touristic benefit of the state."[12] Ironically, the only state agency in the United States charged with empowering heritage language speakers would be complicit in the racialization and division of these communities.

According to Québécois researcher Cécyle Trépanier, not only "was French Louisiana ethnically diversified, but compartmentalized geographically. . . . This geographical complexity was reinforced by social differentiation based on class. Given these circumstances, a viable, Louisiana-wide French ethnic consciousness has always been difficult to achieve." Trépanier continues, observing that despite "the fact the Creole identity had always carried a positive image for White and Black francophones of Southern Louisiana, it is under the Cajun label that CODOFIL proceeded to unify the region."[13] What Trépanier is describing is the reification of "Cajun" as a monolithic White identity that structurally and conceptually excludes non-White Creoles and even people of color of Acadian descent from the common narrative about French- and Creole-speaking Louisiana. CODOFIL, unfortunately, was complicit in this process.

Today, the historically Francophone and Creolophone people of Louisiana are often, and tragically, split along racial lines. White Francophones and Creolophones distanced themselves from their cousins of color by calling themselves "Cajun" and, despite the reality of centuries of transracial cultural production (not to mention métissage/Creolization in both Acadia and Louisiana), Black and Native American Francophones and Creolophones in Louisiana (even those with Acadian ancestry) mostly play along in identifying "Cajuns" as "White people."

CONCLUSION

Forged by voluntary and involuntary immigration, international political events, and its eventual transfer to the United States, Louisiana has been the crossroads of Indigenous North American, European, African, and Caribbean cultures since its founding in 1699. Its peoples represent a complex mosaic of the French- and Creole-speaking world where ethno-racial genealogical identity and linguistic identity are often contradictory. Without action, in the form of direct legal intervention, it is only a matter of time before the effects of Americanization, including racial segregation and forced assimilation into English, accomplish the complete erosion of its heritage languages, and the post-Columbian contact Indigenous culture that manifests through those languages.

NOTES

1. Christophe Landry, "A Creole Melting Pot: The Politics of Language, Race, and Identity in Southwest Louisiana, 1918–1945" (PhD diss., University of Sussex, 2015).
2. Rien Fertel, *Imagining the Creole City: The Rise of Literary Culture in Nineteenth-Century New Orleans* (Baton Rouge: Louisiana State University Press, 2014).
3. Alfred Mercier, *L'Habitation Saint-Ybars, ou, Maitres et esclaves en Louisiane* (Shreveport, LA: Tintamarre, 2003).

4 Ulysse Marinoni, "Ma tante Louise," in *Comptes-rendus de L'athénée louisianais* (New Orleans: Imprimerie Franco-Americaine, 1901).
5 Shane Bernard, *The Cajuns: Americanization of a People* (Jackson: University Press of Mississippi, 2003), xviii.
6 See *Official Journal of the Proceedings of the House of Representatives of the State of Louisiana at the First Regular Session of the Legislature* (1916).
7 See *Constitution of the State of Louisiana: Adopted in Convention on June 18, 1921* (Cambridge, MA: Harvard University Press, 1921).
8 Laura Ewen Blokker, *Education in Louisiana* (Greensburg: State of Louisiana Department of Culture, Recreation, and Tourism, Office of Cultural Development, Division of Historic Preservation, 2012), 26.
9 See Sylvie Dubois, Emilie Gagnet Leumas, and Malcolm Richardson, *Speaking French in Louisiana, 1720–1955: Linguistic Practices in the Catholic Church* (Baton Rouge: Louisiana State University Press, 2018).
10 Bernard, *The Cajuns*, xxi.
11 Bernard, 34.
12 Conseil pour le développement du Français en Louisiane, accessed April 20, 2021, www.crt.state.la.us/cultural-development/codofil.
13 Cécyle Trépanier, "The Cajunization of French Louisiana: Forging a Regional Identity," *Geographical Journal* 157, no. 2 (July 1991): 162–64.

CHAPTER 3

ACADIAN/AFRICAN/INDIGENOUS TRINITY

An Identity Mosaic from Nova Scotia to New Orleans

ANNALYSSA GYPSY MURPHY

I am an imposter. A feeling not uncommon among those of mixed heritage, feeling like a fractioned piece of differing complete and competing selves. I am tasked with bringing into the light the memory and truths of peoples whose narratives exist within the very cells of my body but whose stories I did not gain at the hearth of my collective grandmothers. Rather, this knowledge came to me as an academic, reading and researching a path back to my start, attempting to find out who I am by showing who *we* were. Like many people of mixed heritage, I was often expected to select a single portion—as if that were even possible—or desirable. It is my hope that this work, at least in part, helps create space for understanding that people are not fractions of separate wholes but whole unto themselves in their mosaic of selfhood. I am not seeking to conclude anything with my writing, but to inspire more questions and join in the conversations that have been ongoing for generations. While this chapter offers no clear solutions, it rather seeks to offer another voice into the diasporic experiences of mixed-race Indigenous and African descendants in the Americas. I seek to show my personal and ancestral experiences are connected to issues of miscegenation, identity formation, Americanization, and settler-colonial structures and to disrupt the static notion of the vanishing or vanished Native narrative.

My own story is linked in place, culture, and time to multiple starting points. I found my truths in DNA tests linking me to ancestors whose stories I now seek to honor, specifically my Indigenous ancestors whose stories are often eclipsed or enveloped into the narratives of other cultures.[1] Adopted at birth by White Scandinavians whose extended family always made it clear that light was not White—that I was not them or of them or one of them. Long before Omi and Winant's racial formation theory[2] was required reading, first for me as a student and later in most of my ethnic studies classes, I knew two things to be true—race was a myth; and that like many myths we know are fiction, real consequences exist based on how we live with and within these myths. The myth of race did not negate the lived reality and dire consequences of being othered by these racialized constructions. Maybe that is what set me on this journey to find out what or who I am?

Being adopted, having that fail, and ending up in foster care in middle school was as awful as it sounds. Rehoming is devastating for pets; for people it in unthinkable. I had only ever had formal education through eighth grade when at fourteen I ran away from Minnesota to New York City. I would earn my GED as a teen and find a form of salvation in the library at the local community college. It was there that I first began to read myself around the world. I looked in books to find pieces of my own biological narrative to connect my life to the places I knew my ancestors to be connected to and from. I became a mom that first year, but I knew the power of the written word could free me and my baby and so I kept going until I got my PhD. I want to do justice to the people behind the stories that unite in me. Like many adopted people I have pieces of paper that claimed to tell me who I was but it was not until I took the first DNA ancestry test that I began to discover and uncover who I am and how connected I was to the places I already had fallen in love with.[3] As Indigenous scholar and artist T. Shawnee writes in this collection, "Just as one passes on their genetic thumbprint of certain traits to their offspring, it has been found that historical trauma can also alter how our DNA functions." These manifestations of both ancestral trauma and memory resonate within me at the cellular level. I know nearly nothing about how cellular memory works, but finding my own ancestors among the French Africans of early New Orleans after doing my undergraduate honors project on them seems too remarkable to ignore. Knowing my summer home along the coast in West Pubnico, Nova Scotia, sits mere kilometers from the graves of my French and Native ancestors makes the undeniable pull I first felt when I visited somehow make perfect sense. Knowing that all of these ancestors came together in the 1700s in New Orleans makes that place become, for me, one of the many that feel like home. As Indigenous-Creole scholar Jeffery Darensbourg reminds us, New Orleans was and continues to be "Bulbancha, 'the place of foreign tongues,'" where it is and "was a place of diversity, of changes, where people came and went in search of what they needed . . . a complex, multi-ethnic, multi-cultural place." Knowing that as these Native and French ancestors were forced from their Maritime homes to new homes in Louisiana joining and merging with my Creole and African ancestors already living there is remarkable to me.

Place and land have always been a central pan-tribal connection, it is a common theme among all Native peoples across what is now called the Americas. In crafting the narratives of this shifting homeland it often finds the Indigenous pieces erased. This is a false representation of the role and importance Indigenous culture plays and has played in the lives of Cajun, Creole, and Afro-mixed peoples of Louisiana. We have not been a people that dismisses our Indigenous heritage but rather we have always embraced our mosaic identities. Even for those tribal peoples who may not have originated in the region pre-contact, deep roots and connections had been and continued to be forged in the decades and centuries after the first Europeans and Africans began to arrive. As Darryl Barthé (Creole métis) shared with me, "The historical processes of Creolization and métissage that characterized the relations between Europeans and non-Europeans in the territories settled by France in North America emerged in opposition to the process of 'Americanization' that typified Anglo-settler relations to Indigenous people and Africans in North America." The intermarriage and intermixing of Africans and Indigenous peoples is also in part overlooked due to the fact that enslavement of Indigenous peoples is often another point of erasure wherein popular narratives of slavery fail to include Indigenous people. Oftentimes this is also due to miscegenation laws that reclassified some Indigenous peoples as Black and not Native at all, such as the Racial Integrity Act of 1924.

I mention this not only as a ridiculous example of hypodescent (in that it ruled all Natives left in Virginia were in fact Black and thus no Natives were left in the state), but also because this ruling vexed old Virginia White planters who loved the lore in their elite families that linked them to the infamous Pocahontas. Therefore, settler-state governments enacted the "Pocahontas clause"[4] so that the rule was no Natives existed in the state, save those who came from her. I would offer that no other single piece of legislation exists that is so utterly obtuse as this, and that is saying a lot in the vast face of law and policy that sought and seeks to this day to eradicate Indigenous existence by legislating it away.[5] Long before the settler government of the United States introduced the termination and relocation programs of the middle twentieth century, there were a myriad of laws and policies enacted to legislate race to the detriment of Indigenous reality. In most cases it was to steal our land. Always it was to destroy our culture.

Scholars and community members alike often talk of race and culture in terms of negation. For the Cajun and Creole populations it often positions them in terms of the ways one is not the other. While I respect the need to claim space and specificity, I think it is also important to look at the ways these populations intersect and the commonalities between the two. When the Acadian French peoples began to be expelled from Nova Scotia and New Brunswick in 1755, the fact that they were "White" did not protect them from this expulsion and othering by the dominant English who forced their removal. Whiteness is as much of a construction as any of the other more melanin-enhanced classifications and categorizations, and we see the ramifications of othering within Whiteness throughout recorded history. Many of the expelled Acadian French community members had Indigenous connections to the region generations deep at the time. Some were connected through culture, community, and blended families, with the original tribal peoples of the region, specifically the Mi'kmaq and other members of the Wabanaki Confederacy. When the Acadians were expelled so too were the Indigenous family members that were aligned with them by marriage and blended families. In "Decolonizing Antiracism" Bonita Lawrence and Enakshi Dua address this erasure of identity, observing that "a similar ontological assumption about colonialism and Indigenous peoples exists in theories of Atlantic diasporic identities," wherein the narrative of the "French" expulsion often erases or ignores the Indigenous people who were expelled with them.[6] We often hear of the Acadian expulsion as if they were alone in the experience, as if they were not products of métissage, when in fact it goes further back, to the Anglo removal of the original Indigenous peoples of the Maritimes as well.[7] In the aftermath of Indigenous and Acadian removal in the Maritimes, these populations joined with Indigenous peoples already living in Louisiana and would continue culturally and ethnically (i.e., genetically) mixing on the path to becoming métis/méstiz@ populations known as Cajuns, Creoles, and Redbone—post-contact Indigenous communities. As Indigenous scholar-poet Rain Prud'homme-Cranford reminds us in the opening chapter of this collection:

> As a post-contact Afro-Indigenous people, Louisiana Creoles recognize the totality of their ethnic/cultural matrices. These matrices encompass American Indians of the Gulf South (Choctaw, Houma, Caddo, Chitimacha, Tunica, Biloxi, Creek, Atakapa Ishak, Natchez, and others); African Americans; Caribbeans (Afro-Spanish-French-Indigenous-Caribbean); French-Indian (including métissage with the Wabanaki Confederacy, Sac and Fox, Ojibwé, and Miami), and multigenerationally kinshipped tribal groups and landbases in what is now the state of Louisiana.

It is wildly accepted that if we rewind the paths of human existence to the very beginning, we will find our start in present-day eastern Africa. Though we do not know when humans first began to mark one another by distinctions of race, origin, or color, we do know that for most of recorded time it has occurred in one way of another. The metaphor of a braid has always resonated with me. Three parts that join to make a whole. Something new that is not each alone but needs each to be what it has become. Acadian. African. Indigenous. Of all the troubling tropes of colonization and colonial occupation, perhaps the most troubling is the insistence that marginalized people adopt the occupied notion of self in that we allow these forces that sought to erase us to be that which defines us though constructions like hypodescent and blood quantum.

That those who sought to erase us are allowed to be those who define us becomes the pinnacle of this occupation. Fortunately, we have seen, in recent decades, activists and academics pushing back against these narrow definitions of who we are and demanding our own construction. Andrew J. Jolivétte, in his book *Louisiana Creoles: Cultural Recovery and Mixed-Race Native American Identity*, explains, "Questioning who is white subverts the typical power dynamic in racial classification that usually marks as *other* those who are not white."[8] However, Whiteness itself is complicated, a point Jolivétte addresses in his book focusing on the often-overlooked Indigenous heritage and culture of Creole and Cajun peoples. This is in part based on the false assumption of extinction that many tribes, particularly first or early contact tribes, suffer under. This does not negate the genocide that began in what is now called North and South America starting in 1492, but to acknowledge that those Native peoples still exist in the DNA and living cultures of many peoples and populations, including Cajun and Creole communities. This narrative of vanishing or vanished Natives serves not the Indigenous communities nor does it lend itself to the mixed mosaic of our collective identities. Rather, it pretends that these notions of hypo-decent are a truth rather than a cultural narrative motivated by capitalist settler dominance. Claiming a distinct hybrid identity as one of completion and not reduction is key in seeing the ability to self-identify that Native peoples often subscribe to. In general, it has not been a traditional Indigenous worldview to think of mixed culture or mixed ethnic peoples as diminished or less than in terms of being members of Indigenous tribes or communities. This is an imported notion rooted in Eurocentric ideas of social class and ethnic hierarchies and is a frequently overlooked part of the ongoing cultural genocide against Native peoples.

The history of Indigenous peoples being erased into other narratives comes with the false assumption of either extinction or the belief that the colonizer narrative overrides and mutes the Indigenous one. It also supports the narrative of a static past, a marked historical point that does not allow for Indigenous people to be contemporary. As Craig Womack claims, it is the "anthropological assumption that things Indian are always swallowed up by European culture."[9] Central to righting this historic misread and misrepresentation is the idea of intrinsic Indigenous "Peoplehood." This work was originally conceived of by Robert K. Thomas,[10] where he built on the work of earlier scholars and expanded "the three factors that distinguished persistent peoples." Tom Holm, Ben Chavis, and Diane Pearson added "sacred history" to define "Peoplehood" and expanded on this in their work

"Peoplehood: A Model for the Extension of Sovereignty in American Indian Studies."[11] They offer "that it be utilized as the core assumption of American Indian studies." Moreover, Peoplehood was expanded on in Billy Stratton and Frances Washburn's "The Peoplehood Matrix: A New Theory for American Indian Literature," wherein they offer that "the Peoplehood Matrix provides critics with an interpretive tool that can be employed to delineate and clarify the underlying themes and ideas expressed in American Indian literary discourses in a way that enriches meaning through a culturally grounded point of view."[12] Thus, rather than being absorbed or erased by these cultural links, Indigeneity is a linking factor, a pan-tribal synthesis that positions Indigenous identity and culture connecting to land at the center of Cajun, Creole, and Afro-Indigenous communities in Louisiana and across the Creole diaspora. With this reading the Native is not erased, rather, it is a leading force in righting the misread of settler cultures as absorbing the Native rather than the Native being present and even primary.

In telling my story I give voice to those ancestors that merged in me and created something new. As a former foster child and an adopted person, most of what I knew about my family of origin were words on pages such as the very words you are reading right now, words that were disconnected from authentic experience. Descriptions of culture or identity, but like a recipe without instructions, hard to craft to completion. My chapter is an extension of a journey that began before my own birth with all the varied and various people and the narratives that converge in me and is the result of my conscious desire to piece them together, to form the mosaic of myself. Like most Indigenous stories there is not a linear timeline of starting and stopping. There is just story, layers, putting the pieces together, sometime seemingly out of order, but in the end, when the story is all told, it is whole and compete. There is Nova Scotia, the place I married the love of my life, where I gave birth to my second of three biological daughters. A place that was home in my head and heart when I first heard of it but had never been. A place only later would I find out through family records that a branch of my own bloodline started, in the Acadian French of Nova Scotia and those sent to Louisiana, and those who mixed in before they left with the Indigenous communities of the region and those they met along the way. My African, maybe quintuple great grandmother leaving Africa bound for Amsterdam ending up in New Orleans and becoming the mother of one of the first Black women to own land in her own name in Louisiana. In researching Acadian Maritime history synthesized with nineteenth-century mixed-race narratives, I would find my own past and through it, my contemporary voice. My quest for identity took me from GED to PhD, and the birth of each of my three daughters burned brighter my desire to offer them something concrete in the telling of who they are. I offer here not a complete narrative by any means, but a segue into the myriad of conversations ongoing about race, place, and identity and the synthesis of Cajun/Creole/African/Indigenous communities in Louisiana. My piece is offered up in the vast mosaic of our ancestors and I hope offers you the chance to join this discussion, too.

NOTES

1. Identity has always been a challenge for me, at best. And in flux in many ways. In recent years I have come to write, when asked as Natives often are to parenthetically note our tribes, that in terms of tribes I am Blackfeet, Celtic, Gaelic, Ashkenazi, and Cherokee. In part to embrace all of what I was told was "me" but also to subvert narratives on what IS and is NOT a "tribe" and/or tribal peoples and claiming my European heritage as well as embracing my Jewish identity. In the time after my DNA testing and finding these genetic links to the French and Native people of Nova Scotia, where I always felt home and own a home as well as knowing the name of and reading about my Black great (still not sure how many times) grandmother in New Orleans, is both exciting—it feels like a cultural "aha moment," as if my cells always knew. BUT also disruptive, as if I HAVE an identity, I can't / don't want to "change" again after feeling like who I am is all set in a way. I also do not look "Black" and do not want to be seen as appropriating a culture not mine, ever aware that my visually Black younger sister lives a truth I will never know, also not for a moment wanting to deny any of my ancestors. It is, in the end, as complicated as this note.
2. See Michael Omi and Howard Winant, *Racial Formation in the United States: From the 1960s to the 1990s* (New York: Routledge, 1994).
3. As T. Shawnee notes in a chapter within this collection, DNA testing is problematic for mixed-race, multigenerational people. My own experiences with DNA coupled with other forms of discovery (research, narrative, etc.) have worked to help locate myself within the mosaic of a diasporic mixed ethnic experience.
4. Kevin Noble Maillard, "The Pocahontas Exception: The Exemption of American Indian Ancestry from Racial Purity Law," *Michigan Journal*

of Race and Law 12, no. 107 (2007): http://www.doi.org/10.2139/ssrn.871096.

5 Since 1789, when the US government placed Native relations within the War Department, our fate, if not sealed in 1492, was then done in. Congress passed the Act to Regulate Trade and Intercourse with the Indian Tribes in 1790; this was the first of many, some long forgotten, laws, acts, regulations, treaties, and declarations enacted to the detriment of Indigenous peoples. Notable among them, the Dawes Act, the Indian Removal Act, the Indian Citizenship Act, and the ramifications of all the Jim Crow legislation in a post–*Plessy v. Ferguson* world after 1896. Even with the Indian Civil Rights Act of 1968, which seemed to mark a shift that included Native American Graves Protection Act (NAGPRA) and Indian Child Welfare Act (ICWA), Native legal rights have never really gained any substantial momentum.

6 Enakshi Dua and Bonita Lawrence, "Decolonizing Anti-Racism," *Social Justice* 32, no. 4 (2005): 120–43.

7 See John Mack Faragher, *A Great and Noble Scheme: The Tragic Story of the Expulsion of the French Acadians from Their American Homeland* (New York: W. W Norton, 2006); and Brett Rushforth, *Bonds of Alliance: Indigenous and Atlantic Slaveries in New France* (Chapel Hill: University of North Carolina Press, 2014).

8 Andrew J. Jolivétte, *Louisiana Creoles: Cultural Recovery and Mixed-Race Native American Identity* (New York: Lexington Books, 2006), 2.

9 Craig S. Womack, *Red on Red: Native American Literary Separatism* (Minneapolis: University of Minnesota Press, 1999), 12.

10 See Robert K Thomas, *Getting to the Heart of the Matter: Collected Letters and Papers* (Vancouver: Native Ministries Consortium, 1990).

11 Ben Chavis, Tom Holm, and J. Diane Pearson, "Peoplehood: A Model for the Extension of Sovereignty in American Indian Studies," *Wicazo Sa Review* 18, no. 1 (Spring 2003): 7–24.

12 Billy Stratton and Frances Washburn, "The Peoplehood Matrix: A New Theory for American Indian Literature," *Wicazo Sa Review* 23, no. 1 (Spring 2008): 51–72.

COMMUNITY RESPONSE

IT'S NOT THE WEIGHT, BUT HOW YOU CARRY IT

A Prose Poem

KELLY CLAYTON

Black butterfly hinges close their wings, and the door claps the wall. I enter the room, stoop to look under the bed, then crawl to the armoire. No. Not there. I dig through vanity; pull silk scarves from the mouths of drawers. Nothing. I search the white house with the dark green shutters every night. Each arrival, my first. Room leads into room. There are no hallways in the white house. Soon I come to the drawer, the stuck one, and pull hard.

An envelope addressed simply, The Prodigal Daughter

I open it with a pearl handled knife. It says, "Nights when you can bear no more, come to us in silence, out the cypress door, past coops and pens, over by the rope swing in the magnolia. We will come, girl. Wait for us. Leave your bags behind."

Rope swing? Who is we? Who they calling girl? Why can't she bring her bags?

No matter. Don't know what I'm looking for, but this ain't it. I continue the search. Believe I'll know it when I see it. Not before. My bare feet whisper across wood floors velvet with the oils of other feet. Rushing feet, waiting for a baby to get born feet, gone tell mama right now feet, muddy boots feet, clean it up before it sets feet, floors long ago buffed by sliding sock feet.

Under my own soles, a vibration. Thunder rolls through wide cut planks and travels up my legs.

A rhythm fills my belly bowl with desire. To move.

At the French doors, arms spread wide from the opening, I see them. They span the gallery, standing side by side. Satin slippers next to scarlet clogs, leather boots softened by chewing, sturdy oxfords, ankle strap patent, most though simply bare. A mosaic of women, from more sepia to chestnut, and suede, they stomp. A drum, rolled by feet; calls me outside like on Mardi Gras morning. I step onto the porch as one woman moves toward me. Tall, with strong arms looking like a gap tooth oracle. "My wide grin don't mean I like you," she says, "With your dirty bare feet, dry leaf stuck to your ankle. Lemme see what you got." She bows, offers her hand to me. I take it. Her callouses are warm pebbles. I catch the syncopation. The vibration. The Bamboula. They break from the line, gather skirts in fists, and we dance.

I am passed around, living whiskey in an alabaster flask, hands wide on my back, curl

around my waist. I'm held in carnal mama, auntie, sister-love. From a soft neck, I hear a whisper of postpartum sundown. Spinning; I trade round belly laughs with a freckled dervish wearing hibiscus rayon. My pelvis is fancy folk wine circling a stemmed glass. I glide from a child size Creole, black hair swinging, to a mighty woman wearing middle age like armor. My head tips into her open palm, rests for a moment. Our kindred blood flows. A gelatinous glob on my thigh drops to the boards. A foraging bee lands on its gloss black surface, thinking it raw honey, only to discover, too late that her legs are stuck in my restless need.

Softness hugs me from behind "Want your wishes granted? Your questions answered?" she asks,

"Then unstrap the satchel from your bird boned back and give it to me. We told you not to bring it. We'll carry that for you." When the weight lifts, ancient hands massage dents left on my shoulders. I bend to accept kiss blessings from a shrunken apple face. She turns me toward the brick stairs, pushes between my wing bones.

I don't move.

She pushes again.

I take each stair toddler style, with both feet. But when I reach the gate I don't look back.

I don't have to.

CHAPTER 4

BULBANCHA IS STILL A PLACE

Decolonizing the Tricentennial of New Orleans

JEFFERY U. DARENSBOURG

PART 1: BIG FRENCH DAY

In 2018 the city where I live was abuzz with the "Tricentennial." Countless events sprung up. Lectures, festivals, concerts, posters, artwork, flags, and shirts proclaimed that this place where I write is three hundred years old. The idea is that three hundred is a number of particular significance, marking the anniversary of Bienville landing around here. The commemorations often, though not always, described his arrival using colonialist lies such as "discovery" and "founding," as if the Indigenous Peoples of the area never existed, as if there were no other people around in 1718 other than Europeans. Those who celebrated the Tricentennial knew there were people here, I suppose, but choose not to focus on it very much, and when they did, they tended to leave out the negative legacy of colonialism. They often don't even know the names of the displaced nations, but they could have, if they had looked. Importantly, they often didn't know that this was already a place, a place with a name, before the first Europeans set sail for the area.

Bulbancha, "the place of foreign tongues," is the original name for this area. (Depending on what orthography one uses for Choctaw language, it could also be spelled "Balbancha," "Bvlbancha," or "Bạlbancha."[1] I use the orthography from Choctaw Chief Allen Wright, the first version I learned).[2] Bulbancha is much older than New Orleans.

It is also closer to the heart of the matter. Before the first Europeans came here, it was a place where people from around forty distinct Native groups crisscrossed, traded, followed game and fish, moved due to rising and falling waters, and interacted with one another.[3] It was a place of diversity, of changes, where people came and went in search of what they needed, including the Chitimacha, Houma, Chawasha, Washa, Acolapissa, Tunica-Biloxi, Bayogoula, Natchez, Taensa, Atakapa-Ishak, and other groups as well. That was Bulbancha then; that is Bulbancha now: a complex, multi-ethnic, multicultural place.

Rather than following a typical White custom of naming places after those with the most power and physical possessions, such as the Duke of Orleans, the Native name honors the various peoples of the area and their complex arrangements. It honors the search by all these peoples for sustenance and interaction.

Three hundred years is not a significant amount of time for the First Nations of the area. It's a good bit of time for Europeans to be somewhere on Turtle Island, what they call "the Americas." Indigenous Peoples recognize that this land has thousands of years of our thoughts, thousands of years of our songs, our care, our living with it, our caring for it. This land has thousands of years of our campfires, our nets, our pots, our baskets, our children, our drums, our love. It contains thousands of years of our bones, and those of our animal cousins, who have traveled this long journey with us. What can we say in response to a Tricentennial greeting?

I offer up something from the Atakapan language, as a member of the Atakapa-Ishak Nation—"Nakit kiwilš yil hiwew tolš hakokino!"—which translates as "Happy Big Powerful French Day!" That's the greeting for New Year's Day for our people, in our language.[4] It is a recognition that some ways of marking time and events are colonial ideas, and not part of how we have lived and thought about our ancestral lands and the time we have spent in them. French days are fine. Many of us speak French. Ancestors I have known spoke it from birth, but there are other aspects of the cultural heritage of the area that get too little attention.

As to whether or not I, as a Native and Creole person, think the Tricentennial is worth celebrating, I must offer a decisive "NO!" The racist legacy of colonialism that caused Bulbancha to be renamed "New Orleans," the ensuing enslavement of people of color, the discrimination, the segregation, the slow violence of denied opportunities and exploitation, a legacy that Hurricane Katrina and its aftermath proved is in no way in the past: that is not worth celebrating, at all. I love this place, Bulbancha, and that Native name captures the great and wonderful aspects of its nature. However, to celebrate the greed and racism of its colonial "founding" is simply beneath me.

PART 2: INDIGENOUS ORIGINS OF BULBANCHA'S CULTURE

An image of *Desseins de sauvages de plusieurs nations* by Alexandre de Batz (1735), a Frenchman living in Bulbancha, is one of the earliest depictions of Indigenous People in the area, or "sauvages" as its painter calls them. I don't object to that term so much, a term related to "savage" in English, because the French version has more of the sense of the original etymology of being a "nature person," from the Latin *silvaticus*, "of the woods."

Note the banks of the Mississippi River. The people depicted probably traveled a good ways to get there. He depicts, left to right, members of the Meskwaki (Fox) Nation, some members of the Illiniwek Confederation, an African child, and, all the way on the right side, looking directly at the viewer and holding a calumet, a gentleman labeled "Atakapas," a member of my own people. The Meskwaki and Illiniwek people might have come through for business with colonial powers. The Ishak fellow—our own name for ourselves, though others have called us "Atakapa"—might have been from the relatively nearby village close to present-day Diamond, Louisiana, a settlement that still exists. It is still a good ways from traditional Ishak centers of power such as present-day Lake Charles, Louisiana. The Natives depicted were people likely to have needed something in Bulbancha, and who went there to get it. The African child takes his place next to these Natives, and the histories of African and Native peoples have intertwined in every way in Bulbancha.

I came to Bulbancha looking for work, but various ancestors in my Creole family have lived here since the time that de Batz did his artwork.[5] When people talk about what makes this place so special culturally, they often discuss Creole jazz or Creole cuisine or other aspects of local culture with the name "Creole" attached. But what are Creole people? The common answer is that Creole people are mixtures of Francophone people with Africans. Other European groups are often mentioned as well, as reflected in common Creole surnames, especially Spanish and German people (e.g., "Darensbourg" is a French version of a Germanic surname). The fact that Creole people are mixed with First Nations is easily proven by both cultural memory and genealogical record. It is mentioned in accounts, but sometimes receives scant attention. Here I'd like to emphasize that Native aspect, based on research from a contributor to this very publication.

Andrew Jolivétte's landmark 2006 book *Louisiana Creoles: Cultural Recovery and Mixed-Race Native American Identity* focuses on the Creole population beyond simply European or African ethnicity. As a large, mixed population, Louisiana Creoles carry the blood, culture, and traditions of the First Nations of the area. Jolivétte notes that many Creole people are aware of our Indigenous heritage. Many of us self-describe as "Creole and Indian," "Creole and Chitimacha," or other similar terms. Some of us are members of historic Native tribes, as I am.

Creole people have often held tight to our Indigenous ancestry and heritage, yet this is often ignored when people talk about the culture and ethnic heritage of Bulbancha. As an example, consider the Tremé neighborhood. It has several "African American Heritage Sites," and it is fitting and necessary to honor the African contribution to local culture. However, it is also wrong to deny the Native aspects of the Tremé's culture. One well-known place in the area is Congo Square, a place where Africans danced and sang together, providing origins for the unique music of Bulbancha. However, even the sign in Armstrong Park, where Congo Square is located, refers to it as ceremonial ground of the Houma Nation, a place where Houma people danced and sang as well. Yet that is too often omitted.

Another example would be St. Augustine Church, located at 1210 Governor Nicholls Street. That church, built by Creole people, is of historic significance. It is also a traditional "African American Heritage Site." Yet a memorial for enslaved individuals buried on the property includes reference to enslaved First Nations people buried there. That Native presence is often, though not always, ignored when people talk about this church.

That sort of omission isn't atypical. Unfortunately, African blood has often been seen as a contaminant in American culture. Any ethnicity mixed with it becomes tainted by Africanness, losing its own identity, according to the racist notion that African people are somehow lesser or poisonous. When mixed, the other parts of the mixture are often ignored. Barack Obama had one African parent and one

European American parent, but he is "Black." Tiger Woods has one African American parent and one parent from Thailand of Thai, Chinese, and Dutch ancestry, but he is almost always referred to as "Black." The situation continues with people of mixed African and Native heritage, as Louisiana Creoles are, with famous American examples being Jimi Hendrix (Cherokee ancestry), Crispus Attucks (who had a Narragansett mother), and Mildred Loving (Cherokee and Rappahannock ancestry). Their Native ancestry is often ignored by others, but that doesn't mean they ignored it themselves.

Another important area in which Native heritage in Bulbancha is often ignored is discussions of cuisine. Just look at traditional Creole and Cajun cuisines, which prominently feature ingredients from Indigenous Peoples: crawfish, cayenne pepper, filé (ground sassafras leaves), tomatoes, sweet potatoes, maize, bell peppers, pecans, persimmons, all sorts of seafood from the Gulf of Mexico, merliton (chayote), red kidney beans, and on and on. It would be impossible to have Louisiana's cuisine without these ingredients. It would be impossible to have the most traditional of Bulbancha's fabled foods without these ingredients, impossible to have red beans and rice, grits, or a crawfish boil. There is much work to be done in reclaiming Indigenous aspects of Louisiana's culture and making these more prominent.

PART 3: FIRST NATIONS IN BULBANCHA NOW

In addition to the Creole population, one encounters other Natives in New Orleans, as in any large city. There are members of historical tribes who grew up here, or have come here for school or work, even from tribes nowhere near Bulbancha. I have met Native musicians here to make it in our thriving scene. I've met Native graduate students at our universities. I've met many Houma, Chitimacha, Mississippi Choctaw, Tunica-Biloxi, and Pointe-au-Chien people.

I've met Diné oilfield workers, a Comanche fortune teller, an Anishinaabe hotel worker. I've seen homeless Natives under the Claiborne underpass. I've seen Native sailors in town for Fleet Week. At a launch party in November 2018 at the Ace Hotel New Orleans for a zine I coedit, *Bulbancha Is Still a Place: Indigenous Culture from New Orleans*, many local Natives attended and expressed a genuine thirst for increased representation locally.

A famous group of Métis people originating in Canada, and famous for their contributions to Louisiana culture, are the Acadians, better known as "Cajuns." Their European heritage is primarily, though not exclusively, French, and their Native heritage in Canada comes especially from various nations of the Wabanaki Confederacy, and especially the Mi'kmaq and Penobscot. In this area of the world they did "more than shake hands"—I thank Dr. David Cheramie for that phrase—with the Atakapa-Ishak, Houma, Chitimacha, Avogel, and other nations, as well as Africans. Even though many Acadian people identify as White—a legacy, perhaps, of choices during the period of legal segregation—many also celebrate their mixed heritage and are reclaiming their métis roots.[6]

One of the larger recent groups of Native people around Bulbancha are people who have moved here from several Latin American countries, especially Honduras. The colonial fiction of the "border" in no way negates the Native heritage of these individuals, who are often of Maya, Aztec, Huichol, or other First Nations.[7]

First Nations people have been more than a footnote here in Bulbancha. Just as Latin American Indigenous People came and rebuilt the city after the Storm, First Nations people have continuously provided the foundational structures for the culture of the area, and often are not given their proper due. Bulbancha is still a place, and that place was originally made what it is by Indigenous People.

NOTES

A version of this talk was delivered as a paper at Tulane University in 2018 at the conference "Indigenous Spaces, French Expectations: Exploring Exchanges between Native and Non-Native Peoples in Louisiana," sponsored by the New Orleans Center for the Gulf South. A published version has appeared in issue no. 1 of the zine *Bulbancha Is Still a Place: Indigenous Culture from New Orleans* (Bulbancha: POC Zine Project, 2018).

1 Cf. Houma writer Hali Dardar's excellent overview "Bvlbancha," *64 Parishes*, Fall 2018, 25.
2 Allen Wright, *Chahta Leksikon: A Choctaw in English Definition* (St. Louis: Presbyterian Publishing, 1880).
3 The best treatment of these interactions is Elizabeth Ellis, "The Many Ties of the Petites Nations: Relationships, Power, and Diplomacy in the Lower Mississippi Valley, 1685–1785" (PhD diss., University of North Carolina, 2015).

4 I credit linguists David V. Kaufman and Justin Southworth, who run the "Atakapa Language" Facebook page (www.facebook.com/groups/371552763511458), for introducing me to this phrase.
5 A study of some of my European ancestors may be found in Reinhart Kondert's *Charles Frederick D'Arensbourg and the Germans of Colonial Louisiana* (Lafayette: University of Louisiana at Lafayette Press, 2008).
6 For nuanced academic interpretations of Acadian culture, one can do no better than Warren A. Perrin et al., eds., *Acadie, Then and Now: A People's History* (Opelousas, LA: Andrepont Publishing, 2014).
7 Becky Beyer and Minzala Mvula, "The Honduran Community in New Orleans," Via Nola Vie, August 14, 2017, www.vianolavie.org.

COMMUNITY RESPONSE

BULBANCHA IS STILL A PLACE

Decolonizing the History of the Present

LEILA K. BLACKBIRD

By the time the first colonizers arrived in Bulbancha, the land they would name New Orleans, they had already been exploiting the Indigenous peoples of the Americas for over two hundred years. French enslavement of Native Americans began in the Lower Mississippi Valley in the shadow of preexisting Spanish and British slave-raiding on the Atlantic seaboard. British raids to take Native slaves, originating from the Atlantic Coast, traveled far into the continental interior and spread epidemic disease; so too did the Spanish raids along the Gulf Coast, coming from Hispaniola, over a century prior.[1]

As a result, the larger, more populous, and centralized nations first encountered by Hernando de Soto and his slaving forces had fragmented into the *petites nations*—the Biloxi, Pascagoula, Mobila, Choctaw, Chickasaw, Bayogoula, Creek, Alibama, Tunica, Natchez, Mougulasha, Chaouacha, Acolapissa, Quapaw, Chitimacha, Houma, Atakapa-Ishak, and others—by the time the French built their first settlement on the Gulf Coast in 1699.[2] The peaceful coexistence of about forty distinct Native groups nestled along the Crescent of the Mississippi for trade and cultural exchange gave Bulbancha its name. Like Cahokia before it, Bulbancha was a place of Indigenous linguistic and cultural diversity.[3]

Meanwhile, colonizers—whether they be French, Spanish, or British—used slavery-induced epidemics along with divide-and-conquer warfare to compete with each other for land and labor.

British slave traders from the Carolinas, for example, armed hundreds of Chickasaw warriors against the Choctaw in 1702, resulting in the murder of eighteen hundred Natives and the enslavement of five hundred more. In the same year, the Spanish raised a force from across their missions in Apalachicola to attack the British-backed Creeks in what became a prelude to Queen Anne's War. In 1704, the British responded with the Apalachee Massacre, killing and enslaving thousands.[4]

In 1706, the Chitimacha responded to French slave-raids against them by killing Jean-François Buisson de Saint-Cosme, a Catholic priest and enslaver, as he descended the Mississippi River from the Great City of the Natchez. In retaliation, French-Canadian soldiers demolished the entire Chitimacha village on Bayou Lafourche.[5] After rounding up and murdering each man, they sold the surviving women and children into slavery. This would happen again thirty years later, when enslaved Black troops were forcibly dispatched by the French to commit ethnic cleansing against the entire Chaouacha population in retaliation for the Natchez Uprising.[6]

The first French governor of Louisiana, Jean-Baptiste Le Moyne de Bienville, waged an all-out war against the Chitimacha, which lasted until the founding of the City of New Orleans. He would continue to sell Indigenous peoples into slavery in the French Caribbean at an exchange rate of two-for-one for enslaved Africans, writing that he believed Native enslavement and removal "accomplishes a great good for the colonists."[7] Although this slave exchange would quickly become discouraged due to the valuation of African labor, these colonial logics continued to inform Indian removal and Black exploitation.

Slavery and slave-based economic models underpinned much of colonial bloodshed, and the captives produced by it formed the core of Louisiana's first enslaved population. Slavery was not only a large component of settlement plans, it also played a central role in French mercantilism from Cap-Français to Montreal. Across the United States, the enslavement of Native Americans was not a small, isolated practice left behind in some distant past. Native people from across Turtle Island and their Black-Native descendants remained in bondage throughout the Antebellum period.[8] After the US Civil War, however, there was no mass emancipation for Indian slaves; in fact, courts frequently interpreted the Thirteenth and Fourteenth Amendments to the US Constitution as solely being applicable to African Americans.[9]

We do not hear about this in the classroom or our history textbooks. To understand why, we must consider the complex history of the nineteenth century, which bound together Indian removal and the growth of plantation slavery in the South and westward expansion with Indian wars and enslavement in the West. American colonial expansion demanded that a genocide policy be enacted east of the Mississippi River to establish the Southern plantation complex, which increasingly placed demand and enacted violence upon enslaved Black people.[10] At the same time, the Annexation of Texas in 1845 and the end of the Mexican-American War in 1848 saw the current US border established without regard to the Native peoples whose lands it crossed.[11] Many saw their lands and families split apart.

The United States rapidly acquired Texas, New Mexico, Arizona, California, Nevada, Utah, more than half of Colorado, and parts of Wyoming and Kansas. The question then facing Congress was whether slavery would be allowed in the West. To maintain the balance between free and slave states, the State of California passed the Indian Act of 1850, which legalized the arrest of Natives and enabled settlers to purchase them for "indenture." This law saw as many as twenty thousand Native adults and four thousand Native children sold in California alone, primarily as domestic servants and farm laborers.[12]

In fact, California, New Mexico, and Utah all legalized the enslavement of Natives in the nineteenth century. Upon his arrival in New Mexico, right after the signing of the Treaty of Guadeloupe Hidalgo, Governor James S. Calhoun, the first Indian agent for the new territory, marveled at the sophistication of the preexisting Spanish Indian slave-markets and helped to perpetuate them. Mormon settlers rapidly turned Utah into slaving grounds. Founder Brigham Young preached to his followers that they should "buy up all the [Indian] children to educate them and teach them the Gospel so that . . . they would become a white and delightsome people."[13] In more remote locations of the borderlands, Native enslavement continued well into the twentieth century, providing the closest ties to and economic models for the contemporary practice of human trafficking prevalent today, including the transnational human rights crisis of Murdered and Missing Indigenous Women and Girls (MMIWG).[14]

At the close of the nineteenth century in Louisiana, Native lands along the Lower Mississippi were developed into sugar plantations, which were dependent on a particularly brutal form of slavery.

Plantations remained operational throughout Reconstruction, and white control over land and labor was maintained through the pervasive use of state-sanctioned racial violence. With the introduction of the North's industrial model, sugar production became streamlined and required the use of fewer individual refineries. When plantations finally collapsed, many were sold directly to corporations as pre-consolidated large tracts of land. Freedmen were displaced and Native polities, such as the United Houma Nation, were systematically denied land rights and federal recognition to facilitate the corporate acquisition of remaining oil-rich lands and waterways.[15]

This gave birth to Louisiana's present-day petrochemical corridor. By 1937, the nation's first offshore oil well was constructed near Louisiana. Today, there are over four thousand oil and gas platforms, rigs, and deep-sea wells here, representing a multibillion-dollar transnational industry, crucial to national security. Extraction from Native lands along the Lower Mississippi continue to produce wealth. To facilitate this, in Cancer Alley—the petrochemical-industrial corridor stretching from Baton Rouge through New Orleans—Black and Native people are now subject to air pollution, unclean drinking water, industrial waste, lead contamination, and forcible landgrabs that have situated landfills and toxic waste near our communities, exposing us to unequal health risks and cancer burdens.

Across the United States, social justice issues are directly connected to the ongoing legacies of settler colonialism, slavery, and genocide and continue to impact Black and Indigenous peoples at a disproportionately high rate. Even our current border crisis involves thousands of Indigenous families separated after fleeing US-induced poverty and violence, and individuals are detained by a for-profit anti-Black carceral system. Furthermore, the establishment of migrant concentration camps would not be possible without the precedents established by US federal Indian law and the creation of the reservation system as prisoner of war camps under the US Department of War.[16] Yet no one is illegal on stolen land.

Colonization is not in the past; it is ongoing. Although Black and Native people may not have the socioeconomic and political power to control or influence industrial giants, lobbyists, and politicians, we will continue to stand up and to speak out from Standing Rock to the Bayou Bridge Pipeline and from Flint to Minneapolis. Together, we will continue to fight as we have for the last five hundred years.

NOTES

Portions of this chapter have been previously been published in Leila K. Blackbird, "Entwined Threads of Red and Black: The Hidden History of Indigenous Enslavement in Louisiana, 1699–1824" (MA thesis, University of New Orleans, 2018), http://scholarworks.uno.edu/td/2559; and *Bulbancha Is Still a Place: Indigenous Culture from New Orleans*, no. 2 (Bulbancha: POC Zine Project, 2019).

1. Preexisting Indian trade routes along the Mississippi River system provided the framework for the French slave-trade network of Indian slaves. See Blackbird, "Entwined Threads of Red and Black"; and Brett Rushforth, *Bonds of Alliance: Indigenous and Atlantic Slaveries in New France* (Chapel Hill: University of North Carolina Press, 2012). For more on Indian slavery, see Andrés Reséndez, *The Other Slavery: The Uncovered Story of Indian Enslavement in America* (Boston: Houghton Mifflin Harcourt, 2016); and Alan Gallay, *The Indian Slave Trade: The Rise of the English Empire in the American South, 1670–1717* (New Haven, CT: Yale University Press, 2002).

2. One of many examples are the Bayogoulas. As early as 1699, a fourth of the population of the Bayogoulas had been killed by smallpox, and they began taking in refugees from other tribes surviving similar fates, such as the Mongoulachas and Quinipissas. Daniel Usner Jr., *Indians, Settlers, and Slaves in a Frontier Exchange Economy: The Lower Mississippi Valley before 1783* (Chapel Hill: University of North Carolina Press, 1992). See also Ruth Lapham Butler, trans., *Journal of Paul Du Ru (February 1 to May 8, 1700): Missionary Priest to Louisiana* (Chicago: Ye Galleon, 1934), 19–22, 52–53.

3. See Jeffery U. Darensbourg, "Bulbancha Is Still a Place: Decolonizing the Tricentennial of New Orleans," and Hali Dardar, "Bvlbancha," both in *64 Parishes*, Fall 2018; and Elizabeth Ellis, "The Many Ties of the Petites Nations: Relationships, Power, and Diplomacy in the Lower Mississippi Valley, 1685–1785" (PhD diss., University of North Carolina, 2015).

4. Charles W. Arnade, "The English Invasion of Spanish Florida, 1700–1706," *Florida Historical Quarterly* 41, no. 1 (July 1962): 29–37; Verner W. Crane, "The Southern Frontier in Queen Anne's War," *American Historical Review* 24, no. 3 (April 1919): 379–95; Steven J. Oatis, *A Colonial Complex: South Carolina's Frontiers in the Era of the Yamasee War, 1680–1730* (Lincoln: University of Nebraska Press, 2004); Gallay, *Indian Slave Trade*. On the Apalachee Massacre, see also Mark F. Boyd, *Here They Once Stood: The Tragic End of the Apalachee Missions* (Gainesville: University Press of Florida, 1999).

5. The Chitimacha Tribe of Louisiana, "Tribal History," accessed July 18, 2018, http://chitimacha.gov/history-culture/tribal-history.

6. Usner, *Indians, Settlers, and Slaves*, 73. See also MPA-FD I (1927), 64–71, Earl K. Long Library Louisiana and Special Collections, University of

New Orleans; and Arnaud Balvay, *La Révolte des Natchez* (Paris: Éditions du Félin, 2008).

7 "Description of the Condition of the Colony of Louisiana: Abstract of Letters from Bienville to Pontchartrain," MPA-FD II (1929), Correspondance générale de la Louisiane I (1706), 252–68, 514–44, Archives nationales d'outre-mer (ANOM); "Bienville to Pontchartrain," MPA-FD II (1929), Correspondance générale de la Louisiane II (1708), 177–91, 201–14, ANOM.

8 Blackbird, "Entwined Threads of Red and Black"; Gwendolyn Midlo-Hall, *Databases of Afro-Louisiana History and Genealogy, 1719–1820*, accessed February 1, 2018, www.ibiblio.org/laslave.

9 Andrés Reséndez, "The Other Slavery," *Ben Franklin's World*, podcast audio produced by the Omohundro Institute with Liz Covart, June 20, 2017, http://benfranklinsworld.com/139.

10 For more on how the newly formed United States constructed the legal basis for the destruction of Native nations and how that resulted in removal during the 1830s, see Tim Alan Garrison, *The Legal Ideology of Removal: The Southern Judiciary and the Sovereignty of Native American Nations* (Athens: University of Georgia Press, 2002). For a broader discussion of Indigenous genocide, see Patrick Wolfe, "Settler Colonialism and the Elimination of the Native," *Journal of Genocide Research* 8, no. 4 (2006): 387–409. On the growth of the Southern economy, see Edward E. Baptist, *The Half Has Never Been Told: Slavery and the Making of American Capitalism* (New York: Basic Books, 2014).

11 Michael F. Magliari, "Free Soil, Unfree Labor: Cave Johnson Couts and the Binding of Indian Workers in California, 1850–1867," *Pacific Historical Review* 73, no. 3 (2004): 349–89.

12 Paul Finkelman, "Slavery and the Northwest Ordinance: A Study in Ambiguity," *Journal of the Early Republic* 4, no. 4 (Winter 1986): 343–70; Michael F. Magliari, "Free State Slavery: Bound Indian Labor and Slave Trafficking in California's Sacramento Valley, 1850–1864," *Pacific Historical Review* 81, no. 2 (2012): 155–92.

13 "James S. Calhoun, Indian Agent, to Orlando Brown, Commissioner of Indian Affairs, Santa Fe, March 15, 1850," in *A Study of the Citizenship Provisions of the Treaty of Guadalupe Hidalgo*, ed. Mary Childers Mangusso (Albuquerque: University of New Mexico Press, 1966), 80–82; John G. Turner, *Brigham Young: Pioneer Prophet* (Cambridge, MA: Harvard University Press, 2012), 215–18.

14 Reséndez, *Other Slavery*, 1–11. Simon Romero, "Indian Slavery Once Thrived in New Mexico," *New York Times*, January 28, 2018; John Burnett, "Descendants of Native American Slaves in New Mexico Emerge from Obscurity," *All Things Considered*, National Public Radio, December 29, 2016; Joel Quirk, "The Anti-Slavery Project," *Human Rights Quarterly* 28, no. 3 (August 2006): 565–98; Shannon Brennan, *Violent Victimization of Aboriginal Women in the Canadian Provinces* (Ottawa:

Statistics Canada, 2011), www150.statcan.gc.ca; Vivian O'Donnell and Susan Wallace, *Women in Canada: A Gender-Based Statistical Report: First Nations, Inuit, Métis Women* (Ottawa: Statistics Canada, 2011), www150.statcan.gc.ca.

15 Leila K. Blackbird et al., "Standing Up on River Road: Activism in South Louisiana," accessed April 19, 2021, http://climatesofinequality.org/story/standing-up-on-river-road-activism-in-south-louisiana; Barbara Allen, *Uneasy Alchemy: Citizens and Experts in Louisiana's Chemical Corridor* (Cambridge, MA: MIT Press, 2003); Steven Lerner, *Diamond: A Struggle for Environmental Justice in Louisiana's Chemical Corridor* (Cambridge, MA: MIT Press, 2004); Matt Black, "Cancer Alley: Big Industry, Big Problems," MSNBC, August 10, 2015. See also J. Daniel d'Oney, *A Kingdom of Water: Adaptation and Survival in the Houma Nation* (Lincoln: University of Nebraska Press, 2020).

16 For the connection between federal Indian law, plenary powers, and migrant detention, see Maggie Blackhawk, "Federal Indian Law as Paradigm within Public Law," *Harvard Law Review* 132, no. 7 (May 2019): 1787–1877, and "The Indian Law That Helps Build Walls," *New York Times*, May 26, 2019.

PART 2

LANDBASE

From Homelands to Food and Health

CHAPTER 5

FILÉ MAN

Creole Food Harvesting and Sovereignty

TRACEY COLSON ANTEE

In his contribution to this collection, John LaFleur II writes, "In Louisiana French and Creole, filé gombo is sassafras-based gumbo (kombo-ashish/litchi) and remains known to all Creoles and Cajuns alike who've grown up with Louisiana-francophone speakers." Filé, a key ingredient Indigenous to the Americas, along with the produce and meat from Louisiana marks gumbo as a signature dish highlighting the Afro-Indigenous-European post-contact blend of Creole cultural cuisine. My father, John Oswald Colson, has been making filé most of his life. His mother and the generations before her all provided the Cane River community with fresh filé, red pepper, and other seasonings. His process of making filé is now considered a folk art, and the special flavor that seems so rich to his filé, is the story in the hands that create it. Colson's dedication to this traditional practice highlights that "food and its harvesting illuminates deeper notions of nourishment, situating the relationships of the producers of the food as sacred, while also demonstrating how this food, this experience, is tied to home."[1]

The stories, practices, and production of traditional foodways for Louisiana Creole people are tied to land and cultural sustainability. John Oswald Colson, known as the "Filé Man," represents both the stories of the Creole people and the practices of maintaining food sovereignty toward cultural sustainability in Cane River. As Joanne Wadden writes, "Food is political. It may be used as a lens to discuss issues of power and resistance, sustainability and social justice."[2] For the Cane River Creole community, and many other Louisiana Creole communities, food harvesting reinforces family, land ties, and helps solidify a clear social and political identity. This chapter explores the importance of traditional food practices and harvesting as connected to land, familial, and cultural memory through the making of filé. In recent years, with emphasis on ecological and landbase sustainability, there has been an increased effort to recover and implement food sovereignty. In the Cane River community of Louisiana, John Oswald Colson has been making filé since his mother taught him at age eight. Harvesting and processing sassafras for filé (used as a seasoning and thickening agent in gumbo and other foods) and tea (also used medicinally) is a traditional part of Creole practice traced to Choctaw, Caddo, and Ishak roots within Creole culture.

My father, John Oswald Colson, is known by many names and has lived a colorful life to say the least. He is full of stories and traditions of Cane River, but most importantly he carries the stories of our people. Born in 1937, John lived on Cane River until, like so many others in the area, he left for better opportunities. He moved to Chicago as a young man, cutting hair and doing odd jobs but mostly following his dream. He was in Chicago during the magical time of Cadillac Records and sang and played the guitar at local clubs and bars. He brought swamp pop, an easy smile, and his stories to Chi-town and later moved on to California for a while.

Quoting Keith Basso, Nathalie Kermoal writes, "Among Aboriginal peoples, place is inseparably intertwined with cultural identity and sense of self. . . . 'Knowledge of places is therefore closely linked to knowledge of the self, to grasping one's position in the larger scheme of things, including one's own community, and to securing a confident sense of who one is as a person.'"[3] In this respect, the Creole community of Cane River is like any other community of Indigenous People.

Dad always returned home, back to Cane River. Sometimes he would come for a visit; sometimes to stay a bit longer. After battling a long illness and coming back to full capacity he realized how much of the "old ways" and traditions were leaving with each generation. The role of sassafras and its harvesting in Creole food reminds us that "food cannot be disentangled from people and relationships; consuming, producing, and foraging for food all have meaning because they facilitate the strengthening of community bonds."[4] So, in an effort to maintain tradition and preserve Cane River Creole culture, Dad put on his straw hat and started finding sassafras trees taking their rich green leaves, to dry, process, and teach the old way of making filé. Using a traditional pilon, a large tree hollowed out much like a giant mortar and pestle, he pounds the leaves into the fine, fragrant, bright green seasoning known as filé. Soon after coming home, he was demonstrating at conferences, festivals, and educational events, teaching and preserving the art.

Sassafras has a long history as both food (spice) and medicine among the Indigenous populations on Turtle Island. Sassafras trees are Indigenous to the eastern United States, growing as far west as Texas and Oklahoma. "The leaves could be made into teas and poultices, while the root bark was either chipped or crushed and then steeped in boiling water . . . to reduce fevers; soothe chronic rheumatism, gout, and dropsy; relieve eye inflammation; ease menstrual and parturition pain; help cure scurvy and various skin conditions; and act as a disinfectant in dental surgery."[5] Some of the earliest trade items in Louisiana included Choctaw women who would come to market selling sassafras and bay leaf (laurel leaves).[6] According to the Choctaw Nation of Oklahoma:

> In the early 1700s, when the French, with their African slaves, began establishing permanent settlements in the Choctaw homeland, the sharing and blending of ethnic foods lead to the creation of a whole new style of cuisine, known today as Cajun food. In the creation of Cajun cuisine, the French contributed their traditional stews and wheat flour. The Spanish contributed onions, garlic, tomatoes, and peppers. African chefs contributed okra and field peas. Choctaws contributed several essential elements, including an intimate knowledge of local fish, shell fish, and native plant and animal foods. Choctaw people gathered sassafras leaves and sold or traded them in towns to produce filé, a traditional Choctaw stew thickener, and a vital ingredient in Cajun gumbo.[7]

While "Cajun" is used here, this is a description of Creole food practices. As Rain Prud'homme-Cranford shared with me during one of our many conversations about Creole identity, "Louisiana Creoles belong to a *culture*, one that is a product of métissage/méstizaje tied to the

FIGURE 5.1. Father and daughter: John Oswald Colson and Tracey Colson Antee preparing filé from sassafras leaves. Photograph courtesy of Tracey Colson Antee.

landbase of Louisiana" and as "as a post-contact Afro-Indigenous people, Louisiana Creoles recognize the totality of their ethnic/cultural matrices." As a culture that incorporates elements and inheritances of our African, Native American, and European inheritance into our own unique Creole culture, it is what I have described as a culture . . . a roux of the intermingling of flavors that were Native to this land and new to this land.

In her work on the environmental and foodways knowledge of Métis women in Canada, Nathalie Kermoal writes, "Even though consultation processes, including those that surround environmental impact assessments, typically stress the need to recognize and respect traditional ecological knowledge, Métis contributions to that knowledge remain relatively unexplored."[8] I would argue that this is true of the environmental foodways and cultural practices of Louisiana Creoles. That is not to say Cane River Creoles are equivalent or interchangeable with Canadian Métis, however. As Prud'homme-Cranford reminds us, Louisiana Creoles *"are not Métis, as in the Métis Nation (Métis National Council) of Canada. They are a métis, méstiz@ ethnic-cultural group."* Indeed, this is the connection that LaFleur emphasizes in his contribution to this work.

He notes that "scholars, including historians and early food writers, share the same studied and well-documented view that Louisiana's Creole cuisine evolved from cross-cultural marriages/relations between the Euro-French, Acadian-Canadian, Gulf American Indian tribes, and later Afro-Caribbean, Spanish, and German peoples." Cane River harvesting practices are a study in the kinship and cultural confluence of the African, French, and Spanish progenitors of our community who cultivated and maintained interdependent relationships, and kinship connections, with the Indigenous people of Louisiana, whose landbase knowledge would prove integral to Creole culture, from Creole foodways, to medicine, to land stewardship.[9]

The traditional practice of making filé belongs to the Indigenous Peoples of Louisiana and a part of Louisiana Creole culture because of our ties, kinship, and landbase knowledge. In October 27, 2018, the Office of Lieutenant Governor, Billy Nungesser, presented my dad with a proclamation making him an Honorary Louisiana Tradition Bearer, a celebration of his efforts to maintain and honor the traditions of Louisiana folklife and Creole culture. The presentation was held at the Louisiana Sports Hall of Fame museum in Natchitoches and was followed by a demonstration by my dad and a panel discussion where his planned induction into the Folklife Hall of Fame was also announced. As Rachel Vernon observed, for "many Native communities . . . food is the sinew that holds communities together. Food helps build cultural knowledge and practice, satisfies health holistically by satisfying emotional and physical needs, and brings people together through the act of producing, consuming, and distributing foods."[10] This was a huge honor, not only for my dad, but for our family to see him recognized for all of his hard work. Robin Wall Kimmerer (Citizen Band Potawatomie) in her book *Braiding Sweetgrass: Indigenous Wisdom, Scientific Knowledge, and the Teachings of Plants*, writes, "We need to unearth the old stories that live in a place and begin to create new ones, for we are storymakers, not just storytellers. All stories are connected, new ones woven from the threads of the old."[11] Cane River Creole stories, Louisiana Creole stories, and the importance of our traditional food practices and harvesting connect us to land, familial, and cultural memory. It is an expression of our unique ethnicity and culture, marking us as "an offspring of the Old world [Native] and the New [African, European]."[12] This was our story; it is unapologetically Creole.[13]

FILÉ

Making filé with Daddy to
Constant rhythmic pounding, comfort
Thump, beat, thump on my feet
Only other sounds our breathing
oddly in rhythm with this thumping
This sound pulls deep breaths out of lungs,
Makes tense shoulders relax, clears my mind.
My blood remembers simpler, easier, times
When this pounding was natural daily sound
Mixed in with the call of birds, lap of river water,
Language of Tunica, Choctaw, French, Spanish, and
The whisper of breeze through hair black curly coarse,
To perfectly coiffed and fair.
Looking at old weathered pilon[14] I wonder
how many hands have touched, how many
great, great cousins, aunts, uncles, grandparents
crushed dried strong smelling sassafras leaves
in this hollowed cypress log. I wonder at hands
that have rubbed along its hard dried surface to get
bright green powder of pounded leaves off tired
fingers and calloused hands.

These hands with many stories told over this pounding rhythm, turning something flourishing wild along this river, not unlike us, into something to make my gumbo taste just right. A perfect blend of flavors, just like our people. Stories flow naturally when someone stands over the pilon, finds that perfect rhythm, pressure, and flow to make these dried leaves into filé. Memories, old and new, some kindled in the thump and rhythm of blood set to pilon drift into tired minds, spill out as beautiful "'member when" and "my Grandma used to tell me" tales. Stories 'bout climbing down riverbank on ancestral Cane River, leaning far out over the water to get that sassafras tree with the big roots. Daddies and brothers walking two miles and back to the bayou, hunting the trees with big leaves, hauling branches all way back to the house. Mamas and daughters stripping dried leaves from stems and telling stories, their laugher spilling into the sassafras, familial ingredients . . . the story in the stew.

We, my father and I, do it all now like our ancestors did it then. A intergenerational summer task searching as family to find sassafras, stripping leaves, drying, destemming, and finally pounding it into our Creole gold. We make the perfect filé. No machines or electricity needed, just strong hands and that rhythm. It's the rhythm, the memory in the pilon and the hands that makes it so good, so fresh and real. What we add to these small, perfectly lined up bottles of filé are our stories, they move from our blood, to our memory, told over and over in each heart-like pound of the pilon. Some stories are simple, family dinners, what Papa caught or killed that day, stories about Daddy chasing the cows out of his garden, and what this or that one's sister had on when she came to collect a bottle of filé from Grandma. Some are older, and speak in language of land, rhythm, and blood, pumped in a perfect blended balance. Stories flow down into that soft green powder and the pounding eases and relaxes a mind and I remember sitting on Grandma's lap. She stringing red peppers and saying "Now don't touch my baby it will burn your precious hand." Thoughts drift and ebb like floating on Cane River listening to the lap of the water.

> Pounding and thumping stops, big heavy
> pilon leaned over emptied of green gold.
> Fine powder spills out. Rather than go into
> amber colored beer bottles like Grandma put
> her filé and red pepper in, Daddy and my filé
> glows green in little plastic clear bottles, labeled
> for sale. Customers pick them up, smell, exclaim
> over the strong richness and bright green color,
> always wondering: "how long did this take?"
> The answer is always, "well as long it takes."
> So, the pounding starts again, my thoughts ease
> as memories and stories go into every little bottle.

NOTES

Portions of this chapter were originally posted on the blog *GumboLife*, July 12, 2017, www.gumbolife.com/the-file-man.

1. Rachel Vernon, "A Native Perspective: Food Is More Than Consumption," *Journal of Agriculture, Food Systems, and Community Development* 5, no. 4 (2015): 139, www.doi.org/10.5304/jafscd.2015.054.024.
2. Joanne Wadden, "De-linking from Dependency: Indigenous Food Sovereignty Brings Together Land, Food and Health," *Briarpatch Magazine*, September 9, 2010, https://briarpatchmagazine.com.
3. Nathalie Kermoal, "Métis Women's Environmental Knowledge and the Recognition of Métis Rights," in *Living on the Land: Indigenous Women's Understanding of Place*, ed. Isabel Altamirano-Jiménez and Nathalie Kermoal (Athabasca, Alberta: Athabasca University Press, 2016), 115.
4. Vernon, "Native Perspective," 138.
5. "Sassafras Uses in Herbal Medicine and Cooking," *Mother Earth News*, July 1983, www.motherearthnews.com.
6. For more see Daniel H. Usner, *American Indians in the Lower Mississippi Valley: Social and Economic Histories* (Lincoln: University of Nebraska Press, 2003).
7. "History and Development of Choctaw Food," Chahta Anumpa Aiikhvna School of Choctaw Language, accessed July 1, 2019, https://choctawschool.com/.
8. Kermoal, "Métis Women's Environmental Knowledge," 109.
9. For the Choctaw, Quapaw, and Ishak, among others, sassafras was harvested to make tea. This tea was used to clean or thin the blood in springtime, and again toward the end of fall to thicken the blood. See Wayland D. Hand, *American Folk Medicine: A Symposium* (Berkeley: University of California Press, 1980); and "History and Development of Choctaw Food." See also Robin Wall Kimmerer, *Braiding Sweetgrass: Indigenous Wisdom, Scientific Knowledge, and the Teachings of Plants* (Minneapolis: Milkweed Editions, 2015) for more on "blurring the line between food and medicine" in Indigenous foodways.
10. Vernon, "Native Perspective," 1.
11. Kimmerer, *Braiding Sweetgrass*, 175–76.
12. Janet Ravare Colson, *THE Creole Book* (Natchitoches, LA: Creole Heritage Foundation, 2012), 7.
13. The following poem, "Filé," first appeared in the Fall 2012 issue of *Yellow Medicine Review: A Journal of Indigenous Literature, Art, and Thought*, guest-edited by Chip Livingston.
14. In Louisiana Creole and Louisiana Indian culture, a pilon is the hollowed-out log used as a pestle to grind and pound, sometimes referred to as *pilet et pilon*, the "pintail and the pestle" for the elongated mortar used in the pilon/pestle.

COMMUNITY RESPONSE

COLSON'S CREOLE-INDIGENOUS CULTURAL CONTINUITY

Filé Man

ROBERT B. CALDWELL JR.

Louisiana foods are at once transatlantic foods and Indigenous foods. Gumbo is an often-used example, fusing local seafood and spices, okra with African origins, European sausage and flour for the roux. While the food's origins are global, they have been creolized and adopted by the Indigenous peoples of the state. But among these foods, filé—derived from the leaves of the sassafras plant—is special, in that it is both an Indigenous food of Louisiana and a first food of Louisiana's Indigenous peoples.[1] The plant's roots are used in making sassafras tea as well as root beer, and the small tree's trunk can be used to make beanpoles, as wood for grilling, or as the key component for making a smoking rack.[2]

There is no better representative of the Louisiana sassafras tradition than John Oswald Colson. The "Filé Man" is a Louisiana Creole elder full of traditional wisdom. He has been making filé most of his life. He is the undisputed "Sassafras King," with knowledge of use of all parts of the plant. In addition to carrying the oral traditions of the Cane River Creole people, including specialized knowledge regarding food sovereignty, Colson has seen, lived, and knows the last seventy-plus years of what it is to be Cane River Creole. That includes his traditional knowledge in bousillage construction technique, his avocation repairing and caretaking for the *poteaux-en-terre* Badin-Roque House, and even his youthful sojourn north to Chicago as a musician.[3]

He engages with so many people, both within and far beyond his own community. He is proud of his culture and to share his knowledge with those who seek it. Oswald regularly does demonstrations where he explains his method of selecting and gathering the sassafras leaves and pounds the destemmed leaves into fine bright green filé powder. His daughter Tracey and other family members often accompany him on these demonstrations. For a dozen years or more, he has been working closely with Dustin Fuqua, Chief of Resource Management at the Cane River Creole National Historical Park, National Park Service, teaching "Dusty" the secrets of sassafras. Mr. Fuqua is a native of Spring Bayou in Avoyelles Parish and has lived in Natchitoches for fifteen years, and last year, Mr. Fuqua received the Creole Peoples Award. Both Tracey and Dusty, younger members of the "Sassafras Society," will mentor others, passing the tradition to future generations.

Sassafras came to Creoles from both their own Indigenous roots, and their European and African-born ancestors who learned it from the Native peoples of the region. Mr. Colson continues to honor this legacy by integrating sassafras history into his presentations. This legacy is also made apparent in the material culture of pounding filé: he often uses a mortar and pestle (pile and pilon) made by Coushatta (Koasati) craftsman Bell Abbey.

Louisiana Creole foods reflect a long history of cultural convergence, especially in the eighteenth and early nineteenth centuries, to create a distinctive cuisine that crossed ethnic and linguistic boundaries. Many of these foods depend on homegrown and wild harvested ingredients. Anthropologist Hiram F. "Pete" Gregory and researcher Dayna Lee have argued that the Creole cuisine of northwestern Louisiana differs from that of New Orleans in that unlike in New Orleans, where individual cultures fastened their own distinct neighborhoods to preserve multiple identities, Cane River Creole culture represented a fuller synthesis because of the smaller numerical presence of each ethnic group in the area.[4]

There are numerous similarities between the foodways of the Cane River Creole community of Natchitoches Parish and the Choctaw-Apache Community at Ebarb. Tamales are made and eaten in both communities.[5] Mr. Colson's mother dried and provided the Cane River community with fresh filé, red pepper, and other seasonings. My mother still makes sassafras tea, and my great grandmother dried and sold red pepper for Sabine Parish tamale makers. This parallel is just one of many reasons I feel such strong affinity for "Oz."

Honored throughout the state, and known beyond among specialists, John Oswald Colson has been featured at the Southern Food and Beverage Museum, named as a Louisiana Tradition Bearer by the Louisiana Folklife Commission in 2018, and inducted in the Louisiana Folklife Center's Hall of Master Folk Artists at the Natchitoches-NSU Folk Festival in July 2019. He is loved on Cane River: his eightieth birthday party had well over one hundred attendees. While he is well known in certain niche circles, he is less known to the general public in adjacent parts of central and Northwest Louisiana—including my own tribe, the Choctaw-Apache—than he should be.

Tracey Colson Antee has done a great service in popularizing the cultural contributions of her father in "Filé Man: Creole Food Harvesting and Sovereignty." Her chapter, coupled with the irresistible smells and tastes of the aromatic fresh green powder that it invites readers to sample, will undoubtedly inspire even more songs, poetry, creative writing, visual images, and other creative works. Certainly, Louisiana filé and this master maker of it deserve a book and film of their own!

I have had the pleasure of knowing this humble man and living treasure for more than ten years; I sincerely hope "Oz" will grace us for at least ten years more. He has reacquainted Louisiana with locally gathered and sustainably harvested filé. In doing so, he reconnected us with good food, which is good medicine. For that his legacy will live far beyond all of us.

NOTES

1 Here, "first foods" are differentiated from other indigenous foods as being precolonial. For additional clarification of this distinction, see Robert Caldwell, *Choctaw-Apache Foodways* (Nacogdoches, TX: Stephen F. Austin University Press, 2015), 21.
2 Caldwell, 73.
3 The Creole diaspora has a large footprint. Mr. Colson's moves first north to Chicago and later west to California reflect the larger pattern of migration of Afro-Indigenous Creoles from Louisiana. For more on the diaspora, see Andrew J. Jolivétte, "Examining the Regional and Multigenerational Context of Creole and American Indian Identity,"

in *Cultural Representations in Native America*, ed. Andrew J. Jolivétte (Lanham, MD: AltaMira Press, 2006), 73–92.
4 For more on Cane River Creole cuisine, see Robert Caldwell, "Historical Roots of Cane River Creole Cuisine," paper presented at "Hispanic Roots in Creole Culture" (Creole Heritage Center, Natchitoches, LA, 2013).
5 Caldwell.

CHAPTER 6

TELLING IT RIGHT

In Search of the Ishak

JEFFERY U. DARENSBOURG

On November 5, 1961, a bronze statue was dedicated at the site of St. Martin of Tours Catholic Church in St. Martinville, Louisiana, a monument attempting to commemorate the original inhabitants of the area, the Ishak, known more commonly as the "Atakapa" (in various spellings).[1] The statue is located in a town that was a centerpiece of the Attakapas District under French and Spanish rule, and of Attakapas County early in the Orleans Territory after the so-called Louisiana Purchase. (As an Indigenous person, I refuse all legitimations of this act or its foundational idea, the Doctrine of Discovery.) This statue, based on a 1735 watercolor by French colonial polymath Alexandre de Batz, *Desseins de sauvages de plusieurs nations* (Sketches of savages of various nations), among the earliest images of First Nations in Louisiana by a European, has a plinth reflecting a typical sentiment about the Ishak, my people: "a roving savage tribe who settled here prior to the French, partly Christianized and civilized by missionaries."[2]

This banner event featured many local inhabitants wearing "at least an Indian headband with a cocky feather." It also included "Indians who still live in the area," namely, people from the federally recognized Chitimacha Nation, as well as members of the Coushatta Nation, a decade before their own federal recognition. The keynote address was given by former New Orleans mayor deLesseps Morrison, at the time the Kennedy administration's ambassador to the Organization of American States. Notably absent in Morrison's remarks, which centered on the triumph of the interests of the United States in Latin America, or in any published account of the ceremony, are the Ishak ourselves.³ Apparently, we had ceased our existence, something we had been doing for a while, allegedly disappearing some decades previous.

During my Monroe Fellowship through the New Orleans Center for the Gulf South at Tulane University during the 2018–19 academic year, my goal was to craft the basis of a book-length monograph on the Ishak. In doing this I have had three goals. First, I have desired to get the historical record straight in terms of how and where Ishak have lived. History is not the only way to look at Native People, but we do have a history, and that history is quite often ignored.⁴ That has led to the second goal, to chart the ways in which Ishak People and our legacy have been ignored or, in some cases, deliberately destroyed in Louisiana. My third goal has been to center an understanding of Ishak People on the current population, which is overwhelmingly comprised of people who can also, accurately, consider themselves Louisiana Creoles, Acadians, or combinations thereof.

John R. Swanton and Samuel Gatschet from the Bureau of American Ethnology visited us and produced official government accounts of our culture and language.⁵ The tribe appears in colonial accounts from the likes of Milton, who depicted an Ishak bison hunt in the eighteenth century.⁶ We are likely the "Han" people described by the shipwrecked Cabeza de Vaca, who even witnessed both an aversion to cannibalism as well as what would later be called "same-sex marriage" among us: "During the time I was with them I saw a devilish thing, and it was that I saw a man married to another man, and these are effeminates . . . and go about covered like women."⁷ There are, of course, archeological accounts as well, which of necessity treat of earlier times, but that does not excuse the tendency of writers to consign us to history rather than recognizing our current existence as Ishak people.⁸ In 1959, a few "degenerate descendants"—ouch—were reported to be living in Franklin, Louisiana.⁹ Later publications would simply skirt the question of living Ishak altogether.¹⁰ In 1996, under the leadership of Hubert Singleton, a major reorganization of Ishak People took place in Prairie Laurent, Louisiana.¹¹ The result was the formation of what is currently the largest organized Ishak group, the Atakapa-Ishak Nation of Southwest Louisiana and Southwest

Texas. Despite the existence of this and other groups, and the ability of a quick internet search to reveal contact information, it was still possible in 2004 to ignore living Ishaks in an academic publication about us.[12]

While a revised historical account exceeds this discussion, I must note some of what I have learned about Ishak places in Louisiana, places where we lived, including mounds in our traditional lands.[13] Not being an archeologist, I have little to say about the dating of physical objects and the like, other than that civilizations have aspects of importance other than physical culture. Cultures with advanced technology and food production in which large portions of the population are excluded from the benefits of such advancements are quite "primitive" from an Indigenous point of view. What I have learned is something different, and that is how the mounds have been viewed by locals in the past, and how they are thought of nowadays, which is a window into area views about us Ishak.

One site visit I went on, with fellow researcher Joshua Clegg Caffery of the University of Louisiana at Lafayette, took us to a location at Butte La Rose in St. Martin Parish. Harold Schoeffler had described the site to me in great detail, and we found ourselves in front of a nice looking home with a mound in the yard, out of which sprung a sizeable live oak. The owner came out, and after we explained why we were there, he walked us around the place in disbelief. "I thought that was fill dirt from when they put in the road one hundred years ago," he told us. The owner's comment was, I would find, fairly indicative of Native sites in the region, and of Native culture in the United States generally: often hiding in plain sight, and ignored by the surrounding culture. He had multiple earthworks around the outskirts of his home. After learning what these were, he told us he had wanted to cut down a small berm to build a deck, but had changed his mind after speaking with us. He had respect for regional Native culture, and was gracious, even if he didn't know how recognize Indigenous artifacts.

Worse than being ignored, however, is being erased. Pecan Island and environs in Vermilion Parish was a large settlement site of Ishak People leading up to European colonization of the area. The remains of a major complex of earthen mounds and shell middens can be found there. Some of the dirt and shells from this complex, encasing the bodies of human beings, were used to pave area roads in the late

1920s, causing human bones to be found littering the roadside.[14] In 1930 a writer in the *Abbeville Meridional* opined about the value of the shell middens and the bones within as they were processed for road use: "The former camping site of the 'noble red man' has been demolished in the interest of progress—of a superior people. His bones stood between us and the dollar, and the poor bones had to go. They make good surfacing material, however."[15]

Regarding contemporary Ishak People, I must note that current tribal members are not tribal "descendants," as one white anthropologist referred to us at a conference in which I participated a few years ago. We are, in fact, the Ishak. Our ancestors called themselves that name because their ancestors did, and likewise, so do we. We are also French and Spanish, Cajun and Creole, residents of Texas and Louisiana, and, of course, mixed with all other sorts of people. In that regard, we are a microcosm of the Gulf South itself. We are especially Creole, though. That is, perhaps, one reason Ishak existence has been ignored, under the assumption that people who are of African descent can't also be considered Native. In fact, Louisiana has a long history of classifying Natives as "Free People of Color" or "mulatto," instead of "Indian" or related terms, when convenient.[16] Andrew Jolivétte, himself a Louisiana Creole and member of the Atakapa-Ishak Nation, argues that tribes that are heavily creolized "still exist, only now they exist as complex populations with important historical, political, social, and cultural relevancy to understanding mixed-race Native Americans in contemporary US society."[17] A deep study of contemporary Ishak People requires an understanding of what it means to be of mixed ethnicity in the United States.[18]

The 1961 statue dedication in St. Martinville could have had an Ishak presence, had its organizers known where to look in their own part of Louisiana. They might have invited some zydeco musicians of Creole and Ishak heritage such as Fernest Arceneaux.[19] They might have recognized that people in the area classified on birth certificates as "negro," as my own parents are called on the first document of my own life, have more complicated histories than that term implies. Such is the work of studying Ishak People going forward, the work of complicating the story in order to make tell it right. We are Ishak. We exist. It is time for our story to be told.

NOTES

1 "Thousands Brave Inclement Weather to Join in Indian Day Celebration in St. Martinville Last Sunday," *Teche News*, November 9, 1961, 1.
2 David Bushnell, *Drawings by A. de Batz in Louisiana, 1732–1735* (Washington, DC: Smithsonian Institution, 1927), 9–10. For my own, personal take on this image, see Jeffery U. Darensbourg, "Traveling Light," *Situate*, June 2016, www.situatemagazine.com.
3 de Lesseps Morrison, "Attakapa Indians Monument Dedication—St. Martinsville, Louisiana, 1961 November 5," box 211, folder 3, Organization of American States, 1961–1963, deLesseps S. Morrison Papers, Special Collections Division, Tulane University.
4 The essential text for any discussion of this sort is Roxanne Dunbar-Ortiz's *An Indigenous Peoples' History of the United States* (Boston: Beacon Press, 2015).
5 Swanton's *Indian Tribes of the Lower Mississippi Valley and Adjacent Coast of the Gulf of Mexico* (Washington, DC: Smithsonian Institution, 1911) has a cultural account (360–64). Swanton and Gatschet's *A Dictionary of the Atakapa Language Accompanied by Text Material* (Washington, DC: Government Printing Office, 1932) has an important selection of texts in the language, but is poorly organized. A revision of that dictionary by David V. Kaufman was published in 2019. For an overview of the present status of the language, see Jeffery U. Darensbourg and David V. Kaufman, "Ishak Words: Language Renewal Prospects for a Historic Gulf Coast Tribe," in *Language in Louisiana: Community and Culture*, ed. Nathalie Dajko and Shana Walton (Jackson: University Press of Mississippi, 2019), 64–68.
6 Louis LeClerc de Milford, *Milford's Memoir: Or, a Cursory Glance at My Different Travels and My Sojourn in the Creek Nation*, trans. Geraldine de Courcy, ed. John Francis McDermott (Chicago: R. R. Donnelley & Sons, 1956), 61–64.
7 *Castaways: The Narrative of Álvar Núñez Cabeza de Vaca*, ed. Enrique Pupo-Walker, trans. Frances M. López-Morillas (Berkeley: University of California Press, 1993), 85. This account is discussed as part of the general history of same-sex marriage among Indigenous Peoples of the Americas in William N. Eskridge Jr., "A History of Same-Sex Marriage," *Virginia Law Review* 79, no. 7 (1993): 1454.
8 See, for example, Jon L. Gibson, *Archaeological Survey of the Mermentau River and Bayous Nezpique and Des Cannes, Southwest Louisiana* (Lafayette: University of Southwest Louisiana, 1976).
9 Harry Lewis Griffin, *The Attakapas Country: A History of Lafayette, Louisiana* (Gretna, LA: Pelican, 1959), 9.
10 See, for example, Joseph T. Butler Jr., "Atakapa Indians: Cannibals of Southwest Louisiana," *Louisiana History* 11, no. 2 (1970): 167–76.

11 Hubert Singleton, *The Indians Who Gave Us Zydeco*, 3rd ed. (self-pub., 2005), 30.
12 William W. Newcomb Jr., "Atakapans and Neighboring Groups" in *Handbook of North American Indians*, vol. 14, *Southeast*, ed. Raymond Fogelson and William Sturtevant (Washington, DC: Smithsonian Institution, 2004), 659–63.
13 Much of what I found was inspired by interviews with local Lafayette car dealer, activist, and keeper of lore Harold Schoeffler, to whom I am grateful for his generosity and interest in Indigenous Peoples
14 David Lyle, "Tales of 2,000-Year-Old Indian Culture in Vermilion Still Told by Pecan Island Folk," *Abbeville Meridional*, December 4, 1952, 6.
15 "We Visit the Shell Mounds at White Lake," *Abbeville Meridional*, March 15, 1930, 4.
16 An important recent work on this issue, especially as it relates to chattel slavery, is Leila K. Blackbird, "Entwined Threads of Red and Black: The Hidden History of Indigenous Enslavement in Louisiana, 1699–1824" (MA thesis, University of New Orleans, 2018). A detailed critical examination of ethnic categories and effects on the tribal recognition process in Louisiana may be found in Brian Klopotek, *Recognition Odysseys: Indigeneity, Race, and Federal Tribal Recognition Policy in Three Louisiana Indian Communities* (Durham, NC: Duke University Press, 2011).
17 Andrew J. Jolivétte, *Louisiana Creoles: Cultural Recovery and Mixed-Race Native American Identity* (Lanham, MD: Lexington Books, 2007), 2.
18 An introduction to this issue in the United States generally, which of necessity has information about Louisiana, is Gabrielle Tayac, ed., *indiVisible: African-Native American Lives in the Americas* (Washington, DC: National Museum of the American Indian, 2009).
19 The Indigenous ancestry of Arceneaux and other Creole musicians of Southwest Louisiana is discussed in a recent work, Bruce Sunpie et al., *Le Kér Creole: Creole Compositions and Stories from Louisiana* (New Orleans: L'Union Creole, Neighborhood Story Project, and University of New Orleans Press, 2019).

COMMUNITY RESPONSE

COMMENTS ON "TELLING IT RIGHT: IN SEARCH OF THE ISHAK"

JOHN DEPRIEST

Jeffery U. Darensbourg's growing body of work serves as valuable contributions to the fields of Native American studies, historical anthropology, ethnography, linguistics, and the interdisciplinary intersections of these fields. His chapter "Telling It Right: In Search of the Ishak" is a remarkably condensed summary of ongoing work related to the Ishak people, from both contemporary and historical perspectives. In his words, his goals are to "get the historical record straight in terms of how and where Ishak have lived . . . chart the ways in which Ishak People and our legacy have been ignored or, in some cases, deliberately destroyed in Louisiana . . . [and] to center an understanding of Ishak People on the current population." Darensbourg, as a scholar who is also Ishak, is almost uniquely qualified to undertake and accomplish these goals. My only complaint about the current chapter is that I wish it were longer. While I recognize that it is a preview or a teaser serving to foster curiosity about the full version to come, the issues raised are important, and much more remains to be said.

Darensbourg's goals are to set both historical and contemporary records straight about who the Ishak were, have been, and are, despite attempts to ignore or erase their impact and existence. In my view, his main contributions in this work are (1) compiling a short list of historical references to the Atakapa people; (2) documenting recent examples of both scholars and local residents ignoring the existence of contemporary Ishak people; and (3) providing perspective, both personal and scholarly, on why systems and individuals persist in denying recognition to contemporary Indigenous peoples. My comments on the chapter will be primarily in regard to contributions 1 and 3 above. Regarding contribution 1, our challenge as contemporary researchers is disentangling the word Atakapa from the people it was used to describe. In terms of historical references to Atakapa, it is important to consider that "Atakapa" was a derogatory term in common usage in Mobilian/Choctaw for "cannibal" (Modern Choctaw: "hattak vpa"), and was sometimes applied to peoples living somewhat distantly west of the Mississippi/Atchafalaya basin. I am disinclined to believe that any groups at that time referred to themselves as Atakapa, unless to provide clarification to ignorant Europeans who otherwise did not know what group an individual came from. Further, the historical record of Europeans using the preferred demonyms of indigenous groups is scant, at best. This means that even when historical accounts use the term Atakapa, we cannot necessarily trust that they were all referring to the same group, or even that they were referring to the ancestors of today's Ishak people. Given Narvaez and Cabeza de Vaca's account of the "Han's" disgust and subsequent attack on the Spaniards after witnessing the latter's starvation induced cannibalism, it would stand to reason that the indigenous group neither practiced cannibalism themselves, nor frequently encountered it. If they were indeed Ishak, and the location suggests they may have been (most scholars conclude that Isla Malhado refers to Galveston Island), then we have to wonder why it is that the Ishak eventually came to be known as Atakapa, aside from just living in the area some Choctaws designated as belonging to the Hattak Apa. Regardless, we cannot assume that every historical reference to the Atakapa was also a reference to the Ishak.

In regard to contribution 3, Darensbourg's portrayal of the denial of recognition (or even basic standards of human decency) to contemporary indigenous people is powerful, thoughtful, and personal. No matter how many times the depravity of white supremacy is demonstrated, the depths of its disrespect and injustice, as in Darensbourg's account of ancestral bones being strewn along the highway, remain unfathomable. As a person of mixed ethnicity who is a member of an indigenous nation (Choctaw Nation) that has, since its founding, been multi-ethnic, I can relate to the ways that individuals (or even entire nations) of mixed ethnicity can be denied recognition as indigenous or, more commonly, insufficiently indigenous. There is a perverse (and inverse) relationship between blood quantum and racial classification in the United States, where unless a native person is "full-blooded," then they are not Native, while "one drop" qualifies someone with African ancestry as Black. Sovereign nations determine their own requirements for citizenship, not census designations, but census designations can determine the amount of sovereignty granted to a particular nation. This remains a fraught issue, particularly in Louisiana, since the US government often denies federal recognition to nations with members who have African ancestry. Of course, the limited slate of possible ethnicities to check on a census form fails to represent the vast range of ethnic identities that members of indigenous nations can also claim. To expand on Darensbourg's point, mixed-ethnicity indigenous people (including Ishak) may also claim Acadian, Creole, Asian American, African American, or any number of other nonexclusive ethnic identities.

One chapter cannot explore or expose all of the issues surrounding Ishak identity and history, especially when so much of it has been misconstrued, misrepresented, misinterpreted, or erased. Darensbourg's voice, however, is a valuable contribution, and the issues he raises warrant further study and description, and I look forward to a more complete showcase of his current research in the years to come.

CHAPTER 7

A PERFECT CIRCLE BOUND IN CHAINS

Creole-NDN Health, Historical Trauma, and Settler Colonialism

T. SHAWNEE

> Historical trauma, a collective and cumulative intergenerational wounding resulting from traumatic events targeting a community (e.g., forced removal from homelands), has been posited by Native communities, health practitioners and researchers to have pernicious effects that may persist across generations through a myriad of mechanisms from biological to behavioral and from cell to society.
>
> KATIE SCHULTZ ET AL.,
> "'I'm Stronger Than I Thought'"

NAMING THE CHAINS THAT BIND

Our people of Louisiana are in the midst of a crisis; not only are we fighting to retain our culture, landbases, and languages as Creole-NDN people, but we are fighting to simply stay alive. Afro-Indigenous struggles with systemic wellness issues of diabetes, autoimmune disease, heart disease, mental health disorders, and cyclical domestic and sexual violence are forever chained to our communities through the institutions of colonization, slavery, racism, and Indigenous erasure. These issues will continue to repeat themselves in a perfect circle because our stories are ingrained into our DNA as survivors representing the Indigenous diaspora of the South. Creole-NDN and Freedmen communities have been underrepresented in research and programming in the most typical ways—by focus and by definition. Genetically[1] and culturally complex communities, such as our own, have been "defined out" of studies by not clearly fitting into racial or ethnic assignments that are typically required. Statistical evidence that is utilized to create treatment goals and plans to better serve populations battling global health issues is often regulated to clearly defined white/European populations first, and then the litany of populations of color to follow thereafter, receiving less funding and focus. One does not have to dig deep to find that statistics indicating glaring disparities in overall health impacting African American, American Indian, and Hispanic/Latinx cohorts. Research is progressively delving not only into the genetics predisposing marginalized groups to certain disorders such as diabetes as well as autoimmune and cardiovascular diseases, but some, albeit few, clinical studies have begun to reflect on the impact of historical trauma.[2] Just as one passes on their genetic thumbprint of certain traits to their offspring, it has been found that historical trauma can also alter how our DNA functions. Historical trauma not only impacts the health and socioeconomic wellness of peoples but is believed to now play a role in how genes are read and utilized (transcribed to build proteins), influencing not only the prenatal level but forthcoming generations prior to conception.[3]

Recognizing that the Creole-NDN peoples of Louisiana and the Freedmen[4] populations of Oklahoma are at the crux of the Americas, intersecting survivals from slavery, colonization, ethnic/cultural genocide, and removal/erasure means our converging histories as Afro-Indigenous peoples are poured into our DNA. This predisposes us to the societal and health epidemics that plague African American, American Indian, and mestiz@/Latinx communities. Acknowledging these histories will allow for appropriate treatment and action plans serving our communities. Let this chapter blow down streets, ricocheting off walls of hospitals, reverberating into universities, and crescendo at the federal and state levels so our voices may be heard like a mighty wind demanding that research and health/wellness programs must stop defining our communities out of the equation and feverishly start *defining us in*.[5] This can be done by allowing a focus on multiracial communities (with an emphasis on Red/Black populations) in federal- and state-funded research, where participants are no longer described by a health professional's description of their racial phenotype, but through a self-reported description of their ancestry. This will provide vital information that must be included in predisposed risk assessments and long-term treatment planning.[6] This chapter reviews some of the research and statistics around diabetes, cardiovascular disease, and autoimmune disorders alongside the realities of historical trauma, settler colonialism, and cycles of domestic, sexual, and intimate partner violence (DV/SV/IPV). I offer through this overview of literatures that there is a definitive lack of understanding, awareness, and research/funding within Creole-NDN and Freedmen communities' health and wellness. Therefore, "A Perfect Circle Bound in Chains: Creole-NDN Health, Historical Trauma, and Settler Colonialism" is a defiant call to action to address the health and wellness of Afro-Indigenous communities by aggressively mending shortcomings in representation and research /funding by focusing on self-identification and familial health histories of complex mixed race / ancestry within Indigenous diasporic communities. By utilizing a matrix of programming that has successfully served American Indian, African American, and mestizo@ populations and tailoring it to fit the needs of our community who have been mitigating the historical trauma inflicted from colonization to slavery will and can offer us a holistic and decolonial way forward.[7]

A PERFECT SCORE: RANKING THE BEST OF THE WORST

Louisiana's national health ranking has an impressively high number, scoring a fifty, which is the highest a state can achieve. Oklahoma is almost as equally low, ranking at forty-seven. These numbers put Louisiana and Oklahoma squarely at *the bottom* of all states comparing the global health of their inhabitants. We are ranked as two of the least healthy states in the USA based on a wide collection of data including everything from obesity, diabetes, smoking, air quality, behavioral choices, lack of education, premature death, physical and mental distress, poverty, and deaths due to cardiovascular disease, to name a few.[8] Louisiana ranks forty-sixth in the nation based on premature death. Our ranking as the least healthy state was bolstered by three critical statics adding to our score: highest child poverty rate in the country, prevalence of frequent mental distress reported, and persistently high percentiles of low birthweights posted each year.[9] Children 0–17 years of age in Louisiana are suffering long-term repercussions of living in poverty. Trauma cycles with poverty and health effects and compounds our communities for generations. Louisiana, like Oklahoma, has a high rate of Indigenous, Afro-Indigenous, and African American peoples. These factors influence health rankings and can be linked to marginalized communities' specific statistics (or lack thereof) in regard to diabetes as well as cardiovascular and autoimmune diseases.

A PERFECT STORM: DIABETES, CARDIOVASCULAR DISEASE, AND AUTOIMMUNE DISORDERS

Reflecting on the health and future of our peoples, if we look back far enough, to the cradle of our beginnings, many of our most debilitating conditions were seldom seen. Early ways of life that sustained our tribal ancestors from the Americas to the African continent had kept our bodies and social systems in balance. Gathered and specifically farmed foods were collected at just the right time of year and accessible only during those times; the plant-based diet rotated with the seasons, save for the items that could be dried or ground. Meat and fish were also on cycles balanced with migratory patterns, mating seasons, and times of plenty. The meats were lean, healthy, and preserved by drying or smoking. Constant activity was had in obtaining and processing these foods. This equilibrium was sent into disarray with the garnishing of lands and freedoms, undulating like waves gaining energy before a great storm. When people are forcibly removed from the land that they have lived on for hundreds if not thousands of years, not only are their diets upended, but their access to traditional medicines have been cut off. "Making connections between historically anchored traumatic events and current health inequities among American Indians and Alaska Natives (AIAN) has launched innovative research among AIAN communities and researchers. . . . Indian removal from the Southeast through a sustained policy of forced removal and relocation had devastating impacts on the tribes involved and is now commonly referred to as the Trail of Tears."[10] Additionally as Creoles and/or Freedmen, our African ancestors' abductions disrupted community nomadic systems that utilized rotational camps, thus causing the seasonal system of their bodies and communities to be derailed. These traumas and removals impact the genetics of a population, which are slowly pressured overtime by the demands of the environment in which they reside, to the point where in many hundreds of years a population expresses the traits that have been selected for more frequently within it. Removal/abduction, relocation, and colonization of our ancestors changed our environment, with which our bodies were in sync. Our diets changed dramatically in a short span of time compared to the thousands of years of regulation:

> In the United States, African Americans, Native Americans, and Alaska Natives have endured a history of multiple traumas. From the time the first colonists came to shore on what would come to be known as the United States, Native Americans and Alaska Natives have been subjected to:
>
> - colonization;
> - epidemic diseases brought from Europe;
> - the tradition of extermination and mass homicide;
> - forced marches and displacement from their lands;
> - peace treaties often signed under coercion and later broken;
> - Indian boarding schools in response to the "Kill the Indian, Save the Man" policy;
> - widespread sexual and physical abuse of children; and
> - rates of violence and victimization higher than any other racial group.
>
> African Americans have endured the legacy of:
>
> - being stolen from their native lands;
> - enslaved from 1619 to 1865;
> - systematically abused and denied education;
> - forced "breeding";
> - widespread sexual assault and rape of Black women;
> - the abolition of slavery gave way to indentured servitude;
> - Jim Crow laws;
> - mass lynching;
> - mass incarceration; and
> - homicide rates higher than any other racial group.[11]

Removal/abduction, relocation, colonization, slavery, exploitation, and the violences listed above and experienced by our Native, Black, and Red/Black ancestors along with ecological environmental changes altered our bodies and therefore the DNA structure of our ancestors at a fundamental level. Therefore, within two hundred years the perfect storm was in full force and has not stopped unleashing its wrath.

Within our general population of the United States American Indians have 15.1 percent of the population battling diabetes, non-Hispanic Blacks have a 12.7 percent diabetic rate, with non-Hispanic Whites sitting at a 7.4 percent diabetic rate.[12] With each of these racial/ethnic classifications, location and socioeconomic status is everything. Northern states have much lower diabetic rates than the states of the Deep South such as Louisiana, Arkansas, Mississippi, Alabama, South Carolina, and Texas, including the South tie-in regions of Oklahoma, Kentucky, Tennessee, and West Virginia. In Louisiana and Oklahoma, the diabetic rates have been soaring and bringing with them a deluge of associated health complications, such as cardiovascular disease. The multiracial population in Louisiana (i.e., Creole-NDN and other admixtures) have a diabetic rate higher than the American Indian national average at 15.5 percent,[13] while African Americans in Louisiana have a staggering 16.7 percent rate, and Latinx have a 14.3 percent diabetic rate.[14] On Louisiana's easternmost boundary with Mississippi, the entire parish of Tensas has a diabetic rate of 17.2 percent.[15] In Oklahoma, American Indians are 16.8 percent, while African Americans are at 12.2 rate, Latinx have an 11.1 percent rate, and multiracial populations register a 12.8 percent diabetic rate.[16]

People battling type 2 diabetes are at drastically compounded risks for developing cardiovascular disease in its many forms such as heart disease, peripheral artery disease, and stroke. Diabetes brings with it a triangulation of comorbid factors that feed off of each other; insulin resistance has a positive correlation to hypertension, abnormal lipids levels causing a disorder known as diabetic dyslipidemia, both of which contribute to worsening cardiovascular disease. Diabetic Americans are four times more likely to die from heart disease. Moreover, 68 percent of diabetics age 65 years or older will die of heart disease and an additional 16 percent of those in that age group will die of stroke induced by cardiovascular disease.[17]

As this storm has built energy, the waves have swelled and broke hard against the shore. With our communal equilibrium in disarray, our internal equilibrium has begun a cascade of effects igniting our immune systems. Lupus SLE and rheumatoid arthritis are two of the most prominent and debilitating autoimmune diseases impacting our communities today at ever increasing numbers. Communities of color have the highest prevalence of lupus, with earlier onset and more destructive disease progression, while patients of African ancestry more frequently have the most severe outcomes of end stage renal failure and mortality.[18] Autoimmune diseases can often be overlooked, misdiagnosed, and underdiagnosed for many years, even upwards of a decade. "Rheumatic diseases among American Indian (AI) populations are highly prevalent and oftentimes atypical in clinical presentation and disease course (1–4). Disease tends to be more aggressive and confers higher morbidity and mortality among AI populations (4, 5)."[19] During this precious period of time, if the disease is not diagnosed, long-term damage is accumulating to internal systems that are not readily apparent to the naked eye. Joint inflammation and disease not only damages the joint capsule and causes pain, but long-term untreated or poorly controlled inflammation cycles will cause permanent bone deterioration and can also damage the supportive framework of tendons and ligaments that stabilize joints. Other internal systems of the body can also be targets of attacks causing organ system damage, most commonly to the excretory system, specifically the kidneys, the respiratory system with the onset of interstitial lung disease, nervous system damage, and unfortunately involvement of the cardiovascular system can occur. Quality of life drastically plummets while mitigating a chronic disease, while the resulting disability impacts the capability to maintain economic stability for many individuals. Autoimmune diseases on the whole disproportionately impact females, where international data on lupus SLE shows a percentile spread across racial and ethnic boundaries where women make up 88 to 96 percent of populations treated or diagnosed with the disorder.[20] A median figure of comparison would show that women are impacted by autoimmune disease over men by a rate of nine to one; and if one reflects on the stability of the family structures in our communities of color and considers who carries the majority of the burden raising children as single parents and providing for them, systemic illness most certainly will impact the socioeconomic stability of women and the children who depend on them.

One of the most important factors in treating this epidemic is early identification of the disease to implement treatment before permanent damage. Autoimmune disorders can be causing damage to an individual yet go undetected for a number of years. For many years blood tests were the primary mode of diagnosis, where specific inflammatory antibodies were searched for. This has been problematic for a variety of reasons, one of which has been that the serology of certain patient groups did not match the clearly evident symptoms. The antibody most typically searched for has been ANA (antinuclear antibodies) factors, yet many individuals of Native American ancestry, specifically tribal populations in Oklahoma with aggressive autoimmune diseases, do not flag with the most common ANA antibodies. Some individuals may be seronegative, meaning bloodwork is inconclusive or the antibodies presenting in diseased individuals are atypical, such as anti-CCP or anti-RF IgM.[21] This atypical presentation should also be on the radar when investigating and treating Creole-NDN populations with symptoms that point toward autoimmune disorders but have tested ANA negative. Autoimmune disorders impact our communities at high rates due to their heritability (40–50 percent), while RA inheritance rate is impacted by both genetic and environmental factors, and lupus SLE boasts a hereditary rate of 66 percent based on genetic markers alone.[22] With the highest rates of these disorders found within American Indian, African descent, and Afro-Caribbean communities, our Creole-NDN and Freedmen communities that hail from the intersects of all these peoples means we are in need of specialists and research to tackle this health risk. Systemic health issues such as these impact the caregivers, the rocks, and often times the financial providers of our family structures—the women. Yet the women in our communities are at risk from more than autoimmune disease.

A PERFECT CIRCLE: THE CYCLES OF DOMESTIC/SEXUAL VIOLENCE AND MENTAL HEALTH CRISES

The storm that has been rolling through our communities since contact and abduction has flooded out our most sacred of spaces; our traditional family/communal structures and the aftermath of this disruption to our communities and general health have dramatically eroded our mental health and wellness. A discreet and simplistic statement can be used as a discussion starting point here: trauma cycles with poverty. Poverty can described beyond the basic descriptors of food insecurity, lack of education, low wages, and health disparities; but it can be also be described as what has been stripped from a community that previously allowed it to be healthy and self-sustaining. If we consider the first and second statement along a linear path in time, one can see where the two ends became bound together to create this perfect circle. As the Creole-NDN and Freedmen population came to be in Louisiana and Oklahoma resulting from colonization, removal/abduction, genocide, racism, and the attempts of cultural erasure, factors such as mental distress, premature death from various factors, and child poverty rates tipped the scales toward these states' last place seating at the table of health. This disruption in our natural balance is not just the current tally of today's situation, but the result of deep canyons dug through our homelands from the manmade "storm" that has been churning for hundreds of years.

In the 1990s, reports were being executed to provide data for the National Violence Against Women survey, which ultimately would lead to the legislative efforts and mandates we now refer to as VAWA (Violence Against Women Act), which was first authorized in 1994.[23] This piece of legislation was the first of its kind, where domestic violence and sexual assault were specifically identified as crimes, and could be charged in local and federal courts as such. Astounding, right? It took an act of Congress to say that, yes, in fact it is illegal to beat or rape your intimate partner—they are not your property to do with as you please. But social stigma, societal norms, immigration status, patriarchy, racism, and settler-colonial constructs have played a heavy role in continuing the silencing of women, especially in communities of color. Among these reports, some rather alarming statistical patterns become clear. American Indian and mixed-race women are victims of rape, physical violence, and stalking at significantly higher rates than all other races;[24] almost one out of three American Indian women were reporting an occurrence of rape in their lifetime, and mixed-race women were not far behind at one out of four reporting the same. These two groups also have a physical assault rate approaching two out of every three women, with Black women following closely behind with more half of the women surveyed reporting prior or ongoing physical assaults.[25] Note that this study is almost twenty years old and the data used to support the passage of the Violence Against Women Act, but doesn't fully speak to more recent concerns. Current data is even higher, particularly regarding Native American women: "In the US, violence against Indigenous women has reached unprecedented levels on tribal lands and in Alaska Native villages. More than 4 in 5 American Indian and Alaska Native women have experienced violence, and more than 1 in 2 have experienced sexual violence."[26] When considering violence against men of American Indian, African American, and mixed-race background, these studies also showed a drastic jump in violence against these groups, where close to three out of four men from these communities reported histories of physical assault. Compound this by the knowledge that many of the statistics we rely on have rather small sample sizes, and the general statistics brandished by the CDC and the Bureau of Justice Statistics wildly underrepresent reality due to the fact that 80 percent of sexual assaults and rape go *unreported*.[27] Accuracy of intimate partner violence (IPV) statistics fare no better, whereby some studies estimate that IPV is reported only half of the time,[28] with other projections proposing that 70 percent of such incidents go unreported.

Considering the composition of our Creole-NDN communities of Louisiana and Freedmen communities of Oklahoma as being American Indian and of African descent, these statistics are alarming as they describe the daily struggles with violence as ongoing and oppressive. As Rain Prud'homme-Cranford writes, Louisiana Creole women and Freedmen women "occupy a space in which both the stereotypes and exploitations of Indian and Black women are imposed, creating an environment wherein the worst aspects of sexploitation and labor are visited on the popular perceptions of Louisiana Creole (and Freedmen) women in the historic narrative of the Americas and its modern imaginings."[29] Moreover, IPV has a very real economic impact, where it is estimated that abuse victims lose pay for eight million days of work each year, and that 21–60 percent of IPV victims lose their jobs due to the web of difficulties caused by the abuse.[30] If the economic impact were not enough, especially in a state like Louisiana with the highest child poverty rate in the nation, there are well-founded health detriments beyond the obvious physical injuries resulting from domestic and sexual violence. The National Coalition Against Domestic

Violence states the following regarding the mental and physical impacts of abuse:

- Women abused by their intimate partners are more vulnerable to contracting HIV or other STIs due to forced intercourse or prolonged exposure to stress.
- Studies suggest that there is a relationship between intimate partner violence and depression and suicidal behavior.
- Physical, mental, and sexual and reproductive health effects have been linked with intimate partner violence including adolescent pregnancy, unintended pregnancy in general, miscarriage, stillbirth, intrauterine hemorrhage, nutritional deficiency, abdominal pain and other gastrointestinal problems, neurological disorders, chronic pain, disability, anxiety and post-traumatic stress disorder (PTSD), as well as noncommunicable diseases such as hypertension, cancer, and cardiovascular diseases. Victims of domestic violence are also at higher risk for developing addictions to alcohol, tobacco, or drugs.[31]

The systemic effects of abuse listed by the NCADV sheds even more light on the interconnectedness of past trauma (i.e., historical trauma), current trauma cycles of domestic and sexual violence, and the battle of mental health particularly for women of color. There is no separating these drivers; they are forever bound to each other; they may be defined separately, described with separate statistics, but make no mistake—their pervasiveness in our communities are intertwined and repeating in a perfect circle. This does not conflict with our teachings that time is not linear, that having an ongoing interaction with our past, with our ancestors makes us who we are as a people, as Indigenous people. Therefore, we cannot separate ourselves from the past and current traumas of abduction, colonization, genocide, slavery, pandemics, removals, boarding schools,[32] Indigenous erasure, and racism. These genetic and communal memories/realities have been connected through time and play a role in how our bodies respond to trauma, how our minds respond to trauma, and have had a financial underpinning on our communities since contact.

UNRAVELING THE CHAINS THAT BIND: WHERE WE GO FROM HERE

As this chapter is a call to action regarding the definitions that have excluded our communities from certain studies, or dropped the ball when it comes to identifying the health risks based on our ancestry, there is another layer of assessment and study that desperately begs attention. Reconciling the idea that Louisiana and Oklahoma hold last-place rankings in health is tied to all that has been presented in this chapter and our communities' experience of this is undoubtedly linked to our shared ancestry and experiences as survivors representing the Indigenous/Afro-Indigenous diaspora of the South.

As part of this diaspora there is no coincidence that poverty is pervasive, because as stated earlier, trauma cycles with poverty restricting access to things that make a community healthy such as early and ongoing education, preventative care, behavioral and family health programs, safe communities, traditional knowledge and ways of knowing, and even the most basic necessities like healthy foods. We cry out to have research specifically include us in their studies. Medical professionals must look to patients to describe their ancestry and familial health histories, so that they may be prescreened/identified as high risk for certain disease groups and DV/SV/IPV due to the histories of intergenerational trauma. With this, health professionals and programs may better understand how our unique genetic background and history as Afro-Indigenous peoples of the Americas impact our health and well-being.

Moreover, health professionals must work with our communities to listen, affirm, and allow access in reciprocal relationships that might not just better Creole, Freedmen, and Indigenous populations, but work to create culturally sensitive and educated medical programs. Better preventative programs and early identification and treatment programs can be created to circumvent the onslaught of obesity, diabetes, cardiovascular and autoimmune disease, cancers, cyclical family violence, sexual violence, and pervasive mental health disorders. Multifaceted programs can be piloted that draw on successes that have been had serving other communities of similar history and/or genetics, where modifications should be made based on outcomes described by statistics and by talking to the communities they are designed to serve. The first step in this process was naming the chains that bound our health and histories together, the next was identifying how and why this cycle exists, and the future steps are beginning right now as we educate and call out for representation in medical research and demand efforts in creating programming that actually addresses the root causes of the storm that has been drowning the health of our peoples for hundreds of years. For Creole and Freedmen populations we should look to the innovative decolonial research that has begun within Native American and First Nations such as research toward the impacts of historical trauma and Indigenous health through not only research but community-driven outreach such as work on diabetes, trauma, obesity, and women by Karina L. Waters (Choctaw Nation) and Michelle Johnson-Jennings (Choctaw Nation); substance abuse and HIV by JoLee Sasakamoose (Anishinabe/ M'Chigeeng First Nation); historical trauma and neuro-decolonization by Michael Yellow Bird (Mandan, Hidatsa, and Arikara); maternal-child and reproductive health by Jennifer Leason (Saulteaux-Métis Anishinaabek / Pine Creek First Nation and Duck Bay); diet and decolonization by Devon A. Mihesuah (Choctaw Nation); and Indigenous healing knowledge and Western medicine by Marcia Anderson DeCoteau (Cree- Saulteaux). Ultimately we have learned to survive through our communities and tenacity. In her poem "Love Letter to Lupus," Rain Prud'homme-Cranford (formally Goméz) writes:

> Muscles stage coup. Needles are painful. Pills don't do shit.
>   Break your ankles.
> Take a bat to your wrist.
> Then walk, write—tell me how it feels? I fucking hate you.
> You're a bully.
> Another rapist, slave master, abusive bastard husband—But me—
>   I'm still a bitch.
>
> Fuck off—
> cuz I been walking with bloody steps for centuries.[33]

Our fight is not over. The storm still gathers. But our voices are calling down a softer rain.

NOTES

This chapter's epigraph is drawn from Katie Schultz, Karina L. Walters, Ramona Beltran, Sandy Stroud, and Michelle Johnson-Jennings, "'I'm Stronger Than I Thought': Native Women Reconnecting to Body, Health, and Place," *Health & Place* 40 (July 2016): 21–28, www.doi.org/10.1016/j.healthplace.2016.05.001

1. I would like to point out that my references to DNA and genetic testing are around illnesses, heredity, and historical trauma, not ethnicity. DNA testing is problematic for mixed-race, multigenerational people, and Native DNA results are not always accurate nor are they what constitutes tribal cultural inheritance, citizenship, or community belonging. For more on this subject see Johnathan Marks and Brett Lee Shelton. "Genetic 'Markers': Not a Valid Test of Native Identity," Indigenous Peoples Council on Bioculturalism, accessed October 20, 2020, www.ipcb.org; Rory Taylor, "DNA Tests Are Not an Indicator of Native Identity," Teen Vogue, October 19, 2020, www.teenvogue.com; "Aviva Chomsky, Making Native Americans Strangers in Their Own Land," Tom Dispatch, November 29, 2018, https://tomdispatch.com; Teresa Carey, "DNA Tests Stand on Shaky Ground to Define Native American Identity," National Human Genome Research Institute, May 9, 2019, www.genome.gov; and Kimberly TallBear, *Native American DNA: Tribal Belonging and the False Promise of Genetic Science* (Minneapolis: University of Minnesota Press, 2013).

2. Of particular note on research towards the impacts of historical trauma and Indigenous health includes research and community driven outreach on diabetes, obesity, and women by Karina L. Waters (Choctaw Nation) and Michelle Johnson-Jennings (Choctaw Nation); substance abuse and HIV by JoLee Sasakamoose (Anishinabe/M'Chigeeng First Nation); historical trauma and neuro-decolonization by Michael Yellow Bird (Mandan, Hidatsa, and Arikara); maternal-child and reproductive health by Jennifer Leason (Saulteaux-Métis Anishinaabek / Pine Creek First Nation and Duck Bay); diet and decolonization by Devon A. Mihesuah (Choctaw Nation); and Indigenous healing knowledge and Western medicine by Marcia Anderson DeCoteau (Cree-Saulteaux).

3. Rachel Yehuda and Amy Lehrner, "Intergenerational Transmission of Trauma Effects: Putative Role of Epigenetic Mechanisms," *World Psychiatry* 17, no. 3 (2018): 243–57, www.doi.org/10.1002/wps.20568.

4. As Rain Prud'homme-Cranford notes in this collection, "Freedman, descendants of slaves and Natives from the 'Five Civilized Tribes' (Cherokee, Seminole, Choctaw, Creek, and Chickasaw), and other Red/Black (Native/African) populations and their Native Nations, remind those of us in Indian country of the contested and related relationships, and histories of African American and Native American peoples."

5. As the descendant of two distinct Red/Black communities—Louisiana Creole and Choctaw/Chickasaw Freedmen—my identifying with my

Louisiana Creole/Choctaw-Biloxi and Freedmen ancestry is testimony to the landbases I have been raised and live in: Oklahoma and Louisiana. This in no way diminishes my pride in mother's ancestry nor her father's Cree-Métis experiences and inheritance as a residential school survivor from Alberta, Canada.

6. Richard Witzig and Mark Alain Dery, "Subjectively Assigned Race versus Self-Reported Race and Ethnicity in U.S. Healthcare," *Social Medicine* 8, no. 1 (January 2014): 35–36.
7. The scope of this chapter is an *overview* to highlight the call to action and systemic issues surrounding best practices within Creole-NDN and Freedmen health and wellness. I encourage others in health and medicine, sociology and psychology, and abuse treatment/counseling to add to this work by doing in-depth studies and community outreach on each of the issues addressed in this chapter.
8. As a Louisiana Creole/Choctaw-Biloxi and Freedmen my home states are both Oklahoma and Louisiana. Hence I have chosen to use the collective "we" when addressing both Louisiana and Oklahoma. Statistics accessed July 1, 2019, www.americahealthrankings.org.
9. Accessed July 1, 2019, www.americashealthrankings.org/explore/annual/measure/YPLL/state/LA.
10. Katie Schultz et al., "'I'm Stronger Than I Thought: Native Women Reconnecting to Body, Health, and Place," *Health & Place* 40 (July 2016): 21–28.
11. Michele Andrasik, "Historical Trauma and the Health and Wellbeing of Communities of Color," HIV Vaccine Trials Network, accessed August 4, 2019, www.hvtn.org.
12. Accessed July 6, 2019, www.diabetes.org/diabetes-basics/statistics.
13. It should be noted that despite having both federal- and state-recognized tribes, Louisiana offers no stats on diabetes for the tribal populations—another Indigenous erasure.
14. Accessed July 1, 2019, www.americashealthrankings.org.
15. Accessed July 7, 2019, https://datausa.io/profile/geo/louisiana#health.
16. Accessed July 7, 2019, www.diabetes.org/diabetes-basics/statistics.
17. Accessed July 7, 2019, www.heart.org/en/health-topics/diabetes/why-diabetes-matters/cardiovascular-disease--diabetes.
18. Myles J. Lewis and Ali S. Jawad, "The Effect of Ethnicity and Genetic Ancestry on the Epidemiology, Clinical Features, and Outcome of Systemic Lupus Erythematosus," *Rheumatology* 56, no. S1 (April 2017): i67–i77, www.doi.org/10.1093/rheumatology/kew399.
19. Jasmine R. Gaddy, Evan S. Vista, Julie M. Robertson, Amy B. Dedeke, Virginia C. Roberts, Wendy S. Klein, Jeremy H. Levin, Fabio H. Mota, Tina M. Cooper, Gloria A. Grim, Sohail Khan, and Judith A. James, "Rheumatic Disease among Oklahoma Tribal Populations: A Cross-Sectional Study," *Journal of Rheumatology* 39, no. 10 (October 2012):

accessed August 5, 2019, www.ncbi.nlm.nih.gov/pmc/articles/PMC3468952.
20. Lewis and Jawad, "Effect of Ethnicity and Genetic Ancestry."
21. Gaddy et al., "Rheumatic Disease among Oklahoma Tribal Populations."
22. Lewis and Jawad, "Effect of Ethnicity and Genetic Ancestry."
23. "Violence Against Women Act," NNEDV, accessed July 4, 2019, https://nnedv.org/content/violence-against-women-act.
24. Patricia Tjaden and Nancy Thoennes, "Full Report of the Prevalence, Incidence, and Consequences of Violence against Women," PsycExtra dataset, 2000, www.doi.org/10.1037/e514172006-001.
25. Tjaden and Thoennes.
26. "Ending Violence Against Native Women," Indian Law Resource Center, accessed July 1, 2019, https://indianlaw.org/issue/ending-violence-against-native-women.
27. Cameron Kimble and Inimai M. Chettiar, "Sexual Assault Remains Dramatically Underreported," Brennan Center for Justice, October 4, 2018, www.brennancenter.org.
28. Jeremiah Bourgeois, Dane Stallone, Justice News, and TCR Staff, "Report: Nearly Half of Domestic Violence Goes Unreported," The Crime Report, June 5, 2017, https://thecrimereport.org.
29. Prud'homme-Cranford, Rain. "No Body Sings Blues like a FAT BODY: Gender, Race, and Colonialism." In *Louisiana Creole Peoplehood: Tracing Post-Contact Afro-Indigeneity and Community.*
30. "Statistics," NCADV: National Coalition Against Domestic Violence, accessed July 3, 2019, https://ncadv.org/statistics.
31. "Statistics."
32. Boarding schools were an essential step in Indigenous erasure, enforcing the dissolution of culture, language, and family construct for Indigenous peoples. Boarding school mandates were in place for American Indian children throughout the Americas, and were also implemented for Afro-Indigenous children identified as Creole who spoke Creole-French.
33. Rain C. Goméz (Prud'homme-Cranford), "Love Letter to Lupus," in *Smoked Mullet Cornbread Crawdad Memory* (Norman, OK: Mongrel Empire Press, 2012).

COMMUNITY RESPONSE

CAUGHT IN THE CYCLE

SUMMER WESLEY

When I began reading "A Perfect Circle Bound in Chains," I intended to approach the topic from an academic perspective, objectively focusing my comments on the broader community impact and compartmentalized from my personal experiences. However, I felt my blood pressure starting to rise as I read the descriptions of the physical effects of autoimmune disorders; my breaths became shallow and quick, chest feeling immensely heavy. By the time I reached the end of the first line of "Love Letter to Lupus," a poem by Shawnee's sister, the tears were unstoppable. You see, at that moment, I was in week 2 of wearing braces on my knees, unable to walk normally (and, at some points, not at all) due to inflammation caused by an autoimmune episode. Even as someone who has studied and routinely educates on the connectedness of colonization, trauma, structural disparities, violence, health, et cetera, seeing words on the page describing the damage that I was feeling, quite literally, the pain of and realizing, yet again, the inevitability of continued degeneration felt so personally violating.

In my case, my autoimmune issues began when I was twenty, after experiencing tick fever. We lived in an isolated rural area of Oklahoma at that time, with inadequate healthcare in local hospitals. Our nation's hospital provided competent care but was 1.5 hours' drive from our home—a trip we could not afford. So I stayed home and used plant medicine to cope with the high fever for an entire weekend, only beginning the recommended antibiotics the following week, after my local clinic opened for regular business hours.

At that point we thought it was over. However, I began experiencing unexplained inflammation and seemingly random low-grade fevers. Initially, it was thought that, perhaps, the tick-borne infection had not been completely cleared up. However, lab values seemed to be within my normal ranges and I became pregnant soon after, so many of my symptoms were dismissed as the overreaction of a hormonal pregnant woman or as normal discomfort related to gestation. It would be several years before medical providers would conclude that there was an actual autoimmune issue—one that has still not been specifically identified, even after seventeen years.

Because my condition was unmanaged, I developed systemic candidiasis, which my baby was then also born with. As a result, his immune system didn't work for the first few years of his life and he had allergic reactions to many common substances until we were able to finally get his body in balance enough to keep his candida levels low enough to not cause infection.

Due to my autoimmune issues, however, my battle with the infection in my bloodstream was much different. When he was around a year old, it almost killed me. Somewhere in my home, there is a photo of me and my sister that we took during that time, because we thought it might be the last one we would be able to take together. It is "somewhere," because I cannot bear to look at the extremely underweight me, with gray skin, and remember what it felt like to think that I was going to leave my children behind, so I hid the photo behind another in a frame.

The only reason that I am still alive is because a doctor was willing to risk his license and prescribe a very aggressive regimen of medication, far beyond the dosages recommended by the CDC at the time. He saved my life and I am normally quite grateful. But there are times when the pain is so unbearable that, for a fleeting moment, I wonder if he made the wrong decision.

For many of us, physical health issues can be compounded by mental health. In addition to historical trauma, I have PTSD as the result of individual, violent trauma. During the early years of my autoimmune issues, I was just beginning to understand my acute PTSD reactions, and it would be years before I was self-aware enough to reliably recognize and manage ongoing anxiety and depression. So, I had no real understanding of how it could affect my physical health or that the physical damage of each autoimmune flare up could be permanent. And not a single healthcare provider had ever explained those vital pieces of information to me prior to two years ago, when a psychiatrist wanted to make sure that I was aware of the interdependent cycle of mental and physical health.

Obviously, these psychological struggles lend themselves to neglecting one's physical health and, at times, a disconnect that they create can cause one to not even be fully aware of their own pain, thus ignoring symptoms of physical maladies. Unfortunately, none of the medical professionals that has treated me over the years has ever identified those psychological issues without me explicitly stating it to them, and some have even tried to accuse me of exaggerating symptoms. None has ever been willing to discuss how the mental health struggles can exacerbate or interfere with management of physical health, or how the pain from physical symptoms can increase the anxiety and/or depression, in order to create a holistic approach to managing my health. As such, I am left to manage it as best I can using what I can discern from my own research, as someone with no medical training, and knowledge of natural medicines passed from my ancestors.

Like many from Indigenous communities, my access to healthcare is limited by economic means. While I am fortunate to have insurance, I generally cannot afford to pay my portion for needed treatments at private clinics. As I now live in an urban setting, I no longer have ready access to my Nation's clinics, so must depend on Indian Health Service clinics, which means extremely long wait times in the one near me, or extensive travel to another area. Resultingly, I generally do not receive needed treatments or the specialized testing needed for them to more specifically pinpoint the particular disorder that I'm dealing with. As a social worker and community advocate, I can attest to the fact that this is a common problem among the people with whom I work. The health and welfare of people are being addressed as if their lives are expendable.

Our people are sick, and dying, because of continued colonization and a lack of will among the institutions that are supposedly set up to remedy such issues. This must end now. It's far past time for the needs of Indigenous peoples to be considered on all levels, from policy making to program development, so that the genocidal cycle can finally be broken in our communities.

PART 3

LANGUAGES

Literacies and Bodies

CHAPTER 8

LANGUAGE REVITALIZATION, RACE, AND RESISTANCE IN CREOLE LOUISIANA

OLIVER MAYEUX

Ideologies of language can be leveraged to (re)construct and contest discourses and hierarchies of race and ethnicity.[1] I intend here to scrutinize how this plays out in the context of language revitalization. Specifically, this chapter interrogates the complex, contested, and sometimes contradictory relationship between Louisiana Creole ethnic, racial, and linguistic identities, taking as its lens the language revitalization movements that have emerged in Louisiana since the Civil Rights Act. My view of language revitalization is shaped by the understanding that "struggles over language actually are not centrally about language at all"[2] and that in the context of language revitalization, as James Costa articulates,

> although language is of course the central rallying point, the actions that we are referring to are primarily not about language but about people: people coming together to act in the world, people articulating opinions about how society should be ordered and about who should take part in that order.[3]

With this in mind, and in response to this volume's focus on Louisiana Creole peoplehood, I attempt here to clarify how Creole-identified activists have established a form of Louisiana Creole *languagehood* that acts as a totem for broader social conflicts. By reifying Louisiana Creole as a language in its own right and emphasizing its distinctiveness from Louisiana French, activists seek to reclaim and rearticulate Louisiana Creole peoplehood on their own terms. This, I argue, is a form of resistance to discourses around preserving Louisiana's linguistic heritage, which have overwhelmingly foregrounded "Cajun" French, a linguistic identity that in Louisiana is racially constructed and represented as "white." This focus on Cajun (i.e., white) linguistic identity has served to further marginalize Louisiana's communities of color, through an ideological process of linguistic erasure.[4]

It is wise to begin by considering histories of the Cajun and Creole language revitalization movements in critical perspective. This review uncovers the ideological roots of the Cajun movement among white reactionary responses to civil rights. I then address how creolophone activists of color began to counter this whitewashing of Louisiana heritage. From this basis, I discuss the burgeoning Kouri-Vini movement, a group of "new speakers"[5] of Louisiana Creole whose language revitalization activities explicitly seek to resist Cajunist discourses, and which are oriented around the symbolic usage of the Louisiana Creole language under the moniker Kouri-Vini. I conclude by reviewing these attempts to establish Louisiana Creole languagehood in broad linguistic-anthropological perspective, attending to the resultant theoretical insights for studies of language revitalization, Louisiana Creole studies and, on a more practical level, for the future of this critically endangered language.

WHITEWASHING FRENCH: HOW LOUISIANA FRENCH BECAME CAJUN

> *On s'appelait des Créoles avant cette affaire de Cadjin.*
> We called ourselves Creoles before this Cajun business.[6]

Linguists typically identify two French-related languages in Louisiana: regional varieties of the French language (Louisiana regional French, hereafter LF) and a French-based creole known as Louisiana Creole (hereafter LC; aka Kouri-Vini, see below). Though each of these languages has particular linguistic features, their relationship is complex. LC is only partially intelligible to some speakers of LF, whereas other speakers have full bilingual competence. Further, due to the sociolinguistic dynamics of regional settlement and racial segregation, dialects of LC are linguistically influenced to varying degrees by LF.[7] Most germane to the concerns of this chapter, this complexity is further compounded by what N. A. Wendte has referred to as the tendency for "ethnoglossic isomorphism."[8] Self-identified Cajuns call their language Cajun (French), while self-identified Creoles call their language Creole (French). These self-reported emic labels often do not correspond to formal linguistic structures designated LC and LF by linguists. Emic language-naming practices in contemporary Louisiana therefore have everything to do with ethnic and racial identification, and very little to do with linguistic structure.[9]

The origins of this situation can be found in the process of Americanization of Louisiana, which imposed the English language on the LF- and LC-speaking inhabitants of the territory. Importantly, however, as Darryl Barthé discusses in this volume, it also ushered in the "Jim Crow" racial binary that brought into contention existing racial and ethnic labels. As Nathalie Dajko puts it, "Ethnicity became polarized around race, it appears that language labels shifted as well, to match the new arrangement."[10] During Americanization, Louisiana's prosperous white families began to integrate steadily into Anglo-American society while rural, poor white families remained more isolated. They were often denigrated and marginalized by wealthy white Anglo-Americans and Americanized white Creoles alike, who used the slur "Cajun," which referred to poor, rural, working-class whites and derived from the French term *Acadien* (Acadian), after the some three thousand refugees who arrived in the late 1700s.[11] "A Creole mother would say to her child, '*Tu es habillé comme un Cadien; ça c'est Cadien*' ['You are dressed like a Cajun; that's Cajun'] and that made her point."[12] Nevertheless, by the 1970s, it was under that label that Louisiana was sold to the world: Louisiana was marketed as the home of the Cajuns, speakers of "Cajun" French.

As Marjorie Esman argued in her important 1983 paper, the "Cajun" French revitalization movement has its ideological roots in the activities of white reactionaries seeking to counteract the civil rights movement, who sought to construct themselves as a marginalized ethnic group via the appropriation of the "Cajun" slur:

> Spontaneous Cajun activities can also be seen as reactions to Civil Rights, attempts by the formerly poor Whites to preserve their only claim to prestige. Influenced by the rhetoric and success of

Black Civil Rights, White Cajun ethnic activities were more than imitations: they represent a direct reaction against Black rights.[13]

These discourses are evident in a little-known legal paper authored by the founder and director of the Council for the Development of French in Louisiana (CODOFIL), Jimmy Domengeaux. Domengeaux positions Cajuns as a (white) minority group who ought to be subject to the same legal protections from discrimination as those outlined for people of color in the 1964 Civil Rights Act:

Le titre VII de la loi de 1964 (Civil Rights Act of 1964) avait pour but de supprimer sur les lieux de travail toute discrimination basée sur la race et la lignée . . . un Acadien d'origine peut se prévaloir de la protection de cette loi.[14]

Title VII of the Civil Rights Act of 1964 had as its goal the abolition of all workplace discrimination based on race or descent . . . a native-born Acadian can invoke the protection of that Act.

Domengeaux's opinions on the end of segregation and the place of people of color in Louisiana society are well-documented. Mark De Wolf reports the following anecdote from civil rights activist John Carlton James:

[Domengeaux] said, "I'll walk in blood up to my neck before Negroes vote in the city of Lafayette." And I told him I didn't know anybody who could ever walk in blood up to his neck. They'd swim if they got that deep. For 25 years after that we didn't speak.[15]

Domengeaux was also famously in favor of the adoption of Parisian French rather than the local Louisiana vernacular, which he derided as "redneck" and "chicken scratch."[16] This irony exposes the important role of classism in the early Cajun movement. The disdain for working-class French appropriately complicates the picture of early Cajunist activism, pointing to the appropriation of the "Cajun" label by *la bourgeoisie louisianaise* in general and Domengeaux in particular. This is, in my view, a more accurate and realistic view of the emergence of "Cajun-washing," an alternative to the somewhat paranoid notion of all-out conspiracy among all early Cajun French activists. Indeed, Ducote's important thesis has shown, many of Louisiana's first generation of CODOFIL French teachers—themselves raised in rural working-class francophone homes—actively resisted Domengeaux's stance in their own activism and their classroom teaching. Individual teachers have worked tirelessly to valorize the languages spoken by the people of Louisiana, both people of color and working-class whites alike, and today have in many ways succeeded in reconstructing CODOFIL as a significantly more inclusive and well-intentioned organization.[17]

Nevertheless, in looking back at the Cajun movement, it must be admitted that the choice to brand Louisiana—its food, traditions, and French language—as "Cajun" over "Creole" can "only be interpreted as the desire for the French Louisiana elite to assure for the region a "white" identity."[18] The Cajun movement's influential "revitalization myth"[19] involved constructing Louisiana's white population as a marginalized group under the "Cajun" label. For whites who consciously or unconsciously perceived civil rights legislation and integration as a threat to their power, the newfound status as marginalized Cajuns was an appropriate solution. In practice, the Cajun myth has been justified less by genealogy and more by the collective imaginary of Louisiana's white population. Even in places like Avoyelles Parish, which historically had very little Acadian settlement, it is commonplace to hear whites identify themselves, their food, and their language as "Cajun." Likewise, "Cajun French" is imagined as the continuation of the language brought by the Acadians to Louisiana. This is despite more than a century of French presence in Louisiana before the arrival of the Acadians, the fact that LF has long been spoken across racial and ethnic lines, and linguistic analyses that demonstrate that the Acadian dialect made a relatively small contribution to what we now know as LF.[20] It is therefore easy to see why the label "Cajun French" is unsuitable for academic research: not only is it linguistically inaccurate, it perpetuates the erasure of Louisiana's thousands of francophones of color.

NOUSQUENNE NAISSANCE CRÉOLE: THE CREOLE RENAISSANCE

Tensions and changes in CODOFIL were evident in January 2017 when outgoing director Charles Larroque established the Comité créole (Creole committee), tasked with addressing the LC component of CODOFIL's responsibility. There was a sense among many Creole activists that this initiative was a case of too little, too late. Indeed, the Comité has not continued its meetings, though many Creole activists are sympathetic to the fact that CODOFIL is chronically underfunded, understaffed and overburdened. For many activists, then, CODOFIL's Comité créole only confirmed what they already knew: the best chance for language activism and concomitant social change lay outside state organizations and, instead, at the grassroots of historically creolophone communities of color. Jolivétte emphasizes the importance of the civil rights movement in galvanizing language activism among Creoles of color:

> The shift from viewing Creoles simply as a subgroup within the black category, begun during the 1965–1990 period, happened because of a larger multiracial movement led by groups such as the Association for Multiethnic Americans. Since that time, Creoles have supported the formation of linguistic preservation organisations such as the Creole Institute at Indiana University, which completed the *Dictionary of Louisiana Creole*, and Creole migrants across the United States have begun reconnecting with the diaspora outside of Louisiana through state and national history conferences.[21]

Thus, the separate Cajun and Creole movements can be viewed as two independent responses to the civil rights movement. Clearly, though, these movements were in (sometimes fraught) dialogue. Opposition to the Cajun narrative is obvious in the name of Creole of color activist group the "Un-Cajun Committee." The Cajun movement, in turn, responded to the criticisms of Creoles of color. For example, when Creoles of color criticized the branding of the "Cajundome," Barry Ancelet decried this as an example of "reverse racism."[22] This time of "Creole Return"—in Jolivétte's timeline—was thus a period of ideological confrontation, as both Cajun and Creole activist groups jostled for their place at the table. It was this setting that gave rise to new ideological positions relative to LF and LC. Crucially, as discussed, Cajun activists had already laid claim to the label "French," now branded "Cajun French." For francophones of color, this constituted an erasure in no uncertain terms: now, the only speakers of

"French" in Louisiana were Cajuns (i.e., whites). Creole of color activists could no longer lay claim to "French." Instead, they concentrated their efforts on reclaiming the label "Creole French." In practice, this mostly meant LC, though this was never explicitly articulated.

Recalling the long history of writers of color in Louisiana—discussed by Prud'homme-Cranford in this volume—poets such as Deborah Clifton and Sybil Kein began to explore LC as a creative medium, ushering in what Jolivétte terms the "Creole Renaissance" (1960s–1990s): "Enfin nousquenne naissance créole!" (Finally our own Creole Renaissance!).[23] From its inception, activist groups such as CREOLE Inc. incorporated a strong linguistic component, where language was situated as a core component of cultural identity. CREOLE Inc.'s *Creole Magazine* included Herbert Wiltz's regular column "La Leson Kreyòl" (The Creole lesson) as well as an occasional "Creole Linguistics" column.[24] Language lessons used to be offered at the University of Louisiana at Lafayette by Deborah Clifton, in Pointe Coupée by the organization Les Créoles de Pointe Coupée and, in St. Martinville, Velma Johnson founded Latab Kreyol, a club for LC speakers that still meets regularly in Parks.

CREOLE Inc. also encouraged regional, national, and international exchanges, bringing speakers of LC into contact with creolophones from Martinique, Guadeloupe, and Haiti. These cultural and linguistic exchanges reinvigorated linguistic and cultural reclamation efforts. In their encounter with the Kreyolofoni, Louisiana Creoles of color could move beyond using the Cajunist movement as an opposing point of reference. With a sense of solidarity, they could instead orient themselves relative to their cultural and linguistic cousins in the Caribbean, a narrative that proliferated throughout this period.

KOURI-VINI, AN INDIGENOUS LANGUAGE: THE CREOLE "E-NAISSANCE"

As the elders at the forefront of the Creole Renaissance have retired, a younger group of activists has stepped forward. Their efforts, spearheaded by activist Christophe Landry, now center principally around a network of language activists and learners based on Facebook. Unlike the activists of the Creole Renaissance, the leaders of the "Creole E-Naissance" are primarily "new speakers" of the language. In the recent sociolinguistics literature, the label "new speakers" describes individuals who have "little or no home or community exposure to a minority language but who instead acquire it through immersion or bilingual education programs, revitalization projects or as adult language learners."[25] As scholars of language revitalization have noted, "issues of authenticity, legitimacy, hierarchies and power relations are often at the heart of "new speakerness."[26] Social media offers an important semiotic terrain for identity construction and, for new speakers of endangered languages, a highly salient terrain for such language-ideological concerns to be represented, furthered, and contested.

Here, I dub this community of language activists the Kouri-Vini movement, in reference to one of their high-priority objectives: establishing control over language-naming practices. Contention over language naming practices is often involved in the construction of group boundaries in this way, perhaps most famously in the case of the Balkans and also in other revitalization contexts.[27] In 2015, the movement led a campaign to change the official designation for LC by the International Organization for Standardization and the *Ethnologue*, where LC had previously been designated "Louisiana Creole French." The mission was to underscore LC's status as a separate language from French, thus rejecting the Cajun-Creole binary that has long dominated conversations of language revitalization in Louisiana.[28]

Most recently, online activists have begun to use the term "Kouri-Vini" to refer to LC, a label sometimes encountered amongst creolophones along the Bayou Tèche (sometimes, though not always, in a derogatory fashion). The word "Creole," Landry and others contend, leads to conflation with the contentious ethnic label and invites comparison with other creole languages, which have historically not been treated as fully fledged linguistic systems.[29] "The Kouri-Vini Louisiana Creole Fanpage," the public-facing Facebook page of the online movement, features a banner that reads "Kouri-Vini: Louisiana's Indigenous Creole Language."[30] The incorporation of the Indigenous label—justified in historical-linguistic terms in the sense that creolization took place in Louisiana—emphasizes the Indigenous component of Louisiana Creole identity discussed throughout this volume. This also results in LC being positioned as an Indigenous language, which may allow access to funding and other support intended for Indigenous language reclamation. Like other endangered creole languages in postcolonial settings, LC has fallen between the cracks when it comes to language revitalization because LC has no federally recognized, contiguous Indigenous group for whom it acts as a heritage language. Social media has provided an important forum for the invention, discussion, and proliferation of such discourses.

The Kouri-Vini movement's other activities include the development of a distinctive orthography, especially apt in the unembodied online spaces where, instead, we are "typed into being."[31] Given the visual nature of spelling and how it can be manipulated to construe social meaning[32] it is of no surprise that orthography development in language revitalization may raise any number of "social, psychological, economic, and historical issues."[33] Orthography becomes the "most obvious terrain" for language-ideological debates to be played out,[34] as commonly occurs in the case of minority languages.[35] Spelling represents a vital semiotic strategy for the representation of the Kouri-Vini movement. The group's orthography was devised by Christophe Landry and underwent various permutations, which culminated in the 2016 publication of "Kouri-Vini: A Guide to Louisiana Creole Orthography." The orthography is designed with the explicit intention of marking LC as a language distinct from both French and other French-based creoles, in contrast to the spellings used by activists in the Creole Renaissance.[36] Thus, as with the glossonym "Kouri-Vini," the intention underlying the orthography is the establishment of LC as an autonomous linguistic system, independent from LF and other French-lexifier creoles.[37] These concerns were arguably secondary to activists in the Creole Renaissance movement, who used French-style spelling (e.g., Sybil Kein, Deborah Clifton, Ulysses S. Ricard Jr.) and a more Haitian-style system (e.g., in Herbert Wiltz's *Leson Kreyol*). Most recently, Herbert Wiltz, CREOLE Inc. member and veteran language activist, started his own LC language classes in downtown Lafayette, which moved online during the COVID-19 pandemic. He chooses the orthography of the Kouri-Vini movement—rather than the Haitian-style orthography he had previously used—for his curriculum, testament to the growing currency of the new orthography.

In other contexts of language revitalization, the language of new speakers has been shown to diverge from that of "traditional" speakers, leading some linguists to identify new, hybridized dialects such as Neo-Hawai'ian or Neo-Breton.[38] Elsewhere, I have argued that, on a linguistic basis, the language used by the Kouri-Vini movement does not diverge from contemporary LC in such a way as to justify branding it as a new or "nontraditional" dialect of the language. Nevertheless, some teaching materials—and, subsequently, learners of LC—use linguistic forms that emphasize the boundary between LC and LF. For example, new speakers of LC tend to use a plural definite determiner *-la-yé*, which is placed after a noun—for example, *lamézon-la-yé*, "the houses." This construction is similar to that used in nineteenth-century LC. Today, most dialects of LC tend to use a construction that resembles the LF equivalent—that is, *les maisons*, "the houses." The nineteenth-century LC form has gained ground because it is maximally distant from LF. Like the Kouri-Vini movement's orthography, this is another strategy for erecting boundaries between the two languages.[39]

Thus, unlike the generation of activists who led the Creole Renaissance, the Kouri-Vini movement does not seek to struggle against the promotion of "Cajun French" movement by championing "Creole French." Instead, by constructing a linguistic identity that moves beyond these binary labels, the Kouri-Vini movement seeks to gain control over discourses of ethnolinguistic legitimacy.

LOUISIANA CREOLE PEOPLEHOOD AND LANGUAGEHOOD

I have attempted here to document the relationship between racial, ethnic, and linguistic identities in Louisiana's language revitalization movements from the 1960s to the present day, deconstructing the linguistic-ideological underpinning of these movements in sociohistorical perspective. By way of conclusion, I will take a broader linguistic-anthropological perspective in considering the implications that the growing Kouri-Vini movement—and its claims to LC languagehood—hold for Louisiana Creole studies in particular and studies of language revitalization in general.

As in all revitalization movements, language activists in Louisiana have been jostling "to define the object they strive to revitalise, and to define conditions of participation in the movement—who will be allowed to take part, and who will not, according to what criteria?"[40] The Cajun French movement laid claim to French, which was used by some activists to emphasize the impoverished, marginalized status of rural whites. It has been shown, however, that this claim to minority status was a response to the civil rights movement led by white reactionaries with the intention of preserving white hegemony. In resistance to their erasure, Louisiana Creoles of color led the Creole Renaissance, their attempt to win back their claims to Louisiana heritage.

On a surface level, it might seem that the Kouri-Vini movement replicates the binary opposition that has emerged whereby racial and linguistic identities are conflated and essentialized: in brief, "Cajun French for the (white) Cajuns; Creole for Creoles (of color)." The undertaking of the nascent Kouri-Vini movement is, however, to effectively deconstruct this binary and, subsequently, to reconstruct a new, twenty-first-century relationship between LC identity, language, and history. The Kouri-Vini movement positions itself as the resistance to an Americanized, racially essentializing reading of Creole identity that has been promoted by the Cajun movement. In so doing, its supporters contend that they are reestablishing historical continuity with Louisiana before Americanization, when the ethnic label "Creole" was applicable to those born in Louisiana, regardless of race. The Kouri-Vini movement moves beyond this, however, including *all* practitioners of Louisiana Creole culture—including those in the diaspora, as exemplified by the remarks of Prud'homme-Cranford in this volume.

Instead of race and place, language has become the rallying point of the Kouri-Vini movement. Through laying claim to LC as a language distinct from LF and, thus, independent of Cajunist discourses, the Kouri-Vini movement are effectively "retelling"[41] peoplehood and who counts as a legitimate Creole in Louisiana. From a Bourdieusien perspective, the Kouri-Vini movement seeks not only to accrue their own cultural capital, rival to that of the Cajunists, but also to redefine what forms of cultural capital are considered powerful, relevant, and legitimate. The Kouri-Vini movement is actively problematizing and disrupting the field of (racial) power that runs horizontally through the field of language revitalization and its contingent fields (policymaking, education, community-building).

The continuation of these efforts will undoubtedly see the proliferation of the kind of language-centered conflicts observed in other minority language communities. First, efforts to maintain and revitalize the LC language have been spearheaded exclusively by Creoles of color, who have acted as guardians for the language through individual and community efforts in the fields of creative expression and activism. Eschewing race from the history of the creation, maintenance, and revitalization of LC would be entirely counterfactual, sorely so for a language that originated among enslaved peoples in a society structured around racial violence. As a white speaker-learner of LC who sometimes has positioned that language as one of my "heritage languages," I can only admit that the contemporary LC language revitalization movement risks (at least partially) whitewashing the language and disillusioning many native speakers if creolophones of color are not positioned at the core of language revitalization efforts. Second, it remains to be seen whether LC's recent formulation as an Indigenous language will help or hinder the revitalization movement. Since the Creole identity is multivalent (cf. Jolivétte and Prud'homme-Cranford in this volume) and, for many Creoles of color, encompasses a strong element of Indigenous identity, the equivocation of LC language revitalization and Indigenous language revitalization risks replicating some of the mistakes of early CODOFIL activism—that is, the subtle erasure of, and ideological conflict with, Indigenous communities such as the Tunica-Biloxi, Houma, Atakapa-Ishak, and so forth, who are each building their own language revitalization movements. Third, the online Kouri-Vini movement is still largely unknown in the rural communities where LC is still spoken. It remains to be seen to what extent the online movement will continue to rely on a "trickle down" ("trickle offline"?) effect, as has been seen in the case of the adoption of the Kouri-Vini movement's orthography in CREOLE Inc.'s recent LC classes. Perhaps the key challenge facing new speakers of LC is how they will engage with the knowledge-bearers in rural Louisiana communities who, themselves, represent the living repositories of the linguistic, cultural, and oral-historical traditions that the Kouri-Vini Movement intends to valorize and reclaim. The online-offline dialogue will doubtless entail some difficult ideological confrontations. Community members in Parks have suggested to me that a language summer school, bringing together local youth and elders with language activists, would be an appropriate starting point for this dialogue and for community-(re)building in general. The success of master-apprentice programs elsewhere makes this a promising proposition.[42]

How the contemporary LC revitalization movement will respond to these issues will be of vital importance to the future of the LC language as well as future conceptualizations of Louisiana Creole peoplehood. Jane Freeland has argued that "diaspora groups like [Creole peoples] are particularly ill-served by the unitary notions of peoplehood, identity, and language that underpin Western state language policies and minority challenges to them."[43] As Jolivétte has noted in the Louisiana context, "by refusing to accept a monoracial identity, [Louisiana] Creoles represent an important case study on ethnic movements and revitalization."[44] Here, I have attempted to show how Louisiana Creoles have constructed links between language and peoplehood on their own terms, beyond the Anglo-American racial binary. This case exposes the intersection of race and language revitalization, and how social movements that unite around language may mount resistance to racism and social exclusion.

NOTES

I am grateful to Marjorie Esman, Michael Hornsby, Christophe Landry, and Li Nguyen for their feedback on this chapter.

1. H. Samy Alim, John R. Rickford, and Arnetha F. Ball, eds., *Raciolinguistics: How Language Shapes Our Ideas about Race* (New York: Oxford University Press, 2016).
2. Monica Heller, "Analysis and Stance Regarding Language and Social Justice," in *Language Rights and Language Survival*, by Jane Freeland and Donna Patrick (New York: Routledge, 2004), 285, www.doi.org/10.4324/9781315760155.
3. James Costa, *Revitalising Language in Provence: A Critical Approach*, Publications of the Philological Society 48 (Malden, MA: John Wiley & Sons, 2017), 4.
4. Judith T. Irvine and Susan Gal, "Language Ideology and Linguistic Differentiation," in *Regimes of Language: Ideologies, Polities, and Identities*, ed. Paul V. Kroskrity (Santa Fe: School of American Research Press, 2000), 35–84.
5. See Bernadette O'Rourke, Joan Pujolar, and Fernando Ramallo, eds., "New Speakers of Minority Languages: The Challenging Opportunity," *International Journal of the Sociology of Language* 2015, no. 231 (January 2015): 1–20, www.doi.org/10.1515/ijsl-2014-0029; Michael Hornsby, *Revitalizing Minority Languages: New Speakers of Breton, Yiddish and Lemko* (London: Palgrave Macmillan UK, 2015), www.doi.org/10.1057/9781137498809.
6. Anonymous interviewee in Cécyle Trépanier, "The Cajunization of French Louisiana: Forging a Regional Identity," *Geographical Journal* 157, no. 2 (July 1991): 167, www.doi.org/10.2307/635273.
7. Oliver Mayeux, "Rethinking Decreolization: Language Contact and Change in Louisiana Creole" (PhD diss., University of Cambridge, 2019),

www.doi.org/10.17863/CAM.41629; Thomas A. Klingler, "La variation ethnolinguistique en créole louisianais au cours du XXe siècle," in *Sprach- und Kulturkontaktphänomene in der Romania—Phénomènes de contact linguistique et culturel dans la Romania Festschrift für Ingrid Neumann-Holzschuh zum 65. Geburtstag*, ed. Edith Szlezák and Klara Stephanie Szlezák (Berlin: Erich Schmidt Verlag, 2019), 53–68.

8 N. A. Wendte, "Nexus Analysis: A Natural Fit for Linguistic Ethnography" (seminar talk given at the Cambridge Endangered Languages and Cultures Group, University of Cambridge, 2019).

9 Thomas A. Klingler, "Language Labels and Language Use among Cajuns and Creoles in Louisiana," *University of Pennsylvania Working Papers in Linguistics* 9, no. 2 (2003): 77–90.

10 Nathalie Dajko, "Sociolinguistics of Ethnicity in Francophone Louisiana: Language and Ethnicity in French Louisiana," *Language and Linguistics Compass* 6, no. 5 (May 2012): 290, www.doi.org/10.1002/lnc3.333.

11 Carl A. Brasseaux, *Acadian to Cajun: Transformation of a People, 1803–1877* (Jackson: University Press of Mississippi, 1992), 104–5.

12 Thad St. Martin, "Cajuns," *Yale Review* 26 (June 1937): 861.

13 Marjorie Esman, "Internal Conflict and Ethnic Activism: The Louisiana Cajuns," *Human Organization* 42, no. 1 (March 1983): 58, www.doi.org/10.17730/humo.42.1.b5x121h5j5086822.

14 James Harvey Domengeaux, "Native-Born Acadians and the Equality Ideal," *Louisiana Law Review* 46 (1986): 1194.

15 Mark A. De Wolf, "In the Eye of the Storm: Lafayette and the Civil Rights Movement, 1954–1971" (master's thesis, University of Southwestern Louisiana, 1997), 1. I am grateful to Marjorie Esman for pointing this quotation out to me and for her correspondence this topic.

16 Natalie Ducote, "CODOFIL's Ally: Local French Teachers in Louisiana" (master's thesis, University of New Orleans, 2017), 28, https://scholarworks.uno.edu/td/2316.

17 Ducote.

18 Trépanier, "Cajunization of French Louisiana," 164; see also Eric Waddell, "La Louisiane française : Une poste outre-frontière de l'Amérique française ou un autre pays et une autre culture?," *Cahiers de géographie du Québec* 23, no. 59 (1979): 199–215, www.doi.org/10.7202/021434ar; Alexandra Giancarlo, "'Don't Call Me a Cajun!': Race and Representation in Louisiana's Acadiana Region," *Journal of Cultural Geography* 36, no. 1 (2019): 23–48, www.doi.org/10.1080/08873631.2018.1500088.

19 Costa, *Revitalising Language in Provence*

20 Ingrid Neumann-Holzschuh, "'Carrefour Louisiane': Aspects of Language Contact in the History of Louisiana French," *Journal of Language Contact* 7, no. 1 (2014): 124–53, www.doi.org/10.1163/19552629-00701006; Thomas A. Klingler, "Beyond Cajun: Toward an Expanded View of Regional French in Louisiana," in *New Perspectives on Language Variety*

in the South: Historical and Contemporary Approaches, ed. Michael D. Picone and Catherine Evans Davies (Tuscaloosa: University of Alabama Press, 2015), 627–40.
21 Andrew J. Jolivétte, *Louisiana Creoles: Cultural Recovery and Mixed-Race Native American Identity* (Lanham, MD: Lexington Books, 2007), 38.
22 Giancarlo, "'Don't Call Me a Cajun!,'" 14.
23 Ulysses S. Ricard Jr., "Introduction," in *Gombo People: Poésie créole de la Nouvelle-Orléans*, by Sybil Kein (New Orleans: Gosserand Superior Printers, 1981), 1.
24 Albert Valdman, "Introduction," in *French and Creole in Louisiana*, ed. Albert Valdman (New York: Plenum Press, 1997), 1–22.
25 O'Rourke, Pujolar, and Ramallo, "New Speakers of Minority Languages," 1.
26 Hornsby, *Revitalizing Minority Languages*, 3.
27 Robert D. Greenberg, *Language and Identity in the Balkans: Serbo-Croatian and Its Disintegration* (Oxford, UK: Oxford University Press, 2004); James Costa, "Patois, gaga, savoyard, francoprovençal, arpitan: Quel nom pour une langue?," *Langues et cité* 18, no. 6 (2011): 6; Mari C. Jones, "Identity Planning in an Obsolescent Variety: The Case of Jersey Norman French," *Anthropological Linguistics* 50, nos. 3–4 (2008): 249–65.
28 Christophe Landry et al., "Request for Change to ISO 639-3 Language Code" (SIL International, November 17, 2014), www-01.sil.org/iso639-3/cr_files/2015-003.pdf.
29 Michel DeGraff, "Linguists' Most Dangerous Myth: The Fallacy of Creole Exceptionalism," *Language in Society* 34, no. 4 (October 2005): 533–91, www.doi.org/10.1017/S0047404505050207.
30 "Kouri-Vini Louisiana Creole Language Fanpage," Facebook, accessed May 10, 2019, www.facebook.com/Kourivini.
31 Jenny Sundén, *Material Virtualities: Approaching Online Textual Embodiment*, Digital Formations (New York: P. Lang, 2003), 4.
32 Mark Sebba, *Spelling and Society: The Culture and Politics of Orthography around the World* (Cambridge, UK: Cambridge University Press, 2007).
33 Lenore A. Grenoble and Lindsay J. Whaley, *Saving Languages: An Introduction to Language Revitalization* (New York: Cambridge University Press, 2006), 137.
34 Costa, *Revitalising Language in Provence*, 96.
35 See the papers in Mari C. Jones and Damien Mooney, eds., *Creating Orthographies for Endangered Languages* (Cambridge, UK: Cambridge University Press, 2017).
36 Christophe Landry et al., "Kouri-Vini: A Guide to Louisiana Creole Orthography" (Louisiana Historical and Cultural Vistas, 2016), www.mylhcv.com/guide-to-louisiana-creole-orthography.
37 Oliver Mayeux, "Writing Louisiana Creole" (bachelor's thesis, School of Oriental and African Studies, University of London, 2014); N. A. Wendte, "L'identité allographique: Le Cas du créole louisianais" (conference presentation, May 24, 2018), www.academia.edu/36708487.

38 Richard Keaoʻōpuaokalani NeSmith, "Tūtū's Hawaiian and the Emergence of a Neo-Hawaiian Language" (master's thesis, University of Hawaiʻi at Mānoa, 2002), https://scholarspace.manoa.hawaii.edu/bitstream/handle/10125/21194/NeSmith_2002.pdf. Mari C. Jones, "Death of a Language, Birth of an Identity: Brittany and the Bretons," *Language Problems and Language Planning* 22, no. 2 (1998): 129–42, www.doi.org/10.1075/lplp.22.2.02jon.

39 Oliver Mayeux, "New Speaker Language: The Morphosyntax of New Speakers of Endangered Languages" (MPhil diss., University of Cambridge, 2015); Mayeux, "Rethinking Decreolization," 225ff.

40 Costa, *Revitalising Language in Provence*, 41

41 Costa, 41

42 Leanne Hinton, "The Master-Apprentice Language Learning Program," in *The Green Book of Language Revitalization in Practice*, ed. Leanne Hinton and Kenneth Hale (Boston: Brill, 2001), 217–26, www.doi.org/10.1163/9789004261723_018.

43 Jane Freeland, "Linguistic Rights and Language Survival in a Creole Space: Dilemmas for Nicaragua's Caribbean Coast Creoles," in *Language Rights and Language Survival*, by Jane Freeland and Donna Patrick (New York: Routledge, 2004), 103, www.doi.org/10.4324/9781315760155.

44 Jolivétte, *Louisiana Creoles*, 48

COMMUNITY RESPONSE

NOTHING TO MANIFESTO

TANNER MENARD

NOTHING TO MANIFESTO
What you don't understand is when you survive genocide everyone
left
is family.

SMOKII SUMAC

There was a time before I became a member of my tribal council during which

> *The French gave us Andre Breton who in addition to being an anti-fascist*

There is a third voice in this poem

By publicly claiming my Indigenous identity

Created a beautiful tarot deck. As the French are prone to do he wrote

that is speaking to you

I became the subject of a certain type of unmentionable financial discrimination

A manifesto that is worth reading in regard to surrealism

About the ongoing redacted

I came home to the so-called state of my birth

> *The French people in my family were peasants mostly from
> who knows where*

Of the original people

Looking for work in a town full of mansions where getting a job as a dry cleaner

> *All over France likely. Celts & had healing ways which to this day*

This is not a dream or fabrication

Was hard to do & where one should be happy making $9 an hour

> *Maintained in relatively secrecy. I reject the notion that the French*

Let me count you down

I was listening to a lot of self-hypnosis tapes back then

> *Were kind to the Indigenous people that they encountered
> as they colonized*

10 9 8 7

Because separated from Indigenous prayer

> *Louisiana & Canada. Let's get back to Breton & the structure*

Don't fall asleep this is real

To which I had become accustomed I was desperate & I mean

> *Of this poem of this poem. The interesting thing about French society*

6 5 4

321

Truly destitute for the sense that life was not a press for clothes I could not afford

colonial societies in general is that they are so extreme that on one end

This is not a dream

I was an old man leaned against the walls of a cabin

Are armies nuclear weapons space agencies & tendencies towards liberalism

On the southern redacted

Holding a poisonous snake & I prayed the image of baskets

& fascism while on the other end is Dada tarot & postmodernism the latter of which

Indigenous women children trans people men

In my memory I prayed the image of baskets asking that one of my ancestors would remember

Is useful even for a mixed-race Indigenous Creole as they position themselves

Are being held in cages

Deep in the coiling snake of DNA

In a modern colonial society. I don't want to be an extreme

By the same mentality

A snake in memory I was dancing with a snake I was dancing with a snake woman

By the same justification

Winding like a caduceus a doctor from an olden time I prayed myself real

> *But how exactly does one avoid extremes when confronted*
> *with modern life*

Used to exterminate indigenous people

Counted out of hypnosis. In the present tense accused of political radicalism by REDACTED

> *& so my response here is a fracture a form of surrealism*
> *a manifesto of sorts*

Since the arrival of christopher columbus

Associated with oil interests I held on for as long as I could to the notion that Ishak

> *Composed this piece using surrealist techniques of automatic writing*

Since the trail of tears

Language could be unearthed. I found a linguist. He wrote a book & it is being published

> *& wanted to acknowledge that the French did something useful*

Since the concept of manifest destiny

I want future generations of Ishak people to read that book I want us to learn

That there is a soul there that hungers in my opinion for an Indigeneity that was taken

It is a mentality that seeks to erase

To speak our ancient tongue. I want us to disassemble the brain fuckery

By Empire. I remember my aunt teaching me to heal with herbs

Not only bodies

Remember who we are. I want us to form a modern sense of ourselves in this dystopian reality

Ways that I will not discuss here. Her prayers were Catholic but she told me

Cosmologies

Fragments of us left buried inside the bodies of former slaves of acadian colonists

Her mother was mixed. Her family had learned herbs from the people

Languages

We bleed into one another. There were blood baths

Who always resided on the land. I am an uncomfortable mixture of peoples

The essence of what it means to be a people

Bloodbath. I consider myself Creole because it is politically expedient. I consider myself Ishak

This poem is an uncomfortable mixture of ideas. My life is weaving together a fracture

We continue

Because I honor those ancestors the life they left behind the earth they loved

This poem is a basket of river cane a DADAist manifesto.
I don't want it to make sense

To exist

Queer identities they maintained in holy way the cow-people they became the horse-people

I want it to destroy all notions that shackle the human race

I manifest

The prairies the Creole zydeco masters the food they left behind to be appropriated

But of course no poem can do that it can only chip away
at the foundations

Nothing

By a white identity movement called the Cajun Renaissance. When I was little I was told

What I really want is healing. I want my people to know who they are

I Resist

That I was a Cajun but now reject that term. I know who I am not & refuse to ally

With forces that actively marginalize the most vulnerable among us

What was expected of me here is to write something rhetorical but I
prefer a sort of dialogue

All language

Willfully denying genetic connection. Fabricating & appropriating an identity

That poem makes possible. I can blame this on the French too

Used to erase

For the sake of control in their nightmare world. In a year that cannot be remembered

That would be a disgrace to my Atakapa ancestors

Used as weapon

The NDNs who I can only assume to be Ishak

Weaved meaning into all of reality

This is an arrowhead

Hid in what is called the big thicket on the Sabine River

Were poets without paper

Turned backwards as a gift

If you examine the formation of the Atakapa Ishak Nation

Needed no tarot to divine

Which i bestow

You will discover how difficult it is for us to identify ourselves

Did not need a postmodern philosophy to acknowledge multiplicity

A plea lacking pity

Because we did not appear on official documents. Never signed treaties with the eagle

> *Could talk to the weather & make it rain*

Strength

& his flock of bullets. We signed a treaty with the earth that is unbroken

> *Survived the mission schools & enslavement of our people*

A call for justice

& our arms are open to one another we acknowledge the travesty suffered

> *By hiding in the big-thicket*

Hear us

By all NDN people in the prairies of Louisiana

> *By traveling south & mixing with other tribes*

See us

The struggle of the so-called Louisiana NDN

> *By intermarrying with enslaved Africans*

The struggle

When I say that I am a Louisiana NDN

> *By learning French & marrying or being forced into marriage with the French*

That our shared ancestors have endured

What I am acknowledging

> *By becoming poets*

Is the same struggle

Is the forced hybridity

> *By destroying the grammatical syntax of the English Language*

Faced at redacted
The rape in enslavement

> *By finding joy in a life that was inconceivable*

The struggle of the boarding school
The mission schools

By harvesting oil when they could no longer harvest crops

The bayou bridge pipeline

The baptisms

> *By denying their own existence*

The dakota access pipeline

The hiding
That we had to do for me to write this poem. Outside of the library window is a Haboob forming

> *I want you to listen*

Am writing this from Arizona because if I were to say these things in Louisiana the powers

We are not extinct

Women separated from children

Maintain the myth of money & racial superiority would find ways to make my life miserable

Help us save our homeland

Locked in dog cages

Let me say this: Evangeline is lighter fluid. Climate change is real. The State of Louisiana

We don't need more French Education

Sprayed with water in the snow

Is still at war with NDNs. Creole is a colonial language

We need to love the Earth

Forced to drink from toilets

Indigenous people are summarily erased. There can be no cultural revival without *acknowledgement*

We need to love one another

REDACTED

Of Indigenous influence the living spirit. I reject the idea that I should edit this. My life is an edit

But you have to acknowledge the truth

We will survive

WORKS CONSULTED

Alim, H. Samy, John R. Rickford, and Arnetha F. Ball, eds. *Raciolinguistics: How Language Shapes Our Ideas about Race*. New York: Oxford University Press, 2016.

Brasseaux, Carl A. *Acadian to Cajun: Transformation of a People, 1803–1877*. Jackson: University Press of Mississippi, 1992.

Costa, James. "Patois, gaga, savoyard, francoprovençal, arpitan: Quel nom pour une langue?" *Langues et cité* 18, no. 6 (2011): 6.

———. *Revitalising Language in Provence: A Critical Approach*. Publications of the Philological Society 48. Malden, MA: John Wiley & Sons Ltd, 2017.

Dajko, Nathalie. "Sociolinguistics of Ethnicity in Francophone Louisiana: Language and Ethnicity in French Louisiana." *Language and Linguistics Compass* 6, no. 5 (May 2012): 279–95, www.doi.org/10.1002/lnc3.333.

De Wolf, Mark A. "In the Eye of the Storm: Lafayette and the Civil Rights Movement, 1954–1971." Master's thesis, University of Southwestern Louisiana, 1997.

DeGraff, Michel. "Linguists' Most Dangerous Myth: The Fallacy of Creole Exceptionalism." *Language in Society* 34, no. 4 (October 2005): 533–91, www.doi.org/10.1017/S0047404505050207.

Domengeaux, James Harvey. "Native-Born Acadians and the Equality Ideal." *Louisiana Law Review* 46 (1986): 1151–95.

Ducote, Natalie. "CODOFIL's Ally: Local French Teachers in Louisiana." Master's thesis, University of New Orleans, 2017. https://scholarworks.uno.edu/td/2316.

Esman, Marjorie. "Internal Conflict and Ethnic Activism: The Louisiana Cajuns." *Human Organization* 42, no. 1 (March 1983): 57–59, www.doi.org/10.17730/humo.42.1.b5x121h5j5086822.

Freeland, Jane. "Linguistic Rights and Language Survival in a Creole Space: Dilemmas for Nicaragua's Caribbean Coast Creoles." In *Language Rights and Language Survival*, by Jane Freeland and Donna Patrick, 103–38. New York: Routledge, 2004. www.doi.org/10.4324/9781315760155.

Giancarlo, Alexandra. "'Don't Call Me a Cajun!': Race and Representation in Louisiana's Acadiana Region." *Journal of Cultural Geography* 36, no. 1 (2019): 23–48, www.doi.org/10.1080/08873631.2018.1500088.

Greenberg, Robert D. *Language and Identity in the Balkans: Serbo-Croatian and Its Disintegration*. Oxford, UK: Oxford University Press, 2004.

Grenoble, Lenore A., and Lindsay J. Whaley. *Saving Languages: An Introduction to Language Revitalization*. New York: Cambridge University Press, 2006.

Heller, Monica. "Analysis and Stance Regarding Language and Social Justice." In *Language Rights and Language Survival*, by Jane Freeland and Donna Patrick, 283–86. New York: Routledge, 2004. www.doi.org/10.4324/9781315760155.

Hinton, Leanne. "The Master-Apprentice Language Learning Program." In *The Green Book of Language Revitalization in Practice*, edited by Leanne Hinton and Kenneth Hale, 217–26. Boston: Brill, 2001. www.doi.org/10.1163/9789004261723_018.

Hornsby, Michael. *Revitalizing Minority Languages: New Speakers of Breton, Yiddish and Lemko*. London: Palgrave Macmillan UK, 2015. www.doi.org/10.1057/9781137498809.

Irvine, Judith T., and Susan Gal. "Language Ideology and Linguistic Differentiation." In *Regimes of Language: Ideologies, Polities, and Identities*, edited by Paul V. Kroskrity, 35–84. Santa Fe: School of American Research Press, 2000.

Jolivétte, Andrew J. *Louisiana Creoles: Cultural Recovery and Mixed-Race Native American Identity*. Lanham, MD: Lexington Books, 2007.

Jones, Mari C. "Death of a Language, Birth of an Identity: Brittany and the Bretons." *Language Problems and Language Planning* 22, no. 2 (1998): 129–42, www.doi.org/10.1075/lplp.22.2.02jon.

———. "Identity Planning in an Obsolescent Variety: The Case of Jersey Norman French." *Anthropological Linguistics* 50, nos. 3–4 (2008): 249–65.

Jones, Mari C., and Damien Mooney, eds. *Creating Orthographies for Endangered Languages*. Cambridge, UK: Cambridge University Press, 2017.

Klingler, Thomas A. "Beyond Cajun: Toward an Expanded View of Regional French in Louisiana." In *New Perspectives on Language Variety in the South: Historical and Contemporary Approaches*, edited by Michael D. Picone and Catherine Evans Davies. Tuscaloosa: University of Alabama Press, 2015.

———. "Language Labels and Language Use among Cajuns and Creoles in Louisiana." *University of Pennsylvania Working Papers in Linguistics* 9, no. 2 (2003): 77–90.

———. "La variation ethnolinguistique en créole louisianais au cours du XXe siècle." In *Sprach-und Kulturkontaktphänomene in der Romania—Phénomènes de contact linguistique et culturel dans la Romania Festschrift für Ingrid Neumann-Holzschuh zum 65. Geburtstag*, edited by Edith Szlezák and Klara Stephanie Szlezák, 53–68. Berlin: Erich Schmidt Verlag, 2019.

"Kouri-Vini Louisiana Creole Language Fanpage." Facebook. Accessed May 10, 2019. http://facebook.com/Kourivini.

Landry, Christophe, Clifford St. Laurent, Michael Gisclair, Oliver Mayeux, and Eric Gaither. "Kouri-Vini: A Guide to Louisiana Creole Orthography." Louisiana Historical and Cultural Vistas, 2016. www.mylhcv.com/guide-to-louisiana-creole-orthography/.

Landry, Christophe, Albert Valdman, Thomas A. Klingler, Kevin J. Rottet, Oliver Mayeux, Andrew Jolivette, Carolyn M. Dunn, and Darryl Barthé. "Request for Change to ISO 639-3 Language Code." SIL International, November 17, 2014. www-01.sil.org/iso639-3/cr_files/2015-003.pdf.

Mayeux, Oliver. "New Speaker Language: The Morphosyntax of New Speakers of Endangered Languages." MPhil diss., University of Cambridge, 2015.

———. "Rethinking Decreolization: Language Contact and Change in Louisiana Creole." PhD diss., University of Cambridge, 2019. https://doi.org/10.17863/CAM.41629.

———. "Writing Louisiana Creole." Bachelor's thesis, School of Oriental and African Studies, University of London, 2014.

NeSmith, Richard Keaoʻōpuaokalani. "Tūtū's Hawaiian and the Emergence of a Neo-Hawaiian Language." Master's thesis, University of Hawaiʻi at Mānoa, 2002. https://scholarspace.manoa.hawaii.edu/bitstream/handle/10125/21194/NeSmith_2002.pdf.

Neumann-Holzschuh, Ingrid. "'Carrefour Louisiane': Aspects of Language Contact in the History of Louisiana French." *Journal of Language Contact* 7, no. 1 (2014): 124–53, https://doi.org/10.1163/19552629-00701006.

O'Rourke, Bernadette, Joan Pujolar, and Fernando Ramallo, eds. "New Speakers of Minority Languages: The Challenging Opportunity." *International Journal of the Sociology of Language* 2015, no. 231 (January 2015): 1–20, www.doi.org/10.1515/ijsl-2014-0029.

Ricard, Ulysses S., Jr. "Introduction." In *Gombo People: Poésie créole de la Nouvelle-Orléans*, by Sybil Kein. New Orleans: Gosserand Superior Printers, 1981.

Sebba, Mark. *Spelling and Society: The Culture and Politics of Orthography around the World*. Cambridge, UK: Cambridge University Press, 2007.

St. Martin, Thad. "Cajuns." *Yale Review* 26 (June 1937): 859–62.

Sundén, Jenny. *Material Virtualities: Approaching Online Textual Embodiment*. Digital Formations. New York: P. Lang, 2003.

Trépanier, Cécyle. "The Cajunization of French Louisiana: Forging a Regional Identity." *Geographical Journal* 157, no. 2 (July 1991): 161–71, https://doi.org/10.2307/635273.

Valdman, Albert. "Introduction." In *French and Creole in Louisiana*, edited by Albert Valdman, 1–22. New York: Plenum Press, 1997.

Waddell, Eric. "La Louisiane française: Une poste outre-frontière de l'Amérique française ou un autre pays et une autre culture?" *Cahiers de géographie du Québec* 23, no. 59 (1979): 199–215, https://doi.org/10.7202/021434ar.

Wendte, N. A. "L'identité allographique: Le Cas du créole louisianais." Conference presentation, May 24, 2018. www.academia.edu/36708487.

———. "Nexus Analysis: A Natural Fit for Linguistic Ethnography." University of Cambridge, 2019.

CHAPTER 9

NO BODY SINGS THE BLUES LIKE A FAT BODY

Gender, Race, and Eco-Colonialism

RAIN PRUD'HOMME-CRANFORD

> Big fat woman
> With her meat hanging on her bone
> > LEADBELLY, "Big Fat Woman Blues" (1936)

> If you roll your belly like you roll your dough
> People, they's crying, they want some more
> > JOHNNIE "GEECHIE" TEMPLE, "Big Leg Woman" (1938)

THIS BODY IS A SONG: FAT, SEX, AND SETTLER COLONIALISM

Ça fé inavé. I want to give a story. Inhabiting my body is a daily act of war. As a blues singer, spoken word poet, and professor I put myself into potential conflict any time I speak or take up public space. Moreover, as a disAbled PhD woman of color—or in my case a PhatDoctor with light-skin privilege—I am markedly aware that I am an ever-sizeable target. I am a target because fat female bodies are reviled, even in the most enlightened cerebral spaces, and queer women of color (even cis queer women of color) are always subjected to a book of rules and regulations. These rules define both our authenticity and our value based on phenotypic notions of "race," sexuality, and white desire. This is a struggle for many mixed Black/Native peoples, including Freedmen and Creoles.[1] This chapter is story from the personal to the political. I offer that my positionality as a fat, dis-Abled, queer, assault survivor, and Creole-NDN[2] descendant is connected to the histories of my family, ancestors, and the land under settler-colonial violence and exploitation. In the first section I explore personal histories, discrimination, and trauma, while the second section connects these with the very real historical and current epidemic violences against Indigenous women, girls, two-spirit/trans populations, and in turn those violences as connected to eco-colonialism, wherein "violence that happens on the land is intimately connected to the violence that happens to our bodies."[3]

I do not occupy a phenotypically racialized body. My skin gives me a privilege that I must recognize, while still honoring the histories, cultures, and familial experiences that move in my blood, memory, and family. Therefore, my racial body is not "read" visually in the same way as my weight or differently abled body. As a "big fat woman" all too aware of my "meat hanging on [my] bone," each curve, lump, scar, dimple, and keloid are markers. They are notes that when sung together cry a woeful moan from the southern Red River watershed to the Alberta Parkland, from Gulf of Mexico to Red River Valley of the North.[4] I am a chorus of voices from land to the topography of my skin. No body sings blues like my fat body. Blues come from the land and it's no surprise to Native folks that blues is an Afro-Indigenous musical tradition. In my work on Creole and Southeast Native American music I attest that "there is an ecology of sound whereby land, people, and music are intricately connected in a dialectal and reciprocal relationship," and this relationship follows a genealogy or kinship between Zydeco and southern blues with traditional Indigenous stomp music.[5] In the Gulf South, stomp songs shuffle-shook their way into a multiplicity of relationships with African slaves. These relationships took many forms: Indian slave masters, Indian and African Slaves, Blindian (Black and Indian) slaves, *gens de couleur libres* (free peoples of color), Gulf Creoles,[6] and partnerships between Black and Red bodies for survival in both the Antebellum and Jim Crow South. Musical miscegenation, as much as cultural/racial, is a by-product of survival in hostile lands. Into this tradition Delta blues musicians Leadbelly and Johnnie "Geechie" Temple sing odes to the strength of the female fat form in their songs "Big Fat Woman Blues" and "Big Leg Woman." Recognized for their bottleneck slide as much as their emphasis on love, loss, sex, and landscape, both Leadbelly and Temple's songs play with Southeast Indigenous stomp and southern blues call and response (antecedent/consequent) as much as classic Delta blues and swamp rock bottom-string jive.

Louisiana Blindian blues musician Huddie William Ledbetter[7]—"Leadbelly"—moans for the loss of his "big fat woman," calling out "I love my woman and I tell the world I do."[8] Mississippi-born Johnnie "Geechie" Temple explicates on the physical joys of a fat body, calling attention to its curves: "Big leg women sure got something good / Now, if you don't believe me, ask everybody in my neighborhood."[9] The assumption that there would be a collective appeal for a body of size, even in 1930s Gulf Delta, can seem lost on those of us struggling to regain a semblance of ourselves in 2021 as we seek to articulate decolonial relationships to our bodies, our land, and our sexualities.

My body is a dangerous, treacherous, hateful, broken, and beloved thing. I am sewn together veins, arteries, cartographic hills, valleys, and ghost whimpering voices of mothers, fathers, grans and great grandparents. See this smile-smirk, these points on brows, freakish small side wobbly baby toes. Look at these keloid scars on legs, arms, hands, even these "non-Indian" green eyes are beloved markers of a rooted place. Wide hips, heavy breast, *hapullo nia* (fat butt), broad cheeks, and square jaw are familial markers in our sea of siblings and cousins from hues of pale pearl to burnt sienna and brownest soot. Blood worked on Spanish moss draped oak tree bedrock drawing nutrients from this land into Red/Black Latinidad bodies of kaleidoscope shades.[10] This is my beloved body.

My body is big, full, round, fat. So fat that that eyes bore into me in spaces where I am at odds with the population around me. My body is a dangerous, treacherous thing to inhabit. While I may be able to *passe blanc* in my Creole-Indigy light-skin privilege—my ethnicity changes from person to person—Latinx, white, Indian, Turkish, and generically "white and Other."[11] In this sense, I am always a topic of conversation—from the ways in which my ethnicity is deemed an appropriate conversation, even a guessing game, to the notion that my body itself is an invitation for ridicule, advice, and passive-aggressive commentary on feminism (or rather white feminism). Nothing invites commentary like a body of size speaking about genocide, sexploitation, disAbility, and settler colonialism. In the act of opening my mouth to speak I invite feedback—the voices of dissent in my physical being buzz disharmoniously. This is my hated body.

In November 2015, Gillian Brown wrote an article discussing why fat is a feminist issue. Brown writes:

> Anybody who is fat knows well enough that fat people are considered second-class citizens and are treated as such in a number of different ways—such as not having as many clothing options made available to us, not being considered as often for employment, being paid less than our thinner counterparts, being judged and/or mistreated in doctor's offices, and being verbally and physically harassed on the streets. . . . Anybody who has experienced life as a woman knows that we face many of the same issues that fat people face. We are not considered as often for employment, we are often paid less, we are often told that men know more about our health than we do, and so on.[12]

While I agree with many of Brown's key points, what is missing for me are the realities of occupying a fat Afro-Indigenous body (or body of color) in our paracolonial state. Fat and the indoctrination of hatred is a product of settler-colonial white desire. As Roxane Gay (Haitian Creole descent) writes, "My fat body empowers people to erase my gender. I am a woman, but they do not see me as a woman. . . . I am large, but I am a woman. I deserve to be seen as such. We have such narrow ideas about femininity. . . . Race plays a part in this too. Black women are rarely allowed their femininity."[13] For women like me, being with people of color, in my communities, particularly Creoles, Natives, Blindians, and Latin@s, I am surrounded by beautiful women with big asses, breasts, thighs, and bellies. Beautiful women with round faces and cheeks, whose eyes disappear when we smile. We are women with big round sexy bodies and big round sexy laughter, because "Big leg women sure got something good."[14] But outside of these communities we are, as we are with everything, under the subjugation of the colonizer's yoke of "femininity."

Moreover, as I still struggle with severe self-esteem issues, my weight and autoimmune continue to plague my body and complicate the deterioration of my muscles, organs, and bone structure. Embracing the totality of my IndigeQueer sexuality means asserting my space as a queer woman as much as a Red/Black woman—as both my Indigeneity and queerness is often erased through my light skin and cis privilege.[15] For me, my sexuality, my understanding of myself as a desirable person, and my disabilities are all intricately linked together. As much as they are linked to my identity as an Afro-Indigenous woman, into the land that I come from, I can't separate one aspect of myself from the other. Settler-colonial culture has sought to inscribe what I am supposed to be as a woman, as a Creole, as Indigenous—via inscriptions of "Pin-Up Pocahontas Princesses" and "Voodoo Vixens."

Dominant society constructs notions of "normativity" for bodies, sexuality, and race as much as it borders the spaces we live in, mapping our interior and exterior landscapes, using images, media, and the momentum of the Hollywood machine to promote stereotypes, define sexuality, and eroticizing or desexualizing Black and Indigenous-descended women. Therefore, we have been left with scopophilic images from the Land O'Lakes maiden to new-age movement cards sporting generic "brown" women in white buckskin bent over bearskin rugs, to the decadent voluptuous imagery of Creole *plaçage* mistresses, and sexualized, dangerous portraits of Creole voodooienne, such as the eroticized mythos of Marie Laveau. In contrast we also have images such as the desexualized fat "mammy" and the dirty fat Native.[16] These are the imaginative expressions of a white male–dominated fantasy of women of color. The formation of what is perceived as Indigeneity and Afro-Indigeneity and more importantly a woman's Blindian embodied self by the American populous has been controlled by settler-colonial definitions of sex and beauty, and not the realities of our transracial/transnational heritage, cultural practices, and varying phenotypic inheritance in a world forever under the yoke of colonization.

Bodies are markers for trauma. Learning to love all the scars and imperfections of my body means I must embrace not only my pain, but a genealogy of trauma. This means I have more weight to carry. And while in my adult life I have fluctuated between sizes 20 to 30, numbers that make most people cringe, it is also part of a larger inheritance of colonial occupation. "American Indian and Alaska Native adults are 1.6 times more likely to be obese than Caucasians. In addition, almost 33 percent of all American Indians and Alaskan Natives are obese. This obesity epidemic is also disproportionately affecting certain groups in the community. Over half of American

Indian and Alaska Native women are overweight."[17] This is not a dismissal of accountability for my own missteps, but to overview intergenerational trauma, poverty's effect on diets, and the impact of changing food sources is to discount what Indigenous/tribal bodies were designed to process, not to mention these similar histories for Black and Freedmen folks.

My body is a hated and broken thing. It is traitorous in its own infirmity. Where weight doesn't mock, lupus SLE and rheumatoid arthritis have played kickball with my joints, skin, and organs for twenty-six years. "Lupus SLE and rheumatoid arthritis are two of the most prominent and debilitating autoimmune diseases impacting our communities today at ever increasing numbers."[18] Where autoimmune disease has not sought to break me, scars and bits of bone, soul, and wounds are patched together with spit, family, and sheer tenacity in the persistent call of survival—like mother, sister, aunties, friends, and ancestors, bent bodies broken under the onslaught of sexual violence. My survival through sexual violence is nothing new in my family, in my community, or my cultural history. I am a verse, a refrain, in this composition of women singing rhythmic and raw. I have learned to grow through scar tissues of violence, disease, and become an acrobat in the art of love. I have decades of practice learning how to contort, twist, turn, lower lingerie, keeping necessary bits exposed while deflecting hands, light, and touches from belly, upper arms—the mounds, ridges, and cellulite of shame. By the time I took my body back from rape I was bowed under the notion that it was flawed beyond measure. I have vacillated in crescendos and diminuendos of my own choir of self-loathing. Hiding from my ex-spouse, lovers, parents, sister, as an adult woman watching movies with fat heroines quietly in the dark—as if in acknowledging my desire to see a form on-screen that echoed my own I was admitting my fragility to feel acceptance in my bloated female form. Shame is a powerful weapon. I do not and cannot ever embody the notions of beauty that Hollywood says I need to as a woman—let alone a woman of Creole/Native/Freedmen heritage.

Angela Y. Davis has called attention the ways blues singers are social revolutionaries observing "illuminate the politics of gender and sexuality in working-class black communities."[19] Moreover, Eric Porter addresses "working-class African Americans (especially women) . . . migration and urbanization, natural disasters . . . racial and economic exploitation . . . leaving violent, unfaithful, or inadequate male lovers . . . and affirmed lesbian relationships as healthy alternatives to the confines of heterosexuality."[20] When considering the ways blues music has encompassed the interior and exterior body, societal constructs of race/gender, and connections to landbase, the blues emerges as a means of both musical and poetical expressions of rebellion, anarchy, and insurrection practiced by both Black and Indian bodies. Indians, Africans, Blindians, Creoles—we have embodied this resistance: "Indians have ever been active in jazz, blues, and popular music, where they highlight the Red-Black-White color lines."[21] I am a product of these color lines. Furthermore, my body's history is also reflected in the history of the land.

THIS BODY IS LAND: FROM CANADA TO USA, HOMELANDS, GENDER, AND ECO-COLONIALISM

> White supremacy, rape culture, and the real and symbolic attack on gender, sexual identity and agency are very powerful tools of colonialism, settler colonialism, and capitalism, primarily because they work very efficiently to remove Indigenous peoples from our territories and to prevent reclamation of those territories through mobilization.
>
> LEANNE BETASAMOSAKE SIMPSON (Michi Saagiig Nishnaabeg), "Not Murdered, Not Missing: Rebelling against Colonial Gender Violence"

At the end of 2016 I relocated from Harrah, Oklahoma, to Calgary, Alberta. I left my family, communities (in Oklahoma and Louisiana), and landbase. And yet, Alberta (the homeland of my maternal grandfather) is in many ways similar to Oklahoma. In August 2017, local Calgarians found "a bloodied sheet shrouding what looks to be a dead body, laid atop an Indigenous blanket in the middle of a busy downtown Calgary."[22] Conceived by Destin Running Rabbit and Iman Bukhari, the project disrupts the morning flow of the city, placing Indigenous violence front and center in the urban space in an effort "to get people to recognize 'the brutal reality' facing many Indigenous communities—and asks them what they're doing about it," said Running Rabbit.[23] Further, Running Rabbit, twenty-five, said he built this project around his own childhood experiences while growing up on the Siksika reserve.

The "Disposable Red Woman Project" is just one testimony of resistance and accountability that has marked Canada's 150th anniversary. As 2017 began with PR in preparation for Canada's 150th anniversary, social media began to explode with hashtags started by those within First Nation, Métis, and Inuit (FNMI) communities, activist circles, and academe: #Genocide150 #Resist150 #Colonialism#150. In May, Mi'kmaq lawyer Pam Palmater's article in *Now Magazine* bears the headline "Canada 150 Is a Celebration of Indigenous Genocide." As Palmater points out "'Indian policy' was based on acquiring Indigenous lands and resources and reducing financial obligations to Indigenous peoples. The primary methodology was either assimilation or elimination."[24] Moreover, Palmater reminds, or in some cases educates, readers that the TRC, "after investigating the historical record, stat[ed] that the totality of policies toward Indigenous peoples amounted to cultural, biological and physical genocide."[25] Similarly, 2016 marked the 240th anniversary of US Independence. Celebrations of this anniversary, or settler-colonial nation-state "independence" (Fourth of July / Canada Day) is problematic for Indigenous peoples and Black folk (a reason why Juneteenth—June 19—is so significant in our Black and Black-NDN communities). In his essay "Remembering the 4th of July: Indigenous Musings on the American Way," Darryl Barthé notes:

> I am a métis Creole from New Orleans, Louisiana. My ancestors were not a part of the rebellion against Britain that is commemorated on July 4th in remembrance of the United States' Declaration of Independence in 1776. The United States colonized the land of my ancestors after the Louisiana Purchase, a land transfer between Napoleon and Thomas Jefferson, announced to the American people on July 4, 1803. The Louisiana Purchase was a disastrous affair for my people. The Louisiana Purchase Treaty stipulated that all the inhabitants of the Louisiana Territory be incorporated into the US and extended the rights of citizenship.
> However, because the government of the United States did not recognize people of African descent or indigenous people as human beings capable of citizenship, my people—who were of both African and Amerindian heritage—were marginalized from full participation in the political life of the United States . . . the 4th of July makes me think of American tyrants ethnically cleansing Chickasaw Indians from their land at the present-day site of Memphis,

Tennessee on July 4, 1836. The removal of the Chickasaw from western Tennessee was a consequences of the Indian Removal Act of 1830, a fateful piece of legislations signed into law by President Andrew Jackson, which resulted in the atrocity that the Cherokee remember as "ńu na hi du na tlo hi lu I" (in English, "the place where they cried," or, as it is more commonly known in English, "The Trail of Tears"). Roughly 3,000 Creek Indians, 2,500 Choctaw Indians and 6,000 Cherokee Indians died on the Trail of Tears.[26]

Celebrations of the settler-colonial nation-states erase the violent histories of Indigenous peoples and histories of inequality and subjugation enacted on Black and Red bodies for manifestations of white heteropatriarchal and governmental hegemony.

Systemic physical and cultural genocide in Canada and the United States, against Indigenous bodies, and particularly Indigenous women, children, and two-spirit/trans bodies is rooted in the violence of the colonial project. Conversations around capitalistic governments and eco-colonialism are usually framed within twenty- and twenty-first-century conversations. However, the colonization of the Americas is surely a process of exploitation/extraction of bodies, land, and resources (i.e., capital/ism and eco-colonialism). The earliest travel accounts, illustrations, and lithographs of the Americas from the seventeenth century are embedded in a racialized discourse of sexploitation of Native body/fecundity of land, Savage (Native, landscape) versus Civilization (Europeans colonization and use of resources). "Columbus relied on descriptions of the female body to articulate his colonial project, writing the earth was shaped like a breast with the Indies composing the nipple."[27] Early travel narratives to the Americas, such as those of Sebastian Münster, Amerigo Vespucci, and Girolamo Benzoni, utilize "sexualized descriptions and images of Native women as both markers of difference" and metaphors for land.[28] The language of colonization is steeped in the language of sexual conquest, of violence against Indigenous bodies.

Because American Indian and African American women historically occupy a spaces of sexualization, exploitation, and capitalism (labor), there are lived realities for our communities. African American women's sexuality and bodies have been tied to capital and labor, from slavery to film. Listening to the history of Black womanhood means acknowledging histories of rape, exploitation, and spaces where the body is sold, bartered, and "kept" (i.e., *plaçage*/concubinage), effectively colonizing Black bodies as sites of historic violence. "For as long as there has been an America, the bodies of Black folk have been co-opted by language and images meant to distinguish their presence as American citizens—indeed human beings—within the context of global body politic."[29] In other words, the constructs of settler colonialism and white patriarchy have defined bodies of color through language, policy, stereotypes, and imagery, in an effort to subsume our voice and power within political and communal structures. Moreover, as Victoria Bomberry (Mvskoke Creek) reminds us, for "many Indigenous women, the colonial project resulted in a steady erosion of status and rights, and at times, an over attack on womanhood and motherhood."[30] What is perceived as a woman's "Indianness" and "Blackness" has been defined by hetero-male white patriarchal definitions of sex, violence, and white desire—not Indigenous and African realities of heritage, survivance, African and Indigenous slavery, and phenotypic legacies on lands and bodies forever imprinted by colonization.

In *Black Looks: Race and Representation*, bell hooks forces readers to acknowledge that a Black woman's sexuality and reproductive abilities are intrinsically tied to white consumptive practices. Likewise, in *Laboring Women: Reproduction and Gender in New World Slavery*, Jennifer Morgan locates the dependence of slavery on "exploited" African women. Using travel accounts, Morgan explores language that delineates a specific beastly communication establishing a rhetorical precedent that places Africans, and particularly African women, as inferior and sexualized, much as hooks uses both visual and written media tying it to histories of dominance and white inscriptions of representations of Black bodies. Historically, the "interplay between slaveoweners' conceptualization of African women's bodies and the development of racial slavery illuminates the evolving relationship between slaveowners' expectations and the realities of enslavements for Black women" as enacted through commodification, capitalistic labor, sexploitation, and violence.[31] The sexploitation and rhetorical dominance of slavery and its iconography allowed for exploitation of African women in the nineteenth century, thus instilling a narrative of sexualization of Black women, which persisted well into the present era.[32] The rhetoric and language of race has influenced the physical body and conceptions of the physical body. Moreover, Indian women are typically caught in the tropes of whore/seductive deer women or Princess savior á la Pocahontas / Sacagawea / La Malinche. In much literature and iconography of the Americas, Indigenous women were "constructed to perpetuate unrealistic, derogatory ideals which consequently foster attitudes which legitimize rape and other kids of violence."[33] Likewise, Indianness is constructed through a similar hegemonic binary of good/bad or useful/useless as African women, wherein Indigenous people are disempowered, their women sexualized, and their bodies rewritten. Therefore, Louisiana Creole women (and I would add Freedmen women) occupy a space in which both the stereotypes and exploitations of Indian and Black women are imposed, creating an environment wherein the worst aspects of sexploitation and labor are visited on the popular perceptions of Louisiana Creole (and Freedmen) women in the historic narrative of the Americas and its modern imaginings. As Carolyn Dunn writes, "We Creoles are also children of necessity . . . we become a dispossessed people, a people not recognized by government entities as white, Indian, or Black."[34]

In Canada and the United States the destruction of the land is directly linked to colonization and the violence against Indigenous peoples. This system of sexploitation and capitalism is rooted in the commodification and oppression of women and the land. This is evident when we see the high rates of violence against Indigenous women. "In the US, violence against Indigenous women has reached unprecedented levels on tribal lands and in Alaska Native villages. More than 4 in 5 American Indian and Alaska Native women have experienced violence, and more than 1 in 2 have experienced sexual violence."[35] Moreover, while Canada has implemented a (granted very flawed) inquiry into missing and murdered Indigenous Women (MMIW), the United States' statistics are severely inaccurate, as a result of which "the lack of a diligent and adequate federal response is extremely alarming to indigenous women, tribal governments, and communities."[36] There are "at least 1,200 murdered and missing Indigenous women in Canada."[37] The connection of land exploitation and Native female exploitation is glaringly evident in the 2016 KWG Resources YouTube channel commercial. The spot features young FNMI promoting the Ring of Fire mining project in northern Ontario while wearing bikini tops. It blatantly sexualizes women supporting capitalistic mining on Indigenous lands. In response to the video Pam Palmater was quoted as saying "I hope that the national inquiry on murdered and missing Indigenous women and girls takes a close look at the correlation between sexualized violence and mining/oil and extractive industry camps."[38] Similarly, activist and cofounder of L'eau Est La Vie Camp ("Water Is Life," a resistance encampment seeking to stop the Bayou Bridge pipeline in Southwest Louisiana) Cherri Foytlin (Dene/Cherokee descent) says:

> These companies don't take people into consideration, especially if they don't have political clout, but I would probably be remiss if I didn't say that the system was never built in the first place to protect those people—it protects the people it's supposed to protect. And then we have kind of a similar situation in Lake Charles where we are seeing increased rates of violence, especially towards women; the residents have seen a spike in crime.[39]

These experiences highlight that "extractive industries have drilled, mined, and fracked on lands on or near resource-rich Indigenous territories for decades. Although the economic gains have been a boon to transnational corporations and the economies of the US and Canada, they come at a significant cost to Indigenous communities, particularly women and young people."[40]

As discussed above, the earliest colonial descriptions and images of Native women as relational to the fecundity of the land set a president that both women and land were waiting to be claimed by the colonizer. This has led to statistics where Indigenous women are ten times more likely to die a violent death than any other North American citizen. There is a cyclical relationship between Indigenous violence of women, girls, and two-spirit/trans and eco-colonialism—from the violence of forced penetration in fracking, as to rape, to the removal/pollution of vital natural resources (trees, waters, medicines), to the removal of Indigenous women's children to residential schools and white foster care, killing cultural resources in the land and the people, the impact of homophobia and gender binaries on traditional spectrums of sexuality. These settler-colonial constructs that created law and policies over land and mineral rights, boarding and residential schools, Native child removal, and land exploitation and pollution have steadily worked to both erode and undermine Indigenous cultural practice and ways of knowing. The infiltration of companies and settlers in the effort to gain access to natural resources raises the conflict and violence by introducing racist, sexist, and homophobic ideologies and entities within our homelands. Native Minnesota activist Patti Larsen says, "Follow the oil trail, and you'll find the girls."[41] While Larsen is "referring to workers in the Bakken oil fields who abduct, rape, and abuse Indigenous women and girls on the land they've invaded," this is no different than the rise in "man camps" in Fort McMurry, Alberta, St. John / Peace River BC, Southwest Louisiana, or on Fort Berthold Reservation in North Dakota.[42]

Amnesty International's report released in November 2016 "details the myriad effects of large-scale energy projects in northeastern B.C.'s Peace River region, including the influx of temporary workers—a 'shadow population' of mostly young men whose presence contributes to the vulnerability of indigenous women and strains social services."[43] The seventy-eight-page report lists "problems," including temporary workers with "disposable incomes" who "blow off steam" by abusing drugs and alcohol; women's shelters that are in a state of "constant crisis due to a lack of resources; inexperienced and overburdened RCMP officers based far from First Nations communities; women trading sex for drugs, meals and accommodation in an area with high housing and food costs; insufficient or non-existent public transportation, resulting in hitchhiking."[44] While the study links the oil industry, tracing it to the rise of "man camps" created during the Bakken oil boom in North Dakota, it clearly articulates that rates of violent crime against Indigenous women and girls are directly proportional to the extraction of oil, gas, and minerals.[45] In the United States, like in Canada, the link between eco-colonialism and MMIW is a result of companies that are

> sites of chemical manufacturing and waste dumping, while others have seen an introduction of large encampments of men ("man camps") to work for the gas and oil industry. The devastating impacts of the environmental violence this causes ranges from sexual and domestic violence, drugs and alcohol, murders and disappearances, reproductive illnesses and toxic exposure, threats to culture and Indigenous lifeways, crime, and other social stressors.[46]

Failure to recognize these issues and connections in the United States and Canada can still be linked to the ways that MMIW investigations and erasure are dogged by bureaucratic systems compartmentalizing issues in Indian country rather than holistically examining systemic violence and the history and contemporary roles of eco-colonialism on the psychology and lived realities behind violence against Native women/girls, two-spirit/trans.

Moreover, as I affirm that my positionality as a fat, disAbled, assault survivor, and Creole-NDN descendant is connected to the histories of my family, ancestors, and the land, then I must question how do I, my siblings, communities, and our children maintain cultural sustainability as our homelands are being eradicated?

> South Louisiana is experiencing the effects of coastal erosion faster than almost anywhere in the world, losing a football field-size piece of land every 100 minutes. It is projected that by 2100, much of South Louisiana will be under water. As we continue to feel the effects of global warming over the next 50 years, architecture and infrastructure will become the foundation for life along the Louisiana coast.[47]

Further, as Monique Verdin (Houma Nation) and Cherri Foytlin address, not only have oil and gas played a large role in the destruction of Louisiana landbases, but the fallout from these industries impact ocean levels destroy protective natural barriers from extreme weather, and infiltrate food and vegetation.[48] The future of the Gulf South, Louisiana particularly, is fraught with fossil fuel exploitation and land loss resulting from climate change and global warming, which ultimately impacts our reciprocal relationships with our traditional cultural homelands.

MY BODY IS OHOYO TVSKA / FEMM NÓR: RESISTANCE, LOVE, AND DECOLONIZATION

Louisiana

> I taste of southern salt pierced with cayenne
> *a Big Fat Woman with the meat shakin' on her bones*

> My hips roll with the water I carry from Cane River and Indian Creek
>
> *A Big Fat Woman with the meat shakin' on her bones*
> I comb gris-gris maji from my hair to catch whispers on a briny breeze
> *Ev'ry time I moves, make your temp'rature rise.*
>
> I comb gris-gris maji from my hair trace trails of praline whisky sauce on skin.
> *Ev'ry time I moves, make your temp'rature rise.*
> My waters run from sky to earth to womb.
>
> Trace trails of praline whisky sauce on skin, read stretchmarks and divots like music.
> Know I birthed generations rooted in this land.
> *a Big Fat Woman with the meat shakin' on her bones.*[49]

Now, in my mid-forties, after divorce, struggling in the increasingly shallow academic humanities, navigating the COVID pandemic as a fat, differently abled chronically ill body, I have learned the ways my body is both a tool of defiance and a threat. And yet, in the deepest self-hating part of my mind at night lives a fear of spending my life alone—I mean, who would ever want me to "roll [my] belly like [I] roll [my] dough?"[50] Bodies outside the accepted aesthetic, especially obese bodies, are often left in exile when it comes to love, sex, and desirability, and even within our work environs we are perceived as "less than" so-called straight size folks. Yet, I am trying to learn that singing into the chorus of my survival is as act of political resistance that must be met with my body taking back space. Unapologetically.

Seeking to unshackle myself from a populous inscribing my lack of worth as a woman, yet alone a queer Indigenous-descended cis woman, for me, as Kréyol femn gra, ohoyo nia, gordita—and tohbi chohmi or güera—it means more than singing out. It has been and continues to be an act of revolution and reinscription. It is a daily battle for both my voice and my physical person. It is a mêlée to acknowledge the defeats and sources of my self-hatred and the roots and wellspring of my empowerment. I've come to realize that my ability to take up and take back space as a IndigeQueer, disAbled, light-skinned (*passe blanc*), Creole-NDN woman is a political act. My sexuality and not hiding it is a political act as much as not hiding the historical trauma, the fight for our land sustainability, the genocide of the ancestors whose blood—Indian, European, and African—runs through my veins. As I've written before, this act of being is not easily won, and my presence in spaces that have sought to eradicate, exploit, and erase me is an act of rebellion and an act of grace. I am learning that the curve and slide of each note my body sings is a call and response blues made through the southern Red River watershed to the Alberta Parkland, from Gulf of Mexico to Red River Valley of the North, worked from blood through cellulite pulsing on skin. No body sings blues like my fat body.

My physical person defies stereotypes of Creole/Indian female figures—it takes up space—it is a call to arms to exist. And it is an act of war, an uprising against settler-colonial dominance that has sought to define, inscribe, control, name, claim, limit, and form me as a woman while exploiting, naming, claiming, and committing violence against my homelands. To decolonize and assert my terms and right of being is not an act not easily won—it is an act of anarchy.

This is my warrior body, my strong body. Yummut ahli!

NOTES

Epigraphs: "Big Fat Woman Blues," written by Huddie Leadbetter (Leadbelly), 1936. © Folkways Music Publishers Inc., March 11, 1963. "Big Leg Woman," written by Johnnie "Geechie" Temple (popular recording by Muddy Waters), 1938. © Decca Records, April 22, 1938.

1. Freedman, descendants of slaves and Natives from the "Five Civilized Tribes" (Cherokee, Seminole, Choctaw, Creek, and Chickasaw) and other Red/Black (Native/African) populations and their Native nations, remind those of us in Indian country of the contested and related relationships, and histories, of African American and Native American peoples.
2. Red English written slang for "Indian" (i.e., Native, etc.).
3. *Violence on the Land, Violence on Our Bodies: Building an Indigenous Response to Environmental Violence* (Berkeley, CA: Women's Earth Alliance; Toronto: Native Youth Sexual Health Network, 2014) 4, http://landbodydefense.org/uploads/files/VLVBReportToolkit2016.pdf.
4. I mark myself through landbases in acknowledgment that I am a summation of all my ancestries—European, Turtle Island Indigenous, African and Latinx diasporas, and so forth.
5. Rain Prud'homme-Cranford, "Summoning Swamp Songs: Decolonizing Creole-Indigenous Textual Tributaries," in *Swamp Souths: Literary and*

Cultural Ecologies, ed. Kirstin Squint et al. (Baton Rouge: Louisiana State University, 2020), 91–115.

6 While Louisiana Creoles might be the best known of this group, Mississippi and Alabama have established Creole populations, while the modern US Creole diaspora in the Gulf also extends to Texas and Florida.

7 It is believed that Leadbelly's mother, Sally Pugho, was of half American Indian descent. See Laurie E. Jasinski and Casey Monahan, *Handbook of Texas Music* (Austin: Texas State Historical Association Press, 2012).

8 "Big Fat Woman Blues."

9 "Big Leg Woman."

10 My identifying with my Louisiana Creole ancestry does not diminish my pride in all my ancestors. Rather, it speaks to my tie between land/place/culture and identity—having spent my life in the southern Gulf United States and Oklahoma primarily, and being the cultural descendant of two distinct Red/Black communities, although "white" presenting.

11 As a person of Louisiana Creole descent (Cane River, Opelousas, Point Coupee, Marksville) who also works within ethnic/Indigenous/Africana studies I feel it necessary to stress the positionality/culture of Louisiana Creoles. Louisiana Creoles are part of Louisiana Latinidad mestiz@s whose ethnicity encompasses American Indian, African American, Caribbean (Afro-Spanish-French-Indigenous-Caribbean), and European (usually French and Spanish) racial cultural inheritance, and are often and historically classified as "mestizos" and "métis." As an Indigenous scholar/poet/author/activist woman it means stressing that Louisiana Creole Indigeneity is a part of the grander narrative of American Indian survivance, negotiation, and survival, in similar ways that Chicano/a Mestizo and Canadian Métis narratives are part of the Indigenous narratives of the Americas. See Rain P. Cranford Goméz, "Hachotakni Zydeco's Round'a Loop Current: Indigenous, African, and Caribbean Mestizaje in Louisiana Literatures," *Southern Literary Journal* 46, no. 2 (2014): 88–107; Andrew J. Jolivétte and Haruki Eda, "Louisiana Creoles and Latinidad: Locating Culture and Community," in *Converging Identities: Blackness in the Modern African Diaspora*, ed. Julius Adekunle and Hettie V. Williams (Durham, NC: Carolina Academic Press, 2013), 273–84; and Andrew J. Jolivétte, *Louisiana Creoles: Cultural Recovery and Mixed-Race Native American Identity* (Lanham, MD: Lexington Books, 2007).

12 Gillian Brown, "Why Is Fat a Feminist Issue?," The Body Is Not an Apology, January 15, 2018, https://thebodyisnotanapology.com.

13 Roxane Gay, *Hunger: A Memoir of My Body* (New York: HarperCollins, 2018), e-book.

14 "Big Leg Woman."

15 I identify as an Indigenous queer/IndigeQueer female, rather than two-spirit. The way I've been taught to understand two-spirit identity is as sacred responsibility for people who have both male and female balance. For me I know that my energy and my spirit is feminine. Some people might see it as masculine because I'm what you would call Indigenous fem, meaning I can still kill and clean an animal, fix stuff on my car, and own more tools than my ex–cis male spouse. Ultimately the point of attraction for me is masculinity (which is not predicated on the penis), intelligence, humor, and kindness. Concepts of male or female gender, or biological male or biological female genitalia, doesn't factor in what attracts me to a person.

16 Perfect examples of this are Mammy in *Gone with the Wind* and the fat Native "seer" in *The Simpsons Movie*.

17 "Ethnicity and Health in America Series: Obesity in the Native American Community," American Psychological Association, November 2015, www.apa.org.

18 T. Shawnee, "A Perfect Circle Bound in Chains: Creole-NDN Health, Historical Trauma, and Settler Colonialism" (in this volume).

19 Angela Davis, *Blues Legacies and Black Feminism: Gertrude "Ma" Rainey, Bessie Smith, and Billie Holiday* (London: Women's, 1999), xvii.

20 Eric Porter, *What Is This Thing Called Jazz? African American Musicians as Artists, Critics, and Activists* (Berkeley: University of California Press, 2002), 26–27.

21 Ron Wellburn, "A Most Secret Identity: Native American Assimilation and Identity Resistance in African America," in *Confounding the Color Line: The Indian Black Experience in North America*, ed. James Brooks (Lincoln: University of Nebraska Press, 2002), 302–5.

22 Tricia Lo, "'Disposable Red Woman' Art Lays Corpse in Calgary Streets to Depict 'Brutal Reality' Facing Indigenous Women," CBCnews, August 17, 2017, www.cbc.ca.

23 Lo.

24 Pamela Palmater, "Canada 150 Is a Celebration of Indigenous Genocide," *Now Magazine*, March 29, 2017, accessed September 16, 2017, https://nowtoronto.com.

25 Palmater.

26 Darryl Barthé, "Remembering the 4th of July: Indigenous Musings on the American Way," Over De Muur: Voor Historische Vernieuwing, July 4, 2017, https://overdemuur.org.

27 Jennifer L. Morgan, *Laboring Women: Reproduction and Gender in New World Slavery* (Philadelphia: University of Pennsylvania Press, 2004), 17.

28 Morgan, 17.

29 C. E. Henderson, "Guest Editor's Introduction: The Bodies of Black Folk: The Flesh Manifested in Words, Pictures, and Sound," *MELUS:*

Multi-Ethnic Literature of the United States 35, no. 4 (2010): 5, www.doi.org/10.1093/melus/35.4.5.

30 Victoria Bomberry, "Blood, Rebellion, and Motherhood in the Political Imagination of Indigenous People," in *Reading Native American Women: Critical/Creative Representations*, ed. Ines Hernandez-Avila (New York: Altamira Press, 2005), 22.

31 Jennifer L. Morgan, *Laboring Women: Reproduction and Gender in New World Slavery* (Philadelphia: University of Pennsylvania Press, 2004), 17–18.

32 bell hooks, *Black Looks: Race and Representation* (New York: Routledge, 2015), 62.

33 Janice Acoose, *Iskwewak Kah Ki Yaw Ni Wahkomakanak: Neither Indian Princess nor Easy Squaw*, 2nd ed. (Toronto: Women's Press of Canada, 2016), 71.

34 Carolyn M. Dunn, "How I Gots My Gumbo Ghosts," in *Smoked Mullet Cornbread Crawdad Memory*, by Rain C. Goméz (Norman, OK: Mongrel Empire Press, 2012), iv.

35 "Ending Violence against Native Women," Indian Law Resource Center, accessed July 1, 2019, https://indianlaw.org/issue/ending-violence-against-native-women.

36 "Ending Violence against Native Women."

37 "Breaking the Silos: Violence against Women, Resource Extraction, and Climate Change," Battered Women's Support Services, March 2, 2017, www.bwss.org.

38 Jody Porter, "'It's like Indigenous People Are a Joke': First Nations Women React to KWG Resources Sexy Mining Video," CBCnews, August 11, 2016, 2018, www.cbc.ca.

39 "'Good Water in Their Bodies and Good Air to Breathe': A Conversation with Cherri Foytlin," Kairos, June 9, 2018, https://kairoscenter.org.

40 *Violence on the Land, Violence on Our Bodies*, 2.

41 Riayn Spaero, "Follow the Oil Trail and You'll Find the Girls," Longreads, February 13, 2019, https://longreads.com.

42 Spaero; and *Violence on the Land, Violence on Our Bodies*, 1.

43 "Out of Sight, Out of Mind: Gender, Indigenous Rights, and Energy Development in Northeast British Columbia, Canada," Amnesty International, November 3, 2016, www.amnesty.org.

44 "Out of Sight, Out of Mind."

45 The Amnesty report does not single out particular corporations, but it calls on the federal and provincial governments to immediately revoke or suspend all permits and approvals associated with BC Hydro's Site C dam. The provincial Crown corporation released a statement on Thursday highlighting the funding it has provided to local social-service agencies during the first year of the dam's construction. Helen Knott, a social worker in Fort St. John from the Prophet River First Nation who is among the one hundred people Amnesty interviewed for the

report, said such funding "won't go far." She is urging corporations to make internal changes such as creating a work environment that is more welcoming to women and ensuring employees have access to addiction treatment.

46 *Violence on the Land, Violence on Our Bodies*, 2.
47 Virginia Hanusik, "Life Adapts to Louisiana's Disappearing Coast," Climate Home News, March 21, 2019, www.climatechangenews.com.
48 Monique Verdin and Cherrie Foytlin, "Monique Verdin and Cherri Foytlin on the Gulf Coast's Unsound Future/36," For the Wild, July 5, 2016, http://forthewild.world.
49 Translations for this section's subheading: Choctaw, "Warrior Woman"; Creole, "Strong Woman." Rain Prud'homme-Cranford's "Louisiana," from the forthcoming poetry collection *Epidermal Journal*; "Big Fat Woman Blues."
50 "Big Leg Woman."

COMMUNITY RESPONSE

THUNDER THIGHS

A Storm's Brewing / Sorte cette laville avant l'ouragan commence

FRANCES E. HOPSON-CUEVAS

After reading Rain Prud'homme-Cranford's "No Body Sings the Blues . . ." I began to think on how full-bodied people are viewed through the lenses of Creole and Native culture. In particular, I began to think on how "BIG" bodies were perceived in my personal experience of Creole and Native American heritage. When it comes to my lineage, I have always been very happy to talk about it. For so many years, Native American blood within Creole families was not looked highly upon. Most Creoles in the St. Francis Xavier Church in Baton Rouge didn't talk about Indians. Everybody wanted to be John Wayne. The Indians? No one ever wanted to be the Indians, not even the Indians! So if other families did have Indian heritage (which I'm sure was the majority of the area), no one talked much about it. Mama grew up with Decuirs, Chustzs, and Ricards. They all originated from some of the same founding families of Pointe Coupee, Louisiana. Despite the Parish literally being built about less than a few miles from the Natchez, Taensa, Avoyel, Tunica, Koroa, Choctaw, and Chitimacha, many Creoles in my Parish experience, will tell you that they have no Indian blood. All the Creoles in Baton Rouge however, knew that *them* Amars on Myrtle Street had that "mean Indian blood" in them. We ourselves never looked down on our Native heritage because we knew we had people on both sides that helped create Louisiana. We were on the *Le Loire, Le Profond*, and were also longtime Native residents of the New Biloxi area well before 1720.

Mama, my mother, is a perfect specimen of the two cultures combined into one soul. Unlike the typical Creole women who were always slender and precocious, Mama was tall, broad shouldered, and lean. In her teens, her eldest brother, Leroy, would joke to her, "Well, you're finally getting a shape, Blondie! You look just like the letter 'L.'" And yes, my mother really is a black-haired Native American and Creole lady named Blondie.

My mother stands five feet ten, a testament to her Native American ancestry and in blatant disregard for the gentility of her Creole French lineage. She is not dainty nor is she fragile. She is as strong and powerful as her community coffee. My mother grew up just off Government Street in Baton Rouge, the first generation to move away from Pointe Coupee Parish. All of her neighbors there were family from one tree or another, but they were all a community about thirty miles away from their homeland. My grandmother was also not the typical Creole housewife. She worked by choice as a butcher and owned several properties that she rented. My grandmother gave birth to nine children, and even though my grandfather worked for Esso, she kept her own employment as well. My mother often told the story that she gave birth to one of my uncles in her house and went out later the same day to pick strawberries. None of her Creole neighbors could believe that she had already given birth that morning, so people actually followed her home to see the baby.

In order to really capture perceptions of how BIG is seen, you need a firsthand view into our culture. One of the ways to understand Creoles is that we are mostly all devout Catholics. We go to church every Sunday, we eat fish on Fridays, and we buy our Easter dresses almost a month before Palm Sunday. We are family oriented, and these traditions have to be kept to acknowledge and honor our Mothers and Fathers before us. But what separates Creole Catholics from others more than anything else? We are born boasters with an immense level of pride. Even now in 2020, you could go to any Creole get-together, and you will find the same "preposterous apathetic suicidal pride" that George Washington Cable saw in 1880 when he lived in Louisiana. Creoles love to exaggerate the things they are proud of. We love getting some fun out of life because when we love, we love hard. Our family and children are the joys of our life. That's why we brag on them constantly, in an audience that we know understands our comicality and magnifications.

I feel that one has to truly understand just how Creoles exaggerate when it comes to pride when I tell you about how my Creole and Native American experience has taught me to think about big bodies. You will have to forgive me if my story at times sounds a little farfetched, but to my four siblings and me, Mama's word has always been the God's honest truth (even if you only prayed to Mary with your intentions because Jesus will never deny his mother ANYTHING she asks him). For my mama, when it comes to her children, good was always "great." Mama could predict you were going to be the "belle of the ball" before you even stepped out her door. I told my kindergarten teacher, Mrs. Hannah, that I liked "Excellent" better than "Great job!" because I knew that those words made my mother smile bigger.

My mother's hands aren't like the typical European French woman. They are not the delicate Creole hands that pour gourmet coffee during family visits. They are big and strong with veins that trace and dance along her bones like the Mississippi River on the state of Louisiana. Her hands are a testament to the fact that even in the Creole community, she comes from a family with that "mean Indian blood." Her hands were made by a land that existed before 1812, and a people who inhabited it for decades and centuries before the American flag was flown. But Mama's big hands don't scare us. They shape and mold us. They nurture and feed us and they bathe us in a way that tell us the story of who we are without having to utter a word.

When Mama tells us a story about her being challenged, whether at work or in a heated conversation, she always describes herself—"So I stood there with my broad shoulders pointed out"—and she gestures at herself puffing out her chest and casting her eyes down the tip of her shoulder. From that one move we all know the only possible outcome. Mama defeated the enemy. Mama's shoulders are her killer move. She commands that space and the room once she sets her shoulders out. Her soul and the power of seven generations push through as she lands her last sentence to put them in their place. Mama uses her body to command her space and command her audience. She prides herself in being the bigger woman in the room and takes full advantage of all that it has to offer. I have never seen my mother not stand out in a crowd (my mother always stands out in a crowd), unless she is in the company of her six feet four brothers. Even the well-known embellisher, French Catholic missionary priest François

De Montigny, couldn't deny that the Taensa tribe were all "large men, well formed."

For a little background to those that *pas connais*, François De Montigny, he was known to exaggerate his accounts of the Taensa—most notably, when he lied about the number of people sacrificed during a Taensa chief's funeral rites in about 1699. His story doubled the number of deaths to a dozen before his group was able to intercede. This same intercession, or this blatant interference with sacred tradition, however, also was believed to have caused lightning to strike their temple, which burned down a few days later. Shortly after that "misunderstanding," De Montigny left his Taensa mission and moved in with the Natchez. Some might say he was cast out after a storm, but he left no further recordings of the Taensa in his journals and within two months he returned to France.

One of my oldest memories is playing in the kitchen to the smell of seafood boiling in the big pot with newspaper full of the fish guts she cut out sitting on the corner of the kitchen sink. My mother, hands full of flour and old bay, hanging the phone over her shoulder in full conversation—as if the food would cook itself, as she "carried on" with her sister, affectionately called Mama Shirley. Whenever the subject turned to her kids, I would know because Mama would begin the litany of honors and awards received by each child in the order in which they were born. When she got to me, the grades were accompanied by another huge compliment: "And girl, wait until you see this little one over here. She's got them THUNDER THIGHS. She could stomp a mud hole right through you if she wanted!"

Thunder thighs. One of the most beautiful images: celestial and magical, dangerous and mighty. Rain is about as much part of Louisiana as the magnolia flower. There can be a downpour on one side of the street while the grass just across is completely untouched. The rain is what fills our bayous, feeds the turtles for our soup, and is what we wash our hair with after a full moon. Have you ever just sat and listened to the thunder during a hard rain in Louisiana? The earth sounds like it has come alive as the sky rumbles. You might not even have gray skies over your house, but can hear the rumble in the distance and know just what type of storm to expect. "Vous tende le tonnere?" So imagine my mama's pride as she casts her eyes on the storm that fills her daughter's legs. My whole life I took pride in my legs. I liked the way they stomped and shook. I loved my "big fat knees." I prided myself in being able to squeeze the life out of my siblings when wrestling on the ground. I knew that my body held a power that was able to conquer even when it was concealed in a sundress alluding to simple grace. I was the biggest, smallest, youngest daughter. Always first in line, but also always needing my size 4 dresses to be let out in the hips.

Big has always been a marker of my Native American heritage. In all my life, big was a sign of strength. It was an indicator of your soul's energy. It was as sacred as the birthmark you carried from the angel's kiss before you were born.

COMMUNITY RESPONSE

"FATTEN UP, YOU'RE TOO SKINNY"

Body, Color, and Trauma

ANDREW J. JOLIVÉTTE AND JOELLE
JOLIVÉTTE-GONZALEZ (IN MEMORIAM)

I was eighteen, not quite nineteen, yet when my aunt Joelle died in 1994 of leukemia. She is my dad's oldest sister. I always thought she was beautiful. She didn't like taking pictures much. Sometimes we wondered why she didn't smile so much. My dad always called her "noir," which means Black in French/Creole. He called her this because she was the darkest of his white-passing siblings. Sometimes it was simply "Black." It wasn't pejorative I don't think. It was much like the Spanish expression "mi negrita," the little dark one / my dear love. And as I read my coeditor's chapter, "No Body Sings the Blues like a FAT Body: Gender, Race, and Eco-Colonialism" I thought about my own experiences with body, race, color, disability, settler notions of "purity," gender, and masculinity. Her history of trauma both inside and outside of academic spaces reminded me of my aunt Joelle. Her legal first name isn't even Joelle. She didn't like her name. I will respect that and not share it here. My aunt was a bigger woman. She suffered physical and sexual abuse. She survived. She told me once when I was about nine or ten to "fatten up, you're too skinny," and I always thought it was a very sweet thing. I was super skinny as a kid and young adult. Now at forty-five I'm considered obese like my aunt. I'm also the dark one of my parents' biological children together.

When I think about land, place, and peoplehood from Creole and Indigenous perspectives, I realize not a lot has changed since 1994 when my aunt died a death too young, too trauma filled, too violent. When the author of this chapter talks about "eco-colonialism" it makes me think about how women and men and trans people in our communities internalize colonial notions of color and beauty. So, for me this chapter brought up the pain and trauma of my aunt's experience as a "fat," "dark" woman but also my own experience as a "fat," "dark" man in Creole and Indigenous spaces. I never really fit in anywhere. If I go into a Black-specific space I don't quite fit. If I go into a Native or Indigenous space I don't fit. Even in many Creole spaces I haven't always fit. Like my godmother, I've looked for love in men who maybe couldn't love me for me, or perhaps we didn't love ourselves enough at times regardless of our color, weight, and external notions of beauty. My other aunts were always thinner, people commented on how beautiful they were. My aunt Joelle was "skinny or average sized" I think until she gave birth to my cousin. I remember calling her when she told me she was sick and would have to go into the hospital and she asked me if I would visit her. I said of course and then I asked her for advice. I have two older half brothers from my father who have different mothers and I had never met one of them and the older of the two I had only met once. One has blond hair and blue eyes and the other who also has mostly white features was born to a white mom who happens to be half Mexican, which I never knew until about a year ago.

I wanted to reach out to my brothers. I wanted to "find them" but I also knew that sometimes their existence bothered my own mother. I thought it was because my brothers were basically "white" but I'm not entirely sure. My aunt told me you have to do what you feel is right. Those are your siblings. Your family. Your kin. You can have a relationship with them, and those other things shouldn't stop you. This isn't that uncommon in Creole, Native, and Black families—having siblings with different colors—but it's also not uncommon for those with the darkest and lightest skin to be teased the most. My two youngest brothers and I have the same biological parents. They are both much lighter than me. I always thought people thought they were more attractive than me and it was funny because me and my youngest brother look exactly alike, he's just taller and lighter.

As I entered my thirties, I gained more and more weight. I definitely "fattened up," to the point where at times it has impacted my self-esteem and how I have interacted with the men that I've dated and how I have navigated community and academia. The last two men I seriously dated I was engaged to. Both told me I was fat and had become unattractive. One said, "Truthfully, I don't sleep with you because I haven't been as attracted to you since you've gained so much weight," and the other before him who I dated twice said that I was old and fat. I think about how the trauma of losing my aunt, being diagnosed with AIDS, then prostate cancer and losing my mother to breast cancer has impacted my health. As I think about these issues and those raised by Prud'homme-Cranford, I also realize that age is such a complicated process and that colonization has shaped the ways that we as Creole, Native, and Black people understand aging. It isn't about our relationships and kinship formations and bonds at times because we have taken on the ideas of our oppressors about weight, color, age, and beauty. I have internalized these things too. When I think about the men I have dated and the few women many were mixed-race, had lighter complexions, and were pretty "physically fit" from a Eurocentric and homonormative perspective.

When I was still in my twenties, I remember attending my first Creole Studies Conference in New Orleans in 2002. So many of the men were closeted yet flirting. What was different then had everything to do with my age, body, and perhaps even my own sense of self. As time has passed, I think about how my relationship to trauma, death, disease, and body politics as well as color have shaped me. Even as I write this I have recently started "talking to" a new guy who happens to be Creole and I love our cultural connections and shared interests and that we are focusing on getting to know one another slowly as people, and yet in the back of my head I'm still battling my own demons as we FaceTime. I ask myself, why do I look so ugly today? Then I wonder if he will be like the others and think I'm too fat or too old. I learned from my aunt and also from my father to live in joy despite our traumas. Creoles are a strong and a resilient people. I want to do more than be resilient, though. I want to thrive and I want to center my joy and what I do in this life as more than what my body looks like. I want to be healthier. Defining what that means has to start with centering pride in who I am, and that's no small feat as

Prud'Homme-Cranford demonstrates. Academia and society in general is a deeply racist, ableist, ageist, and misogynistic place to work. When I first started my career at twenty-five and even until the present moment, I have always felt judged. Looks of disbelief like, how can he be a professor? So even after twenty years of this work I can still feel the wounds of not quite belonging. And yet where I have felt the most love and the most support as well as acceptance has been among Louisiana Creole people. I think when my aunt told me to "fatten up, you're too skinny" she was really telling me to be good with you no matter how you look and no matter what other people think. She was a caring, loving, hardworking woman who lived an unapologetically brave life. I can only aspire to be as strong as Joelle, my beautiful aunt noir.

CHAPTER 10

DON'T SCRATCH MY WASHBOARD, BUT YOU CAN PULL MY FIDDLE

Negotiating Queerness in the Creole Diaspora

ANDREW J. JOLIVÉTTE

Locating, understanding, and unpacking queerness in the Louisiana Creole diaspora is an unaddressed subject in the contemporary research literature. To begin to understand and document queerness as an identity negotiation across the diaspora, it is important to first frame anti-queerness within the LCD (Louisiana Creole diaspora) as a byproduct of settler colonialism, heteropatriarchy, and what I term "washboard masculinity." The washboard, in Louisiana Creole communities, functions not simply as a musical instrument but as a powerful signifier of male potency: a mixture of hyper-sexuality, patriarchy, and showmanship. To scratch someone else's washboard is to metaphorically expose, subvert, and castrate another man's masculinity. In contemporary zydeco music the washboard remains a central musical instrument with which men will battle one another, whereas the fiddle has become an antiquated or "feminized" instrument that carries not only gendered but also racialized meaning. Zydeco, made popular internationally throughout the late 1970s and early 1980s, incorporated the sounds of the blues to resonate with a broader audience, particularly among African Americans, while the fiddle is primarily heard today in Cajun and bluegrass music. Cajuns, since the mid-twentieth century (some might argue since the late nineteenth century), have been identified with Whiteness, while Zydeco has been deemed, Black music. Each of these designations are simplistic, reductionist, and negate the overlapping histories, genealogies, and cultural convergences of Louisiana Creoles and Cajuns. Further, the impulse to frame these communities as polar opposites and as binary Black-White adversaries (particularly in light of the diverse and multiple Indigenous cultural influences dominant in Louisiana Creole culture) is similar to modes of gender and sexual binaries that deny fluid identity formations.

In my own experience as a descendant of Louisiana Creoles (including Native Americans) and Cajuns (Acadian exiles from Nova Scotia), who grew up outside of Louisiana, queerness was mainly visible in the public sphere, ironically, through the Catholic Church. It was the Catholic Church where it was made clear that Creole men and Creole women were first binary in gender and heterosexual in expectations for "normative" family creation. To uphold one's duty and morality as a devout Creole Catholic, one had an obligation to procreate, abstain from premarital sex, and center family over everything. The centralizing of family over everything has often meant silence around sexuality, gender diversity, and gender oppression within and across the Louisiana Creole diaspora.

To metaphorically scratch another man's washboard (masculinity) as a signifier of emasculation is further visible in thinking about the use of the fiddle as a removed, silent, and unspoken practice in contemporary Creole/Zydeco music. In other words, if a Creole man plays fiddle today, not many people see it, hear it, or empower the history of the instrument in Creole and Cajun music. Thus, the metaphor of pulling another man's fiddle (penis/sexuality) is not seen, discussed, or validated as a mainstream practice. But behind closed doors, in homes, on porches, one might incorporate all kinds of sounds and instruments into contemporary music, but this is not recorded. Queerness is also unrecorded. As long as sexual encounters between men and women of the same sex are not on display and remain a deep, dark unrecorded secret, then there are not public "problems" with same-sex behavior. This chapter explores those secrets and what meaning they have in contemporary life for Louisiana Creoles both in the state and across the vast diaspora, where public spaces have now become virtual and where sexual engagement between same-sex individuals has online, via social media, and at "Creole crossroads" become normalized.

CREOLE SEXUALITIES AND COMMUNITY FORMATION: RECORDING QUEERNESS

> He asked me to record his story. He was abused by many powerful men throughout his childhood. Turns out we are distant cousins from one of Louisiana's largest Creole families. The abuse took place throughout his childhood by multiple men both in the church and in his family. He doesn't want revenge. He just wants the truth to be told. He became a famous local artist and teacher. We still haven't completely written or recorded his story with queerness in the Creole community. He identifies as bisexual and has had many adult relationships with both men and women.[1]

This chapter traces the dominant discourse in settler-colonial Louisiana and its larger diaspora across the United States and the Americas. Over the past seventeen years I have conducted field research primarily through participant observation in personal and professional experiences and encounters with gay, bisexual, and heterosexual identified Creole men to understand the ways that queerness and anti-queer fear leads to community rejection in many cases and a long journey to acceptance for other members of the Creole community. The study includes interactions with at least twenty-five men ranging in age from twenty to sixty-five, most of whom identify as Creole, with some men having a deeper connection to Louisiana Creole culture than others. The men come from Louisiana, Texas, California, Illinois, and Georgia. Situations, events, and other identifying material have been adjusted as necessary to protect the identities of the men that I have interacted with as friends, intimate partners, and professional associates. What follows is the first study to document queer-identified and queer-performing Creole men. By queer performing I mean those men who self-identify as heterosexual but engage in same-sex behavior or intimate relations with other men. As an already hybrid, mixed-race Afro-Indigenous population, Louisiana Creoles struggle over external definitions around racial identity. Through my research and participation in the community I have observed how queerness complicates racial identity and a congruent sense of belonging and a sense of "full-citizenship" within a Louisiana Creole Peoplehood matrix.

The quote above, from a bisexual Creole man in his forties, demonstrates the ways in which sexual violence impacts a sense of belonging and acceptance. Gendered violence can affect belonging because survivors are often expected to remain silent and to prioritize community over the rights of community members, particularly among American Indian women and women of color.[2] Ramirez's analysis can be extended to queer-identified Creole men who are often forced to perform gender identities that are incongruent with their lived experiences. Gender performativity troubles the ways that men, women, gender queer, and transgender individuals can articulate their full subjectivities outside of the confines of settler-constructed notions of nationalism and citizenship.[3] Louisiana Creole Peoplehood as defined throughout the volume includes a connection to land, shared kinship, language, and cultural practices. But as Michel Foucault notes, aligning with multiple communities can in the end negate legitimacy in any one community.[4]

Creole sexualities and queer identities have not been previously recording outside of the settler-colonial contexts of opposite-sex relations and interracial mixing. This therefore means there is a limited analysis of the power relationships involved in antebellum and Jim Crow–era racialized sexual liaisons between White and non-White people. Queer Creole sexualities and community formation must take into account the multiple ways that Creole people have been refused full belonging and recognition based not just on race and phenotype tropes as both Black and Native, but also as queer.

> He had this gaze about him as we exchanged family names and relationships. His family knew mine. He wasn't the only man that I picked up a sexual vibe from. There were at least a dozen Creole men at the Creole conference that I sensed were also queer, but afraid to be identified as such. My sister noticed it before I did. Their flirtations were surprising and powerful for a Creole who grew up in California in the diaspora. There were other men like me. His fame aside he couldn't keep his gaze off of me and we made plans for later evening. My sister came along. I don't know that she approved. He placed his hand on my leg under the table out of the sight of others. He is a famous New Orleans musician. When we entered the club he was asked to perform. He asked me what I wanted to hear and performed a mesmerizing rendition of

"Stormy Monday" that left me a bit weak. But in the weeks that followed while we flirted it became clear that he couldn't jeopardize his place in the Creole community or in the music industry by claiming his queer identity. Our story like many queer Creole stories remains unrecorded.[5]

This international Creole conference in New Orleans was a slippery site for cultural, genealogical, and educational exchanges. I wasn't surprised that there were many politically charged debates over the meaning of contemporary and historic definitions of what it means to be Creole in the twenty-first century. There were many well-known Creole scholars present. There was one man I knew only online and would come to know better over the years for his robust research skill. He would write me privately over the years about queer encounters and experiences but to this day he has never come out to me. My mentor Rafael Diaz, author of *Gay Latino Men and HIV*, has often noted that in Latin-based cultures (like Creole, Cuban, Puerto Rican, Mexican, and Pilipinx) that not naming one's self as queer was a mode of subjectivity that didn't cause rejection.[6] If it wasn't spoken aloud it didn't have to be addressed. It was "normalized" without being "normal" because what wasn't seen or named could still exist. The Creole men I've encountered, both in Louisiana and outside of the state, have had a troubled relationship with queerness as an impediment to community belonging. Thus, queer Creole men have not been able to honestly and openly engage Creole Peoplehood as free sexual beings. As I explore next, Catholicism (a settler religion) has had a powerful impact on queer Creole subjectivities both in- and outside of Louisiana.

CATHOLICISM AND ANTI-QUEER DISCOURSE IN THE LOUISIANA CREOLE DIASPORA

He is an older man in his sixties. He's very religious. The Creole man I was dating told me how he hit on him and used highly sexual and provocative language to entice him. "You want to see that pink pu***?," he asked him. I was jealous but also curious. The man had lived in California for many years, a very accepting area of the state for queer people, but yet religion seemed to hold him back. The irony was deep. My partner and I were having issues and he went to stay with this older Creole man and ended up sleeping with a younger but very openly out queer Creole man in this older Christian man's home. I was hurt when I opened my partner's phone and found their sex videos, but I was also curious how the older man felt knowing these two queer Creole young men that he craved rejected him in his own home. He's older but attractive. I think the rejection was as much about age as it was about a new generation craving freedom from religious rejection to be authentically Creole and queer at the same time.[7]

My grandmother was one of the most devoted Catholic women I ever knew. She was an Indigenous, Afro-Latinx, Creole woman who rejected both her African and at times her Indigenous ancestry in favor of her French, Spanish, and Italian ancestry. She "passed" for White, and while she deeply loved her queer and equally Catholic son (my uncle), she also allowed her second husband to ostracize my uncle and forced him to move out of their shared home. A house that my bastard of an abusive grandfather helped build along with my father, mother, grandmother, aunts, and uncles in the early 1970s. Growing up, religion was a defining feature of my own life. I was an altar boy for nine years and considered becoming a priest. When my grandmother learned of my interest in the priesthood she got me the "good rosary beads" and a St. Joseph's Mass Missal at thirteen to encourage my ambition. The priesthood for young men in Latin-based cultures is one life vocation that can make your family the proudest. I don't think my grandmother ever knew I was queer. She became afflicted with Alzheimer's disease at sixty-four or sixty-five years old, around the same time that I was struggling with coming out as queer.

Anti-queerness within Catholicism is well documented in the Americas and it is also an understudied topic within the Creole community. Three particular stories come to mind when I think of religion and Creole Peoplehood as illustrative of the dissonance experienced by many queer and questioning Creole men. At nineteen, when I came out my mother told me, "You know those people aren't happy. The Bible says that it is wrong," she said. Likewise, one Creole musician I came to know in recent years and became intimate with also told me that God says "it's wrong to be gay," so he couldn't go too far. Additionally, a cousin of mine was thrown out of his family's home because he was queer at the age of nineteen. His family, despite deep Catholic belief in the sinful aspects of queerness in our Louisiana Creole family, has since accepted my cousin.

> Okay TBH the more I'm around you the more its gonna rub off on me then I'm gonna be gay. My mom would die if I was and yes it was good especially at your dad's house. I like you and have a real connection with you, but I just can't do all this because in God's eyes its wrong. I do love you and have these feelings for you but I just can't go there. It would be wrong and my family, my friends, no one would accept this.[8]

Despite stories of religious fear like the one described above there are also stories emerging about acceptance. One of my cousins, who has been proudly out as queer for many years, married his non-Creole partner a few years ago and many of our relatives attended, including his grandmother who is nearly ninety years old. As more and more Creole people articulate both their racial and ethnic subjectivities, there are more Creoles across the diaspora who are also proudly embracing their queerness without relinquishing their sense of belonging in the Creole community. For all of the gay, queer, and bisexual Creole men who are embracing their sexual identities, there are still many more who are unable to articulate their full sexual identities and thus identify as heterosexual but engage in same-sex behavior while attempting to also preserve their socially constructed sense of masculinity.

WASHBOARD MASCULINITIES: ON QUEER ENCOUNTERS ALONG AND OUTSIDE OF THE BAYOU WATERS

> I text him to ask him if he liked massages. He said, "Yeah I love them. In fact I could use one right now." I knew then that he wanted it. I told him to go to my room and wait for me, I'd be right up. I made sure to tell him which room it was. I didn't want my friend who suspected he was queer to know just yet. I went to the room. The lights were off and he was under the covers. When I pulled the covers back I didn't expect him to be fully naked. Now I really was sure. It was going to happen. One of the most "masculine" Creole men I had ever met was now fully exposing

> his secret to me. The surprises didn't stop there. In the dark . . . I could scratch his washboard and he could scratch mine.⁹

> He got on the plane from Texas. We knew it was only a matter of time. We had soul food. Chicken and waffles. He completed his promise. It had been about four years that we had been communicating. His tattooed body pulsated that night like it had three or four years earlier. He throbbed to completion that morning. His secret still secure. But I knew the truth. I wondered if there were others or if he had only done this with me.¹⁰

These quotes demonstrate the ways that Creole men who identify as heterosexual are finding ways to engage with their same-sex desires while also preserving their public identities as "real men" and as "authentic Creoles." To be Creole and queer is to bring into question the legitimacy of one's ability to be accepted and included in the Creole community. Outside the Louisiana geo-spatial and geo-cultural context, Creole men still struggle with identifying with queerness because of toxic definitions of masculinity.

> He came after getting off from work. He had hit me up on Instagram. He was the relative of my ex. He is questioning his sexuality. He cried when we kissed. We were both fully erect. I could sense his nervousness coupled with his readiness to explore further. We had sex that night. I was his first. It went on for about a year. He still seems unsure of what to make of his sexual and racial identity. Not only does he want "light-skinned children," he wants to be seen as a "normal" Creole man. His body says otherwise. He is sexually excited and fully free with me. His freedom, though, is based on the comfort of his secret residing only with me. I still don't know if he will ever tell his family who he is in terms of his sexual identity. And maybe he still doesn't fully know who he is as queer and for that matter as a Creole.¹¹

Creole men more removed from the culture don't often feel the need to necessarily be accepted as Creole from a cultural identity perspective, but if they are subsumed into Black or Indigenous culture they feel a similar pressure to perform masculinity in certain ways as exhibited in the quote above. In other instances, some Creole men who now identify as queer took a longer amount of time to identify as gay or queer because of community expectations. I met an older Creole man about my age online via Instagram. He didn't come out until he was in his thirties and he had many trust issues about gay men and seemed to operate from a homonationalist perspective. We were both interested and attracted to one another, but he couldn't get past trust issues and had a generally negative perception of queer Creole men. In addition to gay-identified Creole men having reservations about engaging in same-sex relationships, there were also heterosexual and bisexual-identified men who were distant with me because they wanted to maintain a public perception about their masculinity.

> We left the going away party. He had asked me for a ride home back to Oakland. Admittedly, I had wanted him since the time that he lived with me three years earlier, but I wasn't quite sure how he felt. On the drive home I took a chance to see how he would respond. I placed my hand on his leg as we crossed the Bay Bridge. He didn't move it. I knew then he didn't mind but I still wasn't sure. As I went for his zipper, he helped me and opened it himself. He was already hard and wet. As we exited the bridge he said let's just pull over and do this and stop playing. So, I did, and we went at it but over the next two years our sexual liaisons would become more intense. He was an amazing lover. We both knew it was taboo, but we kept it going despite who knew. I knew he would never leave his girlfriend or come out directly as gay. I still don't know if he's bisexual or just gay and unable to depart from heteronormative behavior out of fear of being judged. For queer and questioning Creole men, judgment remains a major issue in public displays and acknowledgments of sexuality outside of normative discourse.[12]

The man described above has two biological children. He has been in and out of jail, including for domestic abuse involving another man. He is fairly removed from the Creole culture and yet he always seemed to be seeking validation as authentically Creole and as a man in search of sexual freedom. I knew he loved me and was sexually stimulated by our interactions in ways that he had never been before. But his navigation into Creole and queer spaces was fragile at best. He needed guidance to some extent but was afraid of what others might think and ironically everyone did eventually find out; but that didn't stop us from getting together again for an extended period of time. He, like many of the Creole men who are queer or questioning, felt safe with me because I didn't judge them and because they knew me well. I wasn't the stereotype of a gay man that they held in their heads. There have been other men who were more secure in their identities despite their self-identification as heterosexual or as queer Creole men. Many identify strongly with their Afro-Indigenous cultural roots and see their sexuality as a fluid aspect of who they are as members of the Louisiana Creole community.

AFRO-INDIGENOUS QUEER CITIZENSHIP IN LOUISIANA CREOLE COMMUNITIES

> We drove to Santa Clara for the Zydeco event. We were swept up by the pulsating music. His Indigenous features were very strong. I had never met him in person. He was gorgeous. He first approached me to ask if she was my wife or girlfriend. Then he asked my other friend who is also queer, Creole and strongly Afro-Indigenous identified. My friend and I have also been intimate after many years of friendship. This was his first trip to the Bay Area. We decided to pick up the washboard player. He was after all smoking hot. We became known as the Creole bandits after that. Turns out he wasn't queer even though he has been read as queer for many years. But he is comfortable in his sexuality and racial/ethnic identity. His connection to land, people, and community like my other friend who is queer is all about kinship. All about Peoplehood in a post-contact settler state.[13]

While I have had many same-sex relationships with other Creole men who do not identify as queer or who hide it in public, I have also had some very loving, positive interactions, and serious, long-term relationships with proud Afro-Indigenous, queer Creole men. Dynamics around sexuality and queerness in the Louisiana Creole community and across the diaspora are beginning to open up despite past generational fears. But there are still many fears. A close friend and distant cousin told me about his father's struggle generations ago as a bisexual man, and he also suggested that in telling these stories about queerness and Creole sexuality that I should be careful because there are still many men (and women) who live in secrecy. He literally said:

> You just have to watch to see who gets mad . . .There's a cult of the closet among Creole people. I can tell you now there will be people who are like "I don't believe blah blah blah" and "Oh, this is just lascivious" and "I never knew anybody gay growing up" and all that bullshit . . . But okay, mark my words, any of those three phrases means somebody's been naughty. I guarantee it. I have an uncle we called "Te" growing up. Te was gay and "no one knew" until he died. Then his sister, my grandmother, told everybody.[14]

As I've noted in previous research, community identity formation is based not just on racial ascription but is also deeply embedded in cultural practices and engagements.[15] Being a multigenerational multiracial population, Creoles already struggle with complex questions about ethnic identity, authenticity, and belonging both in Louisiana and across the diaspora. Adding queerness troubles and upsets the already fragile and slippery web of identities that have for more than three centuries of history been associated with questioning the place and location of Creole people: as Native/Indigenous, Black, and White. In addition to earlier discussions about the role of Catholicism on queer navigations across the Creole diaspora, there are also important family considerations that must be taken into account. Many of the parishes (also called villages) of Creole communities are in very small rural towns where everyone knows one another. And even in larger cities like Houston, because Creoles are closely tied to one another, there is still always a chance that "someone will find out." A friend of mine who I had thought was gorgeous and very straight turned out to be bisexual. He's married and has two children. His father is Creole, and his mother is Latinx. As we got to talking online, he confided in me that he was bisexual. We exchanged a few pictures and did eventually meet in person but respected that he was married and didn't go any further. For him his sense of belonging, of "citizenship" (membership in the Creole community), could be brought into question if more people knew. He had only told his wife, mother, and best friends. Guarding and protecting one's role and place in Creole Afro-Indigenous Latinx communities of Louisiana and the diaspora require some critical self-articulation and fight. One of my cousins has not really remained close to his family because of his identity as a gay man. His father never accepted him, but he and his mother are reconnecting. He also has a younger brother who is also queer. As more queer Creole people articulate their right to exist and be fully visible in society, we should see more shifts in the ways that queerness is navigated and viewed by the larger Creole community. As we Creoles continue to unsettle these deeply patriarchal "washboard masculinities," future generations of queer Creole youth and adults will have more access to community and support resources.

UNSETTLING QUEER WASHBOARD MASCULINITIES IN THE QUEST FOR CREOLE BELONGING AND CITIZENSHIP

> The strength of his words moved me. "God is everywhere even beneath the wings of a dove. Congratulations on your good health. Love, Uncle Charlie." This is what my uncle, who is also my godfather, told me when I was diagnosed with HIV/AIDS in 2002.
> He had lived through so much as a gay Creole man in the 1960s, '70s, and '80s. He saw many of the changes that have changed the ways that queer people are viewed in 2019 versus 1969. He and his husband are now married and have been together well over thirty years. He has always represented the complex ways that masculinity and exists in queer and Creole contexts. His voice is soft from his throat cancer surgery. He is also a very strong man who the rest of the family has often depended on. I've noticed this pattern with gay Creole men. Many are the go-to child, cousin, uncle, or brother who navigates the challenges that life brings. This is of course anecdotal and only speaks to my own personal observations. But my uncle dances zydeco better than anyone in my immediate family. He and my father—who is the definition of an old school masculine, Creole gentleman—are very close. They demonstrated to me my entire life what alternative Creole masculinities could look like in the way I respect my partner, my family, and my community.[16]

To unsettle washboard masculinities we have to, from a young age, shift the ways that we represent and teach young boys what it means to be a "man" and to include definitions of masculinity that are inclusive of queer and heterosexual identifications. As José Muñoz writes:

To disidentify is to read oneself and one's own life narrative in a moment, object, or subject that is not culturally coded to "connect" with the disidentifying subject. It is not to pick and choose what one takes out of identification. It is not to willfully evacuate the politically dubious or shameful components within an identificatory locus. Rather, it is the reworking of those energies that do not elide the "harmful" or contradictory components of any identity. It is an acceptance of the necessary interjection that has occurred in such situations.[17]

Today queer, Creole Afro-Indigenous individuals are indeed picking and choosing what they wish to take away from identification with the Creole community. At the same time that Louisiana tribal communities such as the Atakapa-Ishak are seeking recognition and full citizenship, so too are queer Creoles seeking affirmation of their place within the community. As we move toward the future, however, struggles for citizenship must also be assessed within the context of settler colonialism and empire as a system of transit whereby limits are placed on who can belong and who is refused into society.[18] But we must also deconstruct the boundaries of a socially constructed citizenship that still privileges settler over Native, White over Black, and heterosexual over queer and transgender. Thus, as queerness becomes articulated across the Creole diaspora it must also seek to critically interrogate homonationalism and the gendered, sexualized, and racialized scripts that are still being used to admit or deny group membership and acceptance. So in the end the question becomes acceptance at what cost? Are queer Creoles simply looking to assimilate in Western, settler notions of citizenship and belonging, or will they be guided by a deep commitment to articulate a transformative citizenship that is rooted in kinship, land, and culture? A citizenship rooted in Peoplehood, not patriarchy?

NOTES

1 Author field notes, August 2018.
2 Renya Ramirez, "Race, Tribal Nation, and Gender: A Native Feminist Approach to Belonging," *Meridians* 7, no. 2 (2007): 22–40.
3 Judith Butler, *Gender Trouble: Feminism and the Subversion of Identity* (New York: Routledge, 1993).

4. Michel Foucault, *Power/Knowledge: Selected Interviews and Other Writings, 1972–1977*, ed. Colin Gordon (New York: Pantheon Books, 1972).
5. Author field notes, October 2003.
6. Rafael Diaz, *Latino Gay Men and HIV: Culture, Sexuality, and Risk Behavior* (New York: Routledge, 1997).
7. Author field notes, June 2016.
8. Author field notes / social media communication, April 2018.
9. Author field notes, December 2015.
10. Author field notes, April 2017.
11. Author field notes, October 2017.
12. Author field notes, September 2014.
13. Author field notes, March 2014.
14. Personal communication, March 2019.
15. Andrew J. Jolivétte, *Louisiana Creoles: Cultural Recovery and Mixed-Race Native American Identity* (Lanham, MD: Lexington Books), 20–27; Andrew J. Jolivétte, *Indian Blood: HIV and Colonial Trauma in San Francisco's Two-Spirit Community* (Seattle: University of Washington Press, 2016).
16. Author field notes, November 2018.
17. José E. Muñoz, *Disidentifications: Queers of Color and the Performance of Politics*. (Minneapolis: University of Minnesota Press, 1999), 12.
18. Jodi Byrd, *The Transit of Empire: Indigenous Critiques of Colonialism* (Minneapolis: University of Minnesota Press, 2011).

COMMUNITY RESPONSE

BENDING THE STORY

M. CARMEN LANE

She scratched and she pulled. It didn't matter because we were both invisible. They saw what they wanted to see. Her long brown hair caught every man's attention, but her hands told a different story. We were seen together all of the time. They were silent as a means to not complicate things. The elder Black woman down the hall saw my heart. Was old enough to know it wasn't right. "She is older than you and married. She is unhappy and taking advantage that you care about her." Delores didn't know what she was talking about. She was just sad because the person who saw her is long dead. Collected shit to hide her grieving.

I remember her smell. The heat of her body from across the room. She called me her "other husband." I dared not name her. She called me a "man." She liked that I was both Black and an Indian. She could hide her indiscretions by my body being read as Black, young, and new to the ecosystem. She was a half-breed mixed with white and poor. She was cunning but not strategic. When she was sick, I made medicines for her and paid the price. Her vulnerability in her own body made her hold on to anything that would give her power. An old friend said she had "flushed her soul down the toilet" not to be with me. They were being kind. I could never be angry with anything that was done to me and I would do most of what she would ask of me.

Here's the thing: she saw all of me and knew this world would never take me in. She didn't understand that I had no interest in being at the center of anything or chopped into pieces based on a colonial comfort. At the edge of the woods, our teachings tell us this is where I am located, to be honored and acknowledged.

THUNDERBOI

I am not a man.

Woman—
I will spend the rest of my days
with you

your family will not want
me to dance you
into sky
surround you in
mist

you
who are the most beautiful
silken hair
stained by the color
meant for fox

skin like a bowl of mush
against my belly / my own
a blue moist clay

I am not a man.
I will make a way to enter you

cornhusk & a dried offering from one of your sisters
        wrapped in deerskin
        bound with sinew

this will be
& you will teach me
your song

I will envelope you
in the thunderstorm
of my bosom

I will bring you home
with child

here. now.

NOTE

First published *Yellow Medicine Review.* From *Calling Out after Slaughter* (Ontario: GTK Press, 2015).

PART 4

CEREMONIALS AND CULTURAL PRACTICE

From Testimonials to Activism

CHAPTER 11

ON PASSING AND SURVIVAL

Memories of a Choctaw-Apache

THOMAS PARRIE

Throughout my childhood and into my teens and twenties, I had no idea what I was. I mean, I knew *who* I was but *what* I was remained a mystery. Other kids and even some grown-ups would ask "What are you?" and my reply, which came slow because of the shock, since you never get used to being interrogated about your skin color, was always "I'm American." Usually, most would back off and go their own way, but there was always a percentage of inquisitors that scoffed, as if I were lying. But how could I lie about my race when I wasn't even sure what it was? Moreover, what was behind my motivation to lie about my skin color? I wasn't passable with my black hair and my brown skin; hardly anyone was. And no matter how many times elders would claim we were Spanish, I felt like they were hiding or denying what we obviously were. That we were Latinx and "Spanish" was code for it. It wasn't quite Mexican, but it was a close association, like they avoided the label by insisting we were somehow connected to Spain, and by extension, its rigid caste system.

My dad's side of the family has skin of various shades of brown, a skin that inevitably gets browner in the sun. Yet, when I asked what we were, the answer was always "We're Spanish, baby." Sometimes they said we were white, and other times Spanish. It was how you held onto land and stayed connected to the river and its creeks. Accepting settler thought was how you survived. It was what my family and my tribe had been doing since the 1700s—blending in.

And since there had been an influx of Mexican immigrants in town at the time, and since our elders spoke Spanish and were Catholic, we were easily misidentified by everyone who wasn't us. For years, we misidentified ourselves. I would learn later that the Spanish they spoke is a Spanish-based trade language that uses Mississippian Choctaw, Lipan Apache, and Nahuatl loan words. Couple that with how the tamale was a staple food for us and the community, and that added up to a lot of confusion.

But when I was sixteen my dad gave me a tribal ID card. It was a simple white business card with an encircled alligator snapping turtle at the center with the words "Choctaw-Apache Tribe of Ebarb" in red font. Dad told me the turtle was our family crest. That we were, and had always been, Choctaw-Apache. That put an end to the mystery. It was the defining moment. This card not only vindicated me but began a long journey toward my own discovery of Indigeneity. Dad and I would participate in our tribe's powwow a few years later, but only when the MC invited everyone to dance. There was a change in the wind and of attitude. In the '90s it was suddenly in vogue to be Indian. There was this resurgence in our family, an assertion that we were Native. It was a reclaiming of the rights of what generations before me had been denied.

There was something underneath all that denial of what we were, and the answer had been everywhere. It was in our tamales. It was in the stories the elders told us, stories my dad would pass on to me. It was in our tendency to play music on the front porch and all my cousins and aunts and uncles would come over and everything would turn into a reunion even though everyone lived only yards away. It was also in the lake.

When I was eight my dad and my uncles went swimming in Toledo Bend near a bridge. I'm pretty sure it was Pendleton Bridge, but it's been so long I forget the details. I couldn't swim, so I waded out far out as I could, as would any curious kid, until the water was up to my ears. On my way back, I slipped on algae and ending up splashing my way into deeper waters. Dad saw me going under and jumped after me. But he found himself slipping on the algae as well. An alert uncle jumped in after him, pulled my dad back into shallower water, as he pulled me back with him. The experience was terrifying at the time. I had always been afraid of the lake.

Legends abounded of catfish the size of railcars and man-eating alligator snapping turtles beneath the waves of Toledo Bend. There were even rumors of whole towns that had been submerged. Ghost towns that existed underwater. In my kid mind, it was the most likely place where La Llorona, our as my dad called her, The Crying Woman of Grady Hill, lived. I would learn later that those stories held the truth of our history. That the lake itself held our history.

Those stories, along with the reclamation of our culture, was a nugget that would become my first poetry collection, *Toledo Rez & Other Myths* (published by That Painted Horse in 2019). In the book, I recognize how tied my family is, and always has been, to the land and the lake that occupies it. The foodways, the stories, and the language preserved what was left of our indigeneity. Passing for Spanish or even white, while still living on ancestral lands, was linguistic and cultural survival.

CHAPTER 12

LA TO L.A.

Growing Up Louisiana Creole in the Los Angeles Diaspora

CAROLYN M. DUNN

> Ala Tek. Indian Girl. The ghosts of your ancestors will visit you there.
>
> LEANNE HOWE, "Indians Never Say Goodbye"

Many Creoles in the United States trace their direct ancestry back to the mixing of cultures as it began in Louisiana in the early 1600s. The interactions between Native peoples (Atakapa, Choctaw, Tunica Biloxi, Houma, Chickasaw, Creek, Opelousa, and others), former slaves turned "Free People of Color" or *gens de couleur libre*—and the French and Spanish colonizers who came to what would become Louisiana created our unique population who trace our Indigeneity to Louisiana homelands. But what is oft not recognized, or long forgotten, is the earlier forced migrations by the French and Indian populations that grew out of the expulsion of poor French Catholics from France to Canada, whose own interactions with Native communities there (Métis, MiqMaq, Woodland Cree, Wabanaki Confederacy, Iroquois Confederacy) would later migrate to Louisiana via waterways. These mixed French-Indians would be further forced out of Canada and down the rivers through Native and colonial territories, eventually settling in what would become southwestern Louisiana Bayou Country, intermarrying and intermingling (contrary to popularly held

American cultural beliefs) with the Creole population to create the historical and contemporary Creole culture in Louisiana.[1]

These Creole colonies were formed out of interactions with Native, French, Spanish, African, and Acadian peoples, whose cultural, political, and linguistic influences are still present in today's local and diasporic American French and Spanish Creole communities. Forced migrations, guided often by economic and racial divides, continued the diasporic movement of families and communities, into what Renya Ramirez has defined for Native peoples as "hubs"—the creation of space that reflects identity and citizenship of a people away from the space of creation and identity.[2] In this chapter, part ethnography, part autobiography, part cultural history, and all memoir, I examine the expulsion of a people first from France, then from Canada, and from Louisiana to Los Angeles, via Oklahoma and Texas, who came to call the diaspora home—growing up Creole in L.A. (Los Angeles), all the while calling LA (Louisiana) the place of emergence. While Los Angeles became the new home for a significant Creole population, the hub that was formed in Watts around St. Lawrence of Brindisi church and the reification of Creole cultural practices, including language, storytelling, and familial and community ties, created a tri-culturally competent center that never forgot its origins and reified a cultural identity unique to its origins and place within the Creole diaspora. This cross-cultural neighborhood, whose population included Latino, Japanese, and Jewish residents, was not unique to Watts but appeared in other communities of color in Los Angeles.[3] This chapter, part history, part song, part poem, and all love story, is a story of my family in the diaspora that was/is Los Angeles; before Los Angeles she was Puvungna, Harakmongna, Tujungna, and many other village sites of the Tongva people who were born of that place.[4]

BLOODLINE

A place doesn't need to be idealized to still claim the comfort associated with being called home. To be welcomed home with open arms is to match the night's shimmering of stars and feel at one, at peace with oneself and one's place among those stars. Here, at the junction of land and stars and trees and fog and ocean and somewhere else, that trail has grown cold.

A distant fire burns at the rim of the hollow of the eyes of the desperate ones. They listen to the source of the mystery, but answer in a voice that cannot be silenced.

It is the power in the voice of the soul that has been recovered, restored to beauty from the ghost world. The songs that keep hold of the digest of desperation entrenched in the songs of a dispossessed people is part of that world that must be cut away in order to survive.

That which is cut cannot be defined by its other half, its missing piece, its soul wound. The deepest part of night is that piece which cannot be named. Patterns exist in a person's life that were woven long before their first breath is drawn.

Woven in the bone and blood of the Ancestors, it is now a tapestry concerned with keeping of stories, vocalized in song, in whispers, in secret, from stages and from graveyards and birthing rooms around the long pathway of this world to where the next world awaits.

The patterns weave the sky in the tear of a glittering body, a curved leg of the grandmother. In the sky, she rises over misted reflections of rain, of clouds called by jimsonweed, wild alata, and sage. We will remember to look west, and the land where the sun makes her return, we follow out of desire, out of necessity, out of fear. For warmth and blessing and the calling home of our spirits to the place we shall all be reunited with once again.

Crawling out of the earth, reborn into the balance of love and death by the ladder of mud, stone and clouds, our gazes hold with the great mother in the sky, her love mending the torn centered edge, bearing the stars home on the back of her shell, given freely when the time comes for us to be reborn.

I want to tell you a story. *Ma gaanchi mohma chigah. Ici, mantnot.*[5] I want to tell a story of a family's migration from the old country to a new country, a new place, a new name, new tongue. A place that siblings brought with them to a new space, adding their story to the space that already existed, their vices to the voices already there. These brothers and sisters took with them their home and remade it anew, leaving behind their language and planting seeds that would grow and come back. Eventually, because we all return to the place from which we were born. Therefore, my story begins in Louisiana. Growing up, it was my "old country," the place from where my ancestors emerged and remained for a very long time until their way of life was eventually replaced by a newer way of life, a new landscape, which offered them change and the space to plant new seeds.

My grandmother was born Anna Dora Beridon in LeCompte, Louisiana, in 1898. She was one of six daughters of Laurent Beridon and Azelie Dora Carriere. Laurent was the son of an Afro-Indigenous French free woman of color, Arsene Vereuil. Arsenne and her mother, Marie Mingolois, are listed as two of the last known "Indian progenitors" of Louisiana.[6] Dora, as my great grandmother was called, was "that Cajun woman," one of three of my great grandfather's wives. (Dora was one of two half sisters, also of Tunica-Choctaw-Biloxi descent, married young—at the same time—to Laurent, and she was the one who stayed).[7] There were ten Beridon children: August Joseph (A.J.), Mayo, Eugenie (Jennie), Ida, Esau, Laurentia (Laurence), Anna, Albert, Corine, and James. Of those ten, six relocated to California in the 1930s. Uncle A.J. was married to Aunt Mary, and Aunt Mary's people were from the Creek Nation near present-day Okemah, Oklahoma. For twelve years, Uncle A.J. and Aunt Mary lived near Okemah where they owned a general store.[8] My grandfather, Collins Gilmore, lived there with them, saving money that he made traveling back and forth to Osage Nation, where he worked in the oil industry, saving money to send home to my grandmother, Anna Beridon, to whom he was engaged to at the time. (My grandfather returned to Louisiana to enlist in the army during World War I and was sent overseas to France—I like to think that this long engagement was made even longer by Osage oil money and the assassination of an Austrian noble.)

During this time, as the Oklahoma Dust Bowl was approaching, someone (I heard it was Uncle A.J.) convinced his wife, siblings, and in-laws that Los Angeles would be the place they landed next. I'm not sure why Uncle A.J. and Aunt Mary left Oklahoma, or why he convinced his siblings and their spouses to migrate to California, but as I understood economics was at the forefront of that decision and an entrepreneurial spirit was gifted to him. However, instinct tells me the Tulsa Race Riots in 1921 (White folks attacking Black-owned businesses and homes in the Greenwood section of Tulsa) and the promise of land and economic opportunities is what convinced them to leave the state. I'm not sure of the time of this migration of Beridons, spouses and children, but as far as I know it happened like this: Uncle A.J. and Aunt Mary would move first, followed by the rest: newly-weds Anna and Collins (my grandparents), Aunt Laurence and Uncle Gabriel, and Uncle Albert and Aunt Florence. Aunt Corine and Uncle Gaston would join them a little later. But it was a migration of over half the family; Uncle A.J. and Aunt Mary would eventually return to Louisiana, but most the siblings were forced by the Dust Bowl, the Great Migration, and the Depression of the 1930s to try their hands in Los Angeles. They moved to Watts, in South Central Los Angeles, living on a city block where the term "it takes a village to raise a village" was in pure evidence. Beridon cousins came in waves: Aunt Laurence and Uncle Gabe were the most fruitful with eleven children, and the older cousins were often responsible for the younger ones, as is the case in most villages where parents worked two jobs to support their families.[9]

IN SOME OTHER WORLD

> In some other world
> stars shine bright
> upon wounds of our
> ancestors, stored in gates
> leading from one place
> to the next.
> Songs that herald
> passage of time by birth
> still sung as we
> enter into this world,
> dreaming.
> Distant reaches
> of song storied
> in memory
> of my mother's birth
> is history
> recorded time
> upon shells in
> red, deep sunset,

and carried at
the hip as a gesture
of remembrance.

In some other world,
I speak words
of my grandmothers, their
frozen tongues speaking out of turn,
I gaze out from
behind her
eyes, singing her
world back into existence.
My mother's words
pass through my lips, echoing
across flat plains
and oceans of stars
beckons us home
with songs that bring corn.
In some other world,
the first shoot of silk
reaches toward the space
from where we all came.
Like us, they look to sky, wishing to
call back the ones who left.
Like them, a silk tuft of gold
calls the rain cloud.

This sea is strong,
grounds me here,
in space of breath, in faceted turn
of a song, my face turned to sky.
My grandmother's voice, passing
my lips,
escapes the veil
of some other world.

 The first generation of this particular family of Creoles encompassed not only French, Choctaw, Tunica, Biloxi, Atakapa, Avoyel, Ishak, Houma, and African peoples, but French Canadian Ancestors who intersected with métis, Cree, MiqMaq, and Ojibwe peoples and whose French progenitors were exiled from France, then French Canada, and traveled down the waterways into present-day Louisiana. The names intersecting with and creating this Beridon family included Trahan, Marcantel, Prudhomme (Anglicized later as Prudom), LeJeune, Carriére, Collins, Linscomb, Siméon (Anglicized as Simmons), Roque, Ravare, Vereuil, Verdin, Falamahtubby, Pierite, Casenave, and Farve, among others; but these were the names growing up that created who we, as a family group, became. The family encompassed several city blocks of what would become the community of Watts, long before it became the Watts site of resistance so many of us growing up in Los Angeles came to equate with racial injustice and unrest.

The Watts of the 1930s was an intercultural community, my tricultural family connecting with and living among Japanese farmworkers, Filipino tradespeople, and Mexican market owners. The community members became like family, and my grandfather Collins and my Uncle Albert built, starting from the foundation up, the house in which my mother and aunt would be born and grow up. Growing up, the second generation heard the stories of the first, growing up in Los Angeles—learning how to drive on country roads, before freeways from Watts to San Pedro, to the ocean, swimming in the waves at Cabrillo Beach, going to the market for fresh seafood that populated and replicated our Gulf love for fish.

I remember watching *I Love Lucy* with my parents in syndication in the 1970s. There was a comment Lucy made when the gang went to Hollywood to try and boost Ricky's career. From their hotel in Hollywood, Lucy marveled that she could see Catalina Island. Unlike Lucy, who had an unobstructed line of sight, this clear view would later change as Los Angeles grew into the urban sprawl it is today. Growing up after the boom and the revolution of the automobile, resulting in Southern California's love affair with cars, "smog" (fog, pollution, and natural smoke that rose from San Pedro where I grew up), that view of Catalina (called Pimu by the Tongva—Indigenous peoples of the Los Angeles Basin—was often obscured. My parents, aunts, and uncles all remembered those days when that view was always plain; my generation did not. This is the type of L.A. history I loved hearing about: rooted in the landscape, like the stories I grew up hearing about the old country—Louisiana.[10]

STAY

>   Stay,
>   *my funny valentine.*
>   in midst
>   of this chaos
>   is bliss,
>   me and you,
>   him and her
>   and her and she
>   and he and
>   he and you
>   from us two.
>   Who knew
>   in twinkle
>   of ancestral eye,
>   all those years
>   ago,
>   that we would end up
>   at the dawn of the world,
>   breathing an
>   ocean of stars
>   and sound
>   of water returning
>   to this land of
>   falling stars
>   and fallen angels,
>   Small spaces
>   in midst
>   of this newborn
>   and urban
>   sprawling of arms,
>   fingers,
>   galaxies,
>   patterns of stars and rain
>   in dirt trails and washways emptied?
>
>   At mouth
>   of a forgotten river,

an empty and stolen grave
fingers reaching
for what can
never achieve,
you and me
and he and she
and she and they
became us
against darkest
night,
reborn in earth
and stars
they breathe songs,
stolen from
tongues cut from
brick and mortar,
brought back by love
of those
who came before
 and prayers
of the ancestors
who wove the pattern,
that winds us in
a story of rivers—
forgotten and remembered,
forged and forsaken,
in the eyes
of our children,
hurling back words
cut from mouths
watered and fed
by the very rain
that wanted us
dead.

The first casualty of my family's migration was their language. Louisiana French, or Kouri-Vini, is a hybrid language: not one or the other, or others, but a mix of at least three and sometimes more. Creole scholars Darryl Barthé, Oliver Mayeux, and Christophe Landry have traced the etymology of Kouri-Vini and how many of our words are indeed an amalgamation of French, Choctaw, Mobilian trade language, and West African languages.[11] I don't have a memory of that language, other than vague sounds from my early childhood. I remember sitting in the backyard of my aunt's house, where Aunt Corine had moved to help care for her sister, my grandmother, Anna, or Mama as her daughters and granddaughters called her. I must have been about six years old. I remember sitting under the avocado tree, next to the prolific plum tree, and suddenly I noticed I could not understand what they were saying. So I pretended not to listen but I sat fascinated, hearing the words spill and flow out of them. Then I remembered my mother saying that they had spoken only "Creole," which was "like French," until they went to school, and I was being treated to confidante status by listening to them. Years later, I asked my mother why they stopped speaking it, why they never spoke it to their children. "They wanted us to be Americans," she responded. I remember thinking that odd because they WERE Americans; in fact, they were here before there was an America.[12] That they lived off of the land, fishing and hunting for sustenance. That they had to leave school after eighth grade in order to work their father's cotton fields and that none of the ten siblings finished high school. Not because they didn't want to finish, but that they couldn't because they had to help support their family. That they were ridiculed for speaking their language in school, ridiculed for learning how to survive in that landscape, all along the riverways and waterways of southwestern Louisiana, as their Ancestors and their Ancestors' Ancestors had done before them. Years later, I told my mother that Mama and Aunt Corine had spoken French in front of me. "They used to do that when they were gossiping," my mother said. "They probably didn't want you to know what they were talking about." I like to think that they were indoctrinating me into their secret society—their secret Blindian/Creole society—and they allowed me to hear the language they—and I—were born into, but was taken away by the desire to "blend in" and to "Americanize."

So much of their community, like their parishes back home, was integrated through their lives as Catholic migrants through the church they worshiped at. St. Lawrence of Brindisi served as church, school, and community hub for my elders. Religion is also a cultural identifier for Creole peoples, and the type of Catholicism practiced by Creole Catholics is similar to the "new world" Catholicism of the Pueblo tribes in New Mexico, or Catholicism of Latinidad. Like the Creole people, our religious traditions are hybrids of old and new, but distinctly "new world" Catholicism. The blending of religious practices is a metaphor for the blending of cultures that created Louisiana Creole identity: European, mostly French Catholicism, Indigenous cultural and spiritual practices, and African traditions carried through the Middle Passage to colonies. Nearly all of the Beridon siblings' children attended St. Lawrence school through their elementary school years, and many would later attend Catholic Girls High School. Renamed Our Lady of Loretto and now known as Bishop Conaty / Our Lady of Loretto Catholic High School, this was where my mother, aunt, and their female cousins attained their secondary educations. Education was, and continues to be, very important to our family. I remember hearing about how brilliant my Uncle Gabe was, how he was always fixing and inventing different things while applying for patents. My uncle/cousin Philip (Aunt Corine's only child) used to say that because Uncle Gabe was a dark-skinned Blindian, education wasn't afforded to him growing up Creole in Louisiana, and by the time the family had migrated to Los Angeles, his ever-growing Collins branch of the family had to be supported, so he worked instead. "He really should have been an engineer," I remember Uncle Phil saying years ago. "Instead of building planes he should have been designing them." I remember Uncle Gabe's thick as molasses Creole/Cajun accent, his love of storytelling, how he drank coffee with lots of cream and sugar with the spoon still in it, and how he once cried out at the table in his thick accent "Peeeeeeople! She din' give me no bread!" when Aunt Laurence forgot to give him his dinner. I see him in my Collins relatives, his likeness passed down to so many of them that sometimes cousins look more like siblings, but you know they are all Beridon-Collins cousins.

Our Beridon elders tended to not last very long. It seems as though the knot of the curse of dementia (including Alzheimer's and Lewy body dementia) followed these siblings to their new world. Uncle Albert died when I was very young, and I have very vague memories of Uncle Albert, the uncle who wasn't my Uncle Jim, but looked and acted very much like him. Uncle Albert began to show signs of dementia and while out walking in the street was hit by a car and later died from his injuries. He was one of many surrogate fathers to my mother, my aunt, and my cousin (aka Uncle Phillip). After my grandfather Collins died in his sleep of a heart attack when his daughters were five (my mother) and three (my aunt), Uncle Albert took his young nieces on as daughters; true to the matriarchal society that made us, maternal uncles took on strong roles in children's lives, often parental roles, and my Uncle Albert escorted my mother down the aisle to meet my father at their wedding. My grandmother was the next of the California-based siblings to pass: heart disease was the culprit that time. Soon her sister Laurence was next, as the three sisters—Aunt Laurence, Mama, and Aunt Corine—were nearly conjoined at the hip. So many photos exist of the three of them together, as young wives and mothers, later older wives and widows, and later, grandmothers and great aunts to the L.A. Creoles they brought into the world. Uncle Jim would pass in 1976, also of heart disease, and Aunt Corine, the youngest of the siblings, would follow in 1980, of a heart attack after suffering complications to repair her broken hip.[13]

The loss of our matriarchs was difficult for all of us, but the next generation took on that matriarchal role. Strong women make strong bundles, Paula Gunn Allen once said, and the bundles the Beridon sisters made continued through their own children.[14] As time moved on, the family spread out and grew in its diversity. The Barcenas and the Marambas, Filipino naval officers, married into the Beridons. Of profound influence to me as well as her three sons was my cousin/aunt Miyoko Yoshida, a Japanese American, whose family internment at Camp Topaz in Utah, later became part of this extended Beridon family's story, along with Zoot Suit Riots, the construction of the first freeways, Disneyland, and the growth of Southern California as various industries made Los Angeles their center of operations.

Even though Beridon/Carriére/Collins/Linscomb/Gilmore/Bézart/Siméon/Casenave generations made Los Angeles home, the call of our ancestral origins in Louisiana were never far away. I grew up imagining Louisiana with great longing, the way in which we imagine our place of origin with great longing (nostalgia) and a bit of romanticizing. My family's complicated history with Jim Crow–era policies in Louisiana and Oklahoma and with racism as very light-skinned, nearly White-passing anywhere else, except where they were from, to very dark Creole complexions interspersed with Choctaw, Atakapa, Houma, Ishak, Caddo, Cree, métis, MiqMaq, and West African tribes long lost to us as their freed people of color all came together to create the Creole culture, language, and lifeways indigenous to Louisiana. This story of my family's diaspora is not unique for Creole, or Native peoples here on Turtle Island.

Other Creole diasporas than California were created by the movement of our people in search of a better way of life out of Louisiana; and so we Creoles grew up in those traditions, carrying our bundles of memory, culture, and family into old lands that were new lands in this place now called the United States. We may have lost our language early on, but cooking, music, family, and faith were all part of our Los Angeles upbringing that brought Louisiana to life in our imaginations. Food as culture and as art was always part of the family gatherings. Red beans and rice, gumbo, corn cakes, "dirty" rice, stewed chicken, greens, beignets, pralines, strong coffee, all of these things we grew up with and just took for granted. Couscous, the grain that came from Africa, was not couscous to us, it was something entirely different. Our version often confused with the African grain is actually sweet corn cakes in milk made into a mush that we called "cush-cush."[15] Music, singing, and dancing were important to our family growing up, and the social dances of zydeco clubs sprouting up in Southern and Northern California afforded additional cultural touchstones to connect us to our ancestral homeland.[16]

THE KNOT AT THE END OF THE WORLD

Each knot of a curse
formed long before
The Maker of Breath
sang us into life
from a cloud formed in
the crevices of
the Milky Way.
this world repeats
the presence of spirits
and the land that
speaks to the past.
Can we connect
passing dots,
constellation by
constellation,

forming patterns
that the first woman
who fell through it
named into being?
Crossing water
I hear her voice
and I think I must
tear a song
from static
that lives
on the air
at night. She
is no longer there.
This I have forgotten
For the thousandth time
this morning.
So many dreams.
So many graces
I have let slip and
woven into the skylight covering
my head. Entering
into the song, I
raise my hands
to the stars I
have named in her
honor. The same
star she watched
as I sang the oldest story
I knew, the
light leaving when
she was still here
with me
watching the night
sky.

There is a term known as "hiraeth": *Webster's* defines its origin in the Welsh language, and its meaning as "a homesickness for a home you cannot return to, or that never was."[17] Louisiana, LA, was like that for us growing up in Los Angeles, L.A.: the longing, or nostalgia, for a place unknown but known, and a longing for that place in time that can never exist in that exact way again. We grew up with a certain longing for Louisiana, whether a longing to return home to spend time on the land with family who stayed, celebrating and dancing and singing and keeping those traditions alive as they had sprouted from that landscape. Our Ancestors did what Ancestors, displaced and scattered, have done for time immemorial: replicate culture in new spaces and places. I long for those days of seeing Mama, Aunt Laurence, and Aunt Corine together, in the backyard of what was for a very long time my Aunt Dotty's house, speaking that language I only hear now in dreams, when L.A. was LA.

NOTES

This chapter's epigraph is drawn from LeAnne Howe, *Evidence of Red: Poems and Prose* (Cambridge, UK: Salt, 2005).
1. See Andrew J. Jolivétte, *Louisiana Creoles: Cultural Recovery and Mixed-Race Native American Identity* (Lanham, MD: Lexington Books, 2007).
2. Renya Ramirez, *Native Hubs: Culture, Community, and Belonging in Silicon Valley and Beyond* (Durham, NC: Duke University Press, 2007).
3. See Laura Pulido, Laura Barraclough, and Wendy Cheng, *A People's Guide to Los Angeles* (Berkeley: University of California Press, 2012).
4. The poem that follows,, "Bloodline," originally appeared in Carolyn M. Dunn, *The Stains of Burden and Dumb Luck* (Norman, OK: Mongrel Empire Press, 2017).
5. Mississippi Choctaw dialect, "I'm going to say it again"; and Kouri-Vini, "Here, now."
6. Historical Report on the United Houma Nation of Louisiana, UHN application for Federal Recognition, Bureau of Indian Affairs, accessed July 1, 2019.
7. Azelie Dora Carriere and Eulalie Carriere were the daughters of Joseph Carriere, who both married Laurent Beridon Jr. at the same time. Family lore tells of Laurent's three marriages, his first annulled in the Catholic Church and his second legal marriage to Dora Carriere is recorded in parish records of the time. We can assume that his marriage to Eulalie was more of a common-law situation, which Eulalie would leave and later marry into the Prud'homme and Falamatubby families. August Joseph Beridon (aka A.J) was the son of Laurent and Eulalie, raised by Dora after Eulalie left.
8. Many districts in Okfuskee County and Creek County in Oklahoma came to be known as the "sunset towns" and referred to often as the "Black Wall Street." As the federal government continued its efforts to decentralize tribal government structures in Indian Territory in order to pave

the way for Oklahoma statehood, many of the Black towns were populated by Five Civilized Tribes (Cherokee, Creek, Choctaw, Seminole and Chickasaw) Freedmen citizens.

9 The poem that follows, "In Some Other World," originally appeared in Dunn, *The Stains of Burden and Dumb Luck.*
10 The poem that follows, "Stay," originally appeared in Dunn, *The Stains of Burden and Dumb Luck.*
11 See Mayeux's and Barthé's essays in this book; and Christophe Landry's "Kouri-Vini and Its Sister Languages" from the Louisiana Historic and Cultural Vistas blog at www.mylhcv.com/kouri-vini-its-sister-languages.
12 See Oliver Mayeux's essay "Language Revitalization, Race, and Resistance in Creole Louisiana," published in this collection
13 See T. Shawnee's article in this collection, "A Perfect Circle Bound in Chains: Creole-NDN Health, Historical Trauma, and Settler Colonialism," in which she traces the historical and contemporary diseases that affect Creole-NDN and Freedmen families inherited through Afro-Indigenous populations.
14 Paula Gunn Allen, *The Sacred Hoop* (1986; repr., Boston: Beacon Press, 1992).
15 I see this as a modern cultural modification that traces back to traditional Indigenous corn dishes: tanfula by Choctaws, sofky by the Creeks.
16 The poem that follows, "THE KNOT AT THE END OF THE WORLD," originally appeared in Dunn, *The Stains of Burden and Dumb Luck.*
17 *Webster's Modern Dictionary*, 2019 ed.

TESTIMONIAL 1

LOUISIANA CREOLE PEOPLEHOOD

Mixed Race Foodways

JOHN LAFLEUR II

Louisiana Creole people, as a metis people of European, African, and Indigenous ancestry, contribute much to our contemporary understanding of traditional food practices in the Americas. As an Afro-Indigenous and Latinx people, Louisiana Creoles have created very famous dishes, but the current research scholarship and recipes from Louisiana Creole cookbooks tends to ignore, erase, or minimize the contributions of both Indigenous and African peoples who help to make up the Creole community in Louisiana today. This testimonial is an interruption into that literary tradition. I will discuss some of the ways that Creole cuisine gains its unique and world-renowned flavor as a result of Indigenous, African, and European interactions.

I am a Creole. Our Creole is a unique blend of many cultures and is reflected in our food traditions. The proliferation of Métis/Mixed race communities in "New France" and the Louisiana Territory reflects the reality that interracial marriages (or relations) were quite common within French and Spanish colonial territories. Louisiana became a central region where American Indians, Europeans, and Africans came together in ways to create new social and cultural traditions within music, religion, and the culinary arts. Even after the colonial period of French and Spanish occupation, interracial unions continued (legal or not), and in the nineteenth century immigrants from Ireland, Germany, and the Italian states added to rich fabric of Louisiana Creole Peoplehood. Below I will reflect and share a bit about some of the most popular Creole dishes and how they have been interrupted from a cultural perspective.

No dish has been more debated within Louisiana than gumbo. The sassafras leaves from the Choctaw and other local peppers along with spices and techniques from the Africans and Europeans came together to create one of the world's most influential dishes. Filé gumbo is mostly sassafras-based gumbo and remains known to almost all Creoles and Cajuns. Ham was an early French and African choice in New Orleans, and is a recurring flavorful meat used along with almost anything else put into the early Louisiana gumbo pot. In the countryside, however, wild game, fowl, and seafood are all still used to flavor these exquisite gumbos. According to Dr. Carl A. Brasseaux and New Orleans *Times-Picayune* food writer and author Marcelle Bienvenu, "viande boucanée" or "tasaho" (Spanish for smoked pork/beef; it is spelled *tasso* by Creoles) first appears among the parishes of the northwest French-speaking triangle (St. Landry–Evangeline Parishes), where the descendants of the Alabama- and Illinois-French and Choctaw-Creoles ultimately settled, and remains to this day my people.

The French word "boucan" references the Choctaw practice where a wooden scaffold was lined with animals limb to limb and slowly smoked. Our ancestors learned smoking meat from these Indigenous peoples. So, we see the integration, adaptation, or rather the *creolization* of both the Indigenous and Afro-Caribbean foodways in the culinary traditions of Louisiana Creoles.

The process of making gumbo is as rich and varied as the Louisiana Creole people themselves. Making a gumbo, whether it be an okra gumbo, filé gumbo, or seafood gumbo, is a tradition connected to the process, and every family has their own unique techniques and mechanisms; however, what most gumbos share in common is that the land has always been a necessary component for producing the final product. Below are several different recipes that are central to Creole cuisine. Below I share my own recipe for a chicken and sausage filé gumbo.

CHICKEN AND SAUSAGE GUMBO WITH FILÉ

The Louisiana Creole gumbo was and remains a soup. It is not a "stew" and is still cooked as such by the Houma Indians of Louisiana. Many Louisiana Creoles continue to consume baked sweet potatoes as a side dish to filé gumbo, which is served with rice, cornbread, corn, or grits.

Ingredients

- 1 whole chicken, quartered
- 2 cups chicken livers and 2 cups of chicken gizzards
- 1 lb. thin rounds of Creole/Cajun smoked pork sausage
- 1 lb. cubed tasso
- 3–4 tbsp. John LaFleur's Original Creole Herb & Spice (bay leaf, clove, cayenne, thyme, crystallized onion, and garlic)
- 1 chopped yellow onion
- 3–4 bay leaves
- 1 cup parsley
- ½ tsp. thyme
- ½ cut green bell pepper
- 2–3 tbsp. of filé powder (taken from 2–3 cups of dried, finely ground sassafras leaves)
- 1 tbsp. kosher sea salt
- 1–2 cups flour for dredging
- 1–2 cups cooked okra (optional)

Roll chicken, gizzards, and livers in flour/cornmeal infused with crushed bay leaf, thyme, clove, crystallized onion, and garlic. Then cook these in a skillet of hot grease until light brown to seal in the flavors. Remove meats from the skillet and boil the poultry/fowl, gizzards, livers, sausage, and tasso together with the Creole seasonings in a gallon of water in a large stock pot for one hour. Seafood, wild game, fowl, and leftover roasts can all be put in a gumbo. Add onions, herbs, and return to boil until onions are translucent. Turn off heat. Add filé powder, blending into the stock to the desired texture. Of course, you can also add cooked okra to the gumbo to thicken it up and add more delicious flavor and texture. Add another layer of Creole seasonings and salt as per taste. It's a matter of taste and preferences. No rule ever restricts personal choice and tastes. Serve with a ball of white rice garnished with sprigs of fresh parsley stems and a side of baked sweet potato.

FARCE (FRENCH FOR STUFFING)

Farce is the well-known Louisiana "dirty rice" or "dressing." "Farce de pain de maïs" (cornbread dressing) and "maque chou" (stewed-roasted, caramelized corn with peppers and spices) are French in name only. But, in fact, these are Choctaw-inherited dishes. But neither of these delectable; Louisiana Creole and Cajun dishes are French, Spanish, or Acadian.

JAMBALAYA

A long-established Native American single-pot rice-based dish that can include bits of ham, chicken, fowl, wild game, herbs, and spices, jambalaya has frequently been presumed to be of failed Spanish paella origin by uncritical food writers and "authorities" while others have argued its Atakapa-Ishak origins. Similar rice-based dishes abound in the West Indies, Latin America, Africa, and India, once all ports of call across the French colonial world. And the late, great Dr. Fred Kniffen of Louisiana State University extensively wrote about the remarkable diversity and flavors he discovered and enjoyed among the diverse Indigenous peoples of Louisiana whom he so loved.

GUMBO HERBES DU CARÊME LENTEN (GUMBO WITH GREENS)

When we speak of "gumbo herbes" in New Orleans, the only name that comes to mind is the beloved, and now famous, Ms. Leah Chase of Dooky Chase's Creole Restaurant on Orleans Avenue. And although "gumbo herbes," is one of her specialties, which involves five different types of greens, it is one of our many heirloom Louisiana Creole dishes created out of necessity. And, like gumbo, its contents can vary like the tempers of all Creoles, from good to bad!

Courtbouillon—originally a French wine-based stew—in Louisiana refers to a Creole-style fish stew. According to tradition, it was mentioned among other delicacies brought back to Madame's "school" in New Orleans. Interestingly enough, the Creole version of courtbouillon may also have been what eighteenth-century writer André Pénicaut referred to as "fricassée of fish" once prepared by a Choctaw chief for the young French soldiers who were courting Choctaw maidens, near Mobile one night, who had been encouraged to cohabit among the Choctaw by Governor Bienville, himself, as food supplies were dangerously low. The procedure for cooking tougher meats is French in its Louisiana historical context, as indicated in the recipe's name, to be sure. But, as noted above, the selection of Indigenous Amerindian and African spices and herbs, along with the use of rice, transforms it into a unique Louisiana-based Creole "plat d'excellence" of Afro-Caribbean origins in which hot 'n spicy sauces are commonplace. And we all know how much Louisiana loves its rice 'n gravy! Contrary to what some believe, hot 'n spicy is not Spanish, nor is it from Spain. But it is a trait of Native American, North and West African, and Eastern traditions as far away as India. Many of these herbs and spices were eventually absorbed into later French cookery, too. There has been much hidden about the Native American and African contributions to Creole foodways. I hope I have shared some of this in a way that will encourage others to further explore these histories and cultural traditions.

TESTIMONIAL 2

A REFLECTION

DANNY LEE LANDRENEAU-PETRELLA

I am Danny Lee Petrella, age sixty. I've spent all of my adult years living on the Mamou area (northwestern Evangeline Parish approaching Oakdale at Allen Parish), specifically in the Pain Clare (Pins Clairs) area of Mamou, Louisiana.

This area that I lived in was settled mostly by Creole families, and it was the home of the Mamou Choctaw Band. Growing up and living there afforded me an opportunity to get to know the elderly people—both Creole and Choctaw, and including my grandfather, Élice Landreneau, who had a general store in this area during the Depression era.

I've heard a lot of the Creole French language here, and I learned much of it.

I had a small farm and our few neighbors were farmers also. I was honored one evening when a friend of mine introduced me to Mr. John LaFleur II. This was about twenty-seven years ago, and they had come to visit my antique Creole house.

I could tell he was very much into history and culture. Who knew, that by the blessings of social media, we would meet again?

I love to read his writings on the history of the Creole people! The research he has done to back up everything he has written about our Creole-Métis people is fantastic. What surprised me were his tales; his stories of the Creole-Métis people. They are very true.

I'd heard most of the very same statements that Mr. LaFleur has written about our Creole ethnic heritage, folklore, food ways, and language, told to me long ago the elderly people I met and had grown to love. For example, the Creole Métis—especially those with a lighter-colored skin tone—were ashamed to call themselves Creole because of the public association of the word with the African American people.

And the group CODOFIL wanted to call everyone Cajun for some reason. I, myself, did so. You know, this was to make money off ever thing "Cajun"—the language, the foods, et cetera.

And if I would have never met Mr. LaFleur, I would not have ever known that CODOFIL was behind this identity change.

He is very correct in his knowledge of the Creole language and the history, just to name a few things. I have read his cookbooks, and most of the recipes he has written down were cooked not only by my mother and grandparents, but also by myself.

I know a lot of people that have been call "Cajun" who are not (true) Cajun (Acadian descendants), including myself.

I am writing this because he is doing the right thing. We need our ethnicity to be known not only for us; but, for the entire world. I am proud to be Creole-Métis, and very proud to know Mr. LaFleur II.

You can believe that what he has written is the facts. No "Cajun" or Creole around my neighborhood says the word "oui" for yes; we all say "wea" or "oueh." I'm proud to know John, and very proud of what he is doing to help our culture—which is of many shades of color—have the recognition that it very much deserves, and it is long overdue.

I do hereby affirm that the above statements and comments are true and do grant my permission for my comments to be published.

God bless.

> Danny Lee Landreneau-Petrella, Creole-Métis Mamou,
> Louisiana, May 18, 2018

TESTIMONIAL 3

INTERVIEW WITH KENNETH L. JOLIVÉTTE

ANDREW J. JOLIVÉTTE

Kenneth Jolivétte, a descendant of the Jolivétte, Fontenot, Guillory, and Guidry families of Bayou Mallet, Opelousas, and Eunice Louisiana, spoke with me about Louisiana Creole identity and his efforts to ensure its continuation.

Can you tell us a story about your involvement with the Creole Heritage Center or Creole cultural preservation? How do you try to maintain the Creole heritage?

By telling stories about the old Creoles and our cooking and foodways and keeping cooking our Creole foods and going to the dances and zydecos and telling people about them and trying to get people to understand that we have to get the language back. It's a beautiful language. The food, the music, the language are the main components of our people. The language is so important for the young people especially and we have to learn how we are all related and connected. We need this generation to listen to and learn from the elders so I always try to share what I can from the old days so we can keep it going.

Why do think or do you think it is important to assert Louisiana Creole cultural identity?

Because we are a proud people. Everybody should know about Creoles. Our culture and identity is African and Native American and European. It's a big gumbo pot. We are everything and everybody. Creole. What is Creole? Creole is Spanish, Native American, French, African. We have been here for as long as the land and it is in our blood. The world should know that we are here. And that we are here to stay.

Louisiana Creoles have historically been identified as Black, Indian, Mulatto, Mixed, and White. Why do you think Creoles have been described in so many different ways racially?

Because we are so many different people and ethnicities and nationalities. We're not Africans or Caucasians . . . we are all of that. It may also be the divide, to use the old phrase, the house nigga versus the field nigga, but we are so much more than that and we aren't going for that anymore. It doesn't matter if we are lighter or darker. We got the Native American, the African, the Spanish . . . we have a little bit of everything flowing through our veins so they can't call us just one particular race because we are so much more than that . . . we are deeper than that. It's like we are on sacred ground. When we go to our zydeco dances they aren't like other spaces here in California where I have lived. It's family. It's community. It's connection to land and shared history.

Creoles have also maintained dual identities as Black and Creole; Native American and Creole; White and Creole; or have identified with one strain over the others (Black, White, Native, Latino). What factors do you think contribute to the ways that Louisiana Creoles identify?

I don't think they identify like that. I think they claim all of that today. But growing up it was different, it was just White and Black or Acadians (Cajuns) and Creoles. But a lot of this had to do with societal pressure to make us fight one another and to take our rights away from us. My family moved and identified as French Canadian even though we knew we were also Native and Black. Growing up in California I always identified with being a person of color. Today more and more Creoles are able to embrace their complete selves and all of our different identities.

We have argued in this book that Louisiana Creole Peoplehood is maintained through land, kinship, language, religion (including ceremonial practices), and sacred/shared history (community narrative, religious and cultural narratives). How has land and culture contributed to Creole identity from your perspective and experience?

The land, when you had land, you could have your people over for the boucheries and it brought our relations closer together. They smoked meat, made cracklings. The women would cook while the men would slaughter the animals. We would share food and play with our cousins, and without the land and the animals we couldn't have had those times and memories. The land allowed us to be a community. It wasn't just aunts and uncles, it was cousins and just a lot of people and we would do it at different places. We lived off of the land. Without the land we could not have maintained the culture and our sense of culture. I left Louisiana when I was ten but I still remember it all to this day. The power of memory and land is so strong. We would not have had those opportunities without the land and the people.

How do you maintain pride in your Creole identity for you and your children/grandchildren?

Basically it's, you know, telling them the stories and exposing them to the zydecos, the food, music, and the relatives, but mainly through the stories. If you don't know the relatives and the stories and community you lose that . . . so to us Creole culture is so important and we want the next generation to know who their people are . . . you have to keep that togetherness and family intact. We might not see one another for a long time and we go and have a crawfish boil or a BBQ and some of the cousins I hadn't seen since I left Louisiana and it was like I had never left. When you know your kin folks you know them, and when the kids are together like that the culture never dies. Always go and stop and see your cousins. Know your history. Preserve our stories. Preserve our ancestry. All we can do is instill in our kids and grandkids about the culture that it is all intertwined. Through the gatherings we maintain the Creole culture and traditions.

What advice do you have for future generations of Creole people to maintain the culture?

Keep doing what we are doing. Keep socializing and having get togethers . . . having BBQs and zydecos, and crawfish boils and teaching our young kids how to play the accordion and all of that and, as I've said, through the stories. Teach them how to make a sauce piquant, étouffée, jambalaya, you know, all of that. The stewed hen . . . teach them about the history, the land, and the culture. We have a rich culture and it has to be passed down.

TESTIMONIAL 4

REFLECTION

PIERRE BROOKS METOYER

I am William Pierre Brooks Metoyer, born in Chicago, 1959, the result of the union of William Pierre Metoyer of Natchitoches, Louisiana, and Mary Virginia Brooks (Wilson), who was separated at the time from James H. Brooks Sr. Their union as a marriage could not work as both were Catholic, and divorce was not an option, as was excommunication. I am a Metoyer AND a Brooks as a result.

My father, Bill Metoyer, came north in the Black diaspora of the early twentieth century along with twelve siblings from Cane River to Chicago. I grew up in the housing projects of the Chicago Housing Authority, as did many of dispersed Creoles of Louisiana and postwar veterans. With twelve siblings in and around Chicago, the Cane River connection was strong and undeniable and remains so to this day.

My formative years were spent in both Catholic school and Chicago public schools. The village of Dearborn Homes on State St. taught me to respect elders and listen to their stories, to look out for and help others when you can. Both parents taught a love for music that endures and a wondrous outlook on what is our little blue ball we live on.

My first inkling as to my heritage was stirred by my looks, conveyed by playmates as variously "Porto Rican," "Curly Head," "The Little Injun" [sic]. My Creole culture comes from varying degrees of African, French, Spanish, and Caddo Native ancestry.

At about age twelve, my father gave me a copy of *Forgotten People* by Gary Mills. It stirred me deeply, and gave me knowledge of a culture and a place that seemed like home, though I had never been. It stirred me to contact relatives all around the Chicagoland area and eventually the whole nation. What moved me was, almost to a fault, they accepted those who shared those commonalities of names, place, and tradition as one of their own. Mixing food, faith, and family together in a way that was different from mainstream culture, and even from different from Black culture was also something that was apparent from time to time.

I have always identified as African American AND Creole . . . it's like drilling down to a deeper me. The assertion of being Black *and* Creole is important to me, even though I have relatives that identify as White, Native American, Latino, et cetera. My environment was inner city in a Black neighborhood; Creole DNA seems to be able to thrive and meld to the mainstream culture more to our liking than others, but I'm biased. Our range of skin tones is fascinating, as is the language of Louisiana Creoles. Which is why efforts to maintain it are so very important because it is such a diverse group with many definitions but sometimes we can lose that identity if we don't talk and communicate with one another.

The continued efforts to preserve this culture are extremely important and personal for me. I assert that race is an invention of fear. We are one people, this human race, yet there is a place, in my estimation, for diversity of culture, ideas, tradition, and faith that can bring us together, and Creole culture can be a microcosm of what is possible on a larger, worldwide basis.

CONCLUSION

NOUZOT KRÉYOL

Louisiana Creole Peoplehood or All Our Relations Resisting Settler Violence and Indigenous Erasure

RAIN PRUD'HOMME-CRANFORD, DARRYL BARTHÉ, AND ANDREW J. JOLIVÉTTE

This book is a reckoning. For more than the last three and half centuries Louisiana Creoles, as an Afro-Indigenous Latinx community, have fought against Anglo-American settler violence and racial ascriptions that have eroded Indigenous and African identity in ways that separate our various communities and cultural practices from one another. Each section of this book has been a call to action examining specific ways that settler-colonialist erasures and/or violences have attempted to reduce Louisiana Creole experiences to Black/White paradigms without regard to the ways that Creole people have maintained connections to land (territory/foodways), language (embodied/written), history (kinship/politics), culture (religion/ceremony), and community at large. Louisiana Creole resistance has meant examining the intersections between bodies, cultural practices, languages, health, food sovereignty, and everyday lived experiences that are an intervention into the previous research literature that has negated Indigenous culture and practice in Creole communities of Louisiana. In doing so, *Louisiana Creole Peoplehood* contributes to the fields of Native American / Indigenous studies, Black/Africana studies, southern studies, ethnic studies, sociology, history, and American studies as a project that interrupts the traditional binary approaches to studying Afro-Indigenous populations in the United States. The authors in this collection demonstrate the many ways that Louisiana and its Afro-Indigenous peoples have challenged Jim Crow racism and North American racial exceptionalism by presenting real-life accounts of Afro-Indigenous Latinx Creoles (i.e., mestiz@ peoples) in Louisiana and across the Louisiana Creole diaspora who refuse to be categorized within nineteenth- and twentieth-century racial contexts.

Collectively these chapters trace the nuances that supersede colorism and settler violence in an effort to achieve *rem arbitrium* or defined purpose. We understand defined purpose here as the ability of a colonized people to continue to thrive culturally despite acts of war, cultural genocide, and ethnocentrism. Thriving in the context of Louisiana Creole Peoplehood means that our population will continue as a manifestation at the crux of the matrices coalesced and formed out of a specific ethnogenesis resulting from the violence of post-contact experienced by African and Indigenous peoples of Louisiana. Creole peoples therefore not only accept but practice and engage with each aspect of the various cultural groups making up the entirety of our community as post-contact Afro-Indigenous peoples maintaining cultural continuity in the face of settler binary Indigenous erasure and anti-Blackness. By refusing to accept Americanization and settler violence as a final result of interactions with European colonists, Louisiana Creole people are also situating our communities outside of traditional tropes of nationalism wherein whiteness and white bodies are not subjugated to the same regulations as Indigenous peoples and other communities of color.

One of the most common interpretive tropes of nationalism and American cultural studies is that which articulates the United States as a nation of immigrants. It is a deeply problematic and acutely flawed understanding anchored in a disingenuous and obtuse misinterpretation of the word "immigrant" and reflects a deeply racist, colonial sensibility. If "immigration" means "the movement of people living in one country into another country,"[1] then the people of Turtle Island did not "immigrate" to this land as there were no "countries" to "immigrate" from first, which is why they are called First Nations. Hence, the Creole people of Louisiana (including the Cajuns) occupy a unique space as post-contact Indigenous peoples. As the descendants of Indigenous peoples of Turtle Island, Creoles did not immigrate to the United States either.

America came to Creole Louisiana—appropriated, assimilated, and commodified the people it found here and the culture we practice. America brought slaves, further appropriating, commodifying, and assimilating cultural practices and committing violences against Red and Black bodies.

> The Choctaw word for colonization is *binolhichi*. We can trace the formation of this word from the root words *binili* (to sit), *abinili* (a settler or colonist), and *ibabinoli* (a company or community of settlers). In this sense the process of the formation of the word for colonization is an analogy for squatting. A way by which settlers come forth sitting, gathering, taking land, and forming their own space, displacing the original inhabitants in reoccurring patterns, policies, and practices that seek to perpetuate eradication and erasure of enduring Indigeneity. It is a perfect example, to quote J. Kēhaulani Kauanui and Patrick Wolfe, of the ways settler colonialism is a structure, not an event.[2]

These same structural processes have impacted the Creole peoples of Louisiana and the landbases that sustain our culture. In short, the United States not only colonized Louisiana but is engaged in ongoing processes of eco-colonialism, and the effects on the Creole people of Louisiana have been and continue to be devastating, by all measures.

Historically, Louisiana sits at the top of the Gulf triangle. This triangle is transnational, transracial, and multi-tribal. It is Afro-Caribbean-Latinidad-Indigenous (specifically, groups mostly belonging to Muskogean, Atakapan, Caddoan, and Taíno stock).[3] It is a triangle that has been a site, pre-contact, of trade between Indigenous peoples. Post-contact, this triangle played a significant role in both the African and Native American slave trade. It is now a triangle that is home to Louisiana Creoles, both in Louisiana and in the diaspora (Texas and Florida). After the Haitian Revolution it shuffled Creoles of color to and from the Caribbean as well as mestiz@ Latinx Cubans and Puerto Ricans to and from Louisiana and the islands of the Gulf. Louisiana's role pre- and post-contact as a site for both economic and community trade is a result of its geographic location. It sits as a hub of the Gulf Loop Current. "The loop current, one of the most powerful currents of the Gulf of Mexico, flows from Cuba to the Yucatán peninsula, around the Gulf (Texas, Louisiana, Mississippi) and out through the Florida straits. Like the loop current whose influence touches upon the Caribbean, Mexico, and the US Gulf South, this cross-cultural wash of events inhabits the land."[4] This has made the landbase of Louisiana an ecologically rich and diverse environment, and one that the settler-colonial state has exploited.

The Gulf Coast and Mississippi Delta was a rich ecosystem whose Indigenous and Creole populations thrived on the bounty of fish, shellfish, and delicate salt and brackish wildlife. River cane and natural sugarcane, sassafras, witch hazel, muscadine, loquat, and countless medicinals grew along the coastal areas and inland. Mangrove clusters along with natural barrier islands helped to protect the coast. As settlers moved inland the banks of the Mississippi River were lined with plantations producing sugarcane, rice, and other crops founded on both African and Native slave labor. Infrastructure, including interior canals dug for shipping, further pushed and eroded landbases, disrupting brackish wetland systems while offshore drilling has only added to the coast's eradication. In the twenty-first century alone a "collection of uncapped oil wells located 12 miles off the coast of Louisiana has been leaking as many as 700 barrels of oil every day since 2004."[5] Starting when a platform owned by Taylor Energy collapsed in a seafloor mudslide during Hurricane Ivan in September 2004, the oil is still leaking.[6] Further, in April 2010, the BP oil spill began "when the Deepwater Horizon rig suffered an explosion. . . . In its first month, BP spilled 30 million gallons of oil into the Gulf, three times the Exxon Valdez oil spill. Over the next three months, oil leakage in the Gulf of Mexico created the biggest oil disaster in the United States. Scientists estimated 184 million gallons were spilled. This is 18 times the amount spilled by the Exxon Valdez."[7]

Today, many of those old plantations lining the Mississippi River in South Louisiana house heavy industry, chemical plants, and factories that despoil the natural environment. Communities in the surrounding areas—historically francophone and creolophone communities of people who identify as Black, white, Native, and otherwise—experience such high rates of cancer that the region is referred to, derisively, as "Cancer Alley." The people who profit most from that heavy industry, those chemical plants and those factories, do not live in Louisiana. During the antebellum period, it was often the case that plantations were owned by absentee landlords, content to profit from human misery without feeling a need to bear witness to it; time passes and although some things change, some things do not. Despite all this, these dynamics are almost never interpreted as a manifestation of colonial economy or colonial violence.

The traditional historical landbase of Louisiana Creole people is disappearing. Indeed, much of it is, literally, falling into the Gulf of Mexico. This is a concern that Creole people share with our Native cousins of the Houma, Chitimacha, Port au Chien, and Biloxi-Chitimacha-Choctaw. The Biloxi-Chitimacha-Choctaw of Isle de Jean Charles, who are known as "Americas first climate refugees," have turned down the $48 million in relocation money, remarking that the "state has no respect for our culture."[8] Oil exploration, production, and distribution has facilitated the destruction of Louisiana wetlands and undermined the ability of the Gulf of Mexico to produce the natural resources that we as Indigenous peoples (Creole and Native) require for food, cultural production, and sustainability. It is hard to be a fisherman when the fishbeds have been destroyed by oil spills. It is hard for people to build homes and to build communities on land that washes away. As Monique Verdin (United Houma Nation) tells us, her people have been living off the lands and waters of South Louisiana "for hundreds of years" but that she is "inheriting a dying delta."[9] This too is true for our Louisiana Creole people.

The process of Americanization rendered Louisiana Creoles a diasporic people more than a century ago. At the beginning of the twentieth century, Jim Crow and Anglicization propelled Creoles out of Louisiana, disrupting centuries of community continuity and undermining Creole people's linguistic identity, much like the impact of termination and relocation on Native American tribal communities between 1945 and 1965. At the beginning of the twenty-first century, Hurricane Katrina and the economic devastation that followed in the wake of the levee failure of 2005 has propelled Creoles out of Louisiana, again. Unlike a century ago, however, communication technologies have made it possible for the diaspora to maintain connection, across space and time, in a way that would have been inconceivable to our great-grandparents in the 1920s.

This book was conceived at a lunch table in New York by a group of scholars and cousins who were removed from one another by thousands of miles, and who found one another initially through

FIGURE C.1. Louisiana Creole flag designed by Rain Prud'homme-Cranford. Photograph courtesy of Tracey Colson Antee.

scholarship and Facebook. America takes. America gives. As a refusal to accept the historical ways that Louisiana Creole people have been defined within academia and popular culture, this book is a mapping of a new direction for mixed-blood Indigenous peoples in the twenty-first century. As Afro-Indigenous Louisiana Creole scholars we were not satisfied with the lack of research on the connections and material contributions of Louisiana Creoles within the context of Native American, African, Latinx, ethnic, and American studies scholarship. To quote *Beasts of the Southern Wild*'s Hushpuppy, "They think we're all going to drown down here. But we ain't going nowhere."[10] Settlers might think we could be silenced. We could be removed. We could be drowned. They don't get that we are connected—umbilical cords to the land and people who birthed us.

During the summer of 2016 Andrew J. Jolivétte, Darryl Barthé, Jeffery Darensbourg, and Rain Prud'homme-Cranford spent time conversing from our different locations. At the time Rain was shuffling back and forth between Oklahoma and Florida, Andrew was in San Francisco, Darryl in Amsterdam, and Jeff in New Orleans. We Creoles are ever diasporic, ever transnational, and yet ever connected to family and home. We were all unsatisfied with the Louisiana Creole flag designed by Pete Bergeron in 1987, as it perpetuated our Indigenous erasure. We spent time talking about the elements we liked about other tribal flags and the Métis flags in Canada. We also spent a great deal of time talking about Peoplehood. We listened to one another as cousins, scholars, Creoles, and Natives, taking in elements and suggestions, and mocking up designs. Then, after the feedback, Rain would bring drafts to the table. Moreover, both Rain's father "Papa Lyle" and Andrew's father "Papa Ken" would offer suggestions, weighing in on the process. Finally, we arrived at a version we all felt encompassed who we are as a Creole people of Louisiana. A post-contact Afro-Indigenous people tied to land, language, history, and religion.

The ring of the fleur-de-lis represents both the colonization and cultural impact of France and Spain on the Creole population. The sassafras, or kafi/kaji in Choctaw, speaks to the plant and peoples indigenous to the land from which we make our filé using the pilet and pilon pictured—a practice also acquired from métissage with various tribes (Ishak, Choctaw, Caddo, Chitimacha, Tunica, Koasati, etc.). The rice speaks to our history of both food and slavery wherein our African ancestors' ricing expertise was used in the fields, and yet our "swamp seeds" remain a staple in our Creole cuisine. The harvesting, prepping, and eating of cowan (snapping alligator turtle) is tied to both our Indigenous and African roots within Louisiana landbases and a practice that brings family and community together as Creole people. It is very much a Creole dish, and one that is not easily won—it is an act of persistence, like our culture. Grounding the image is the land and water itself, surrounded by feathers of water birds: egret and anhinga, sacred in different ways to different Gulf tribes. These elements bring community, culture, land, and language alongside the ethnic inheritances of African, Indigenous, and European. This flag represents an awakening, but also a remembrance of the old ways and how we are making new traditions and commitments recognizing our self-determining right to exist as a post-contact Afro-Indigenous people. Moreover, we recognize that defining our history in connection to land is connected to our ongoing to struggle to preserve our sacred sites and landbases in the face of eco-colonialism and settler violence. The chapters in this volume are a beginning, not an ending. We hope that other scholars both Louisiana Creoles and other Afro-Indigenous communities will join in conversations about recognition and resistance within Afro-Indigenous and Latinx peoples across the Americas. As population demographics and questions of citizenship and belonging continue to persist, it becomes all the more important that communities and scholars reexamine previous studies that have contributed to Afro-Indigenous erasure and anti-Blackness in the Americas.

As this book began with a group of scholar-cousins and a meal of rice and beans, it is only fitting that it should end, or rather continue, the same way. The year 2020 marked four years since the editors of this collection—Rain, Andrew, and Darryl—gathered together and conceived of this call and response collection. And so, four years after we three sat, laughing, full of love, joy, and a fire to see the full stories, histories, and representations of who we are, we will gather again. There are farms waiting in Louisiana and Oklahoma. There are families waiting with gumbo, red beans and rice, walakshi, tanchi labona, smothered okra, fish croquets, pvlvska, shrimp creole, banaha, and meat pies. There is family waiting, who all eat rice and beans.

It is our hope and intention that this book will inspire more conversations about the everyday realities of race, gender, class, and equity among people of mixed Afro-Indigenous descent in the Americas. There is an old French Creole expression, "les haricots ne sont pas salés." When translated, it means "the snap beans aren't salty," or in other words the food isn't done. And so as we end, we say the work isn't done. The snap beans, the stories, the conversations, and the interventions into the field are still not seasoned or salty enough. May the work continue in a good way . . . *Nouzot tous ki gen rapó.*

NOTES

1 "Immigration," History.com, A&E Television Networks, accessed August 21, 2018, www.history.com/topics/immigration.
2 From Rain Prud'homme-Cranford's upcoming monograph, *Gumbo Stories: Quantum Relation-Making and Decolonizing the Creole South.*
3 These are large groups. For example, the Atakapa Ishak cover costal West Louisiana to East Texas while the Caddo cover central West Louisiana and Texas. The Muskogean groups include the Choctaw, Creek, Seminole, Miccosukee, Apalachee, Koasati, Houma, and others, from

Louisiana through the Gulf states to Florida, while the Taíno includes most of Cuba, Hispaniola (the Dominican Republic and Haiti), Jamaica, Puerto Rico, the Bahamas, and the northern and lesser Antilles. These Indigenous groups do not form an exhaustive list, but are meant to give a representation

4 Rain P. Cranford Goméz, "Hachotakni Zydeco's Round'a Loop Current: Indigenous, African, and Caribbean Mestizaje in Louisiana Literatures," *Southern Literary Journal* 46, no. 2 (2014): 103, www.doi.org/10.1353/slj.2014.0001.

5 "Uncapped Wells Have Been Leaking Oil into the Gulf of Mexico for 14 Years," Yale E360, October 22, 2018, https://e360.yale.edu.

6 "Uncapped Wells."

7 Kimberly Amadeo, "Costs of the Deepwater Horizon Oil Spill," The Balance, updated June 6, 2020, www.thebalance.com.

8 Julie Dermansky, "Isle De Jean Charles Tribe Turns Down Funds to Relocate First US 'Climate Refugees' as Louisiana Buys Land Anyway," DeSmog, January 11, 2019, www.desmogblog.com.

9 *My Louisiana Love* (WORLD Channel), 2012.

10 *Beasts of the Southern Wild* (Icon Films, 2012).

IN MEMORIAM

Reflections on Janet Ravare Colson, Cane River Creole Matriarch

ANDREW J. JOLIVÉTTE, RAIN PRUD'HOMME-CRANFORD, AND CAROLYN M. DUNN

Twenty years ago I, Andrew Jolivétte, walked into Kyser Hall, room 116, with my cousins Beverly and Lori Fontenot. They had driven me from Raywood, Texas, to Northwestern State University in Natchitoches, Louisiana (about a three and a half hour drive) to meet Janet Ravare Colson, who was the director of the Creole Heritage Center. That day changed my life and set me on my career path, and more importantly it connected me more deeply to my Creole culture and to community. Janet took me into her home and introduced me to her daughter Tracey Colson Antee (Mom liked to say "I was her Andrew first"). She drove me back to Lake Charles after helping me for weeks with my dissertation research on Native American cultural influences and impacts on Creole culture. We ate and chatted as family for hours with them and my cousin Phil Honore and his mom, who was also from Cane River. Over the next twenty years Janet became my mentor, my friend, my teacher, my cheerleader, my other mom, my family. Yesterday Janet (Mom, as I started calling her about ten or more years ago) walked on to be with her daddy and mama and other family in heaven. I remember her always telling me "My daddy thought Louisiana was heaven" and so it was for her and for her children and

FIGURE M.1. Mama Janet Ravare Colson and Andrew J. Jolivétte in Opelousas, Louisiana. Photograph courtesy of Tracey Colson Antee.

husband and grandchildren and for me. Janet was a force . . . not just nationally but internationally. She organized many international Creole Heritage conferences from New Orleans to Chicago to Los Angeles, Las Vegas, and beyond, which included participants from the Caribbean, Europe, and Latin America. She did so at a time when our culture was being lost, misrepresented, and her legacy is the revitalization of the Creole people. I wouldn't be who or where I am today without Mama Janet. Last night when I learned that she passed I was devastated, thinking, did I thank her enough and honor and celebrate her enough? How much it hurts to not say or have a proper farewell. I found some of our old messages and realize that she knew how deeply I loved and appreciated her. I hope to one day open a Creole Cultural Center and Museum and name it after her. The state of Louisiana and the entire Creole Nation/country owes her a huge debt of gratitude. Please keep her husband, daughters, grandchildren, siblings, in-laws, and community in your prayers.

Love you always—Andrew

When the phone rang after 11 p.m. at night, I knew what was coming. I knew, because a week before I dreamed this. I knew because I was restless, felt the air heavy with tears, even displaced from homelands here in Calgary. From the moment I hear Andrew's voice, I looked down, I tried not to dissolve into tears, to take a moment and realize the worse thing I could do is barrage her children with calls and emails. But I had to call my sisters. I had to do what Andrew did, suck up my emotion and loss and carry on the phone tree. By the time Andrew and I hung up, our voices were strained from tears, holding in loss, like the pain of having a limb severed . . . for sure we knew we were losing a part of our souls. It was closing in on midnight in Calgary when I rang my youngest sister in Oklahoma, almost one in the morning her time. She picked up on the second ring. By the time I called my sister-cousin also in Oklahoma, I was numb. The violence of loss for those of us whose lives read like keloid scar absences where family should be, have developed ways to maneuver in times of tragedy. In the days and weeks that followed, I railed against COVID-19 and the inability of our scattered families to come together. I railed at cancer, the spirit that has stalked so many of our families. I remembered the last time I was home in Cane River, the summer of 2017. I came bearing "black gold" (aka a large tin of Tim Hortons coffee) and coffee crisp candy bars. Mama Janet, Papa Oz, and I ate fried catfish and fried okra. We had yam cake for dessert. After dinner Mama Janet and I sat at the table talking about one of our family lines. Mama sent me home with Mimi Magnolia magnets, one of which sits on my altar. Papa sent me off with press filé and bay leaves. And now in July of 2020, I am still absent, missing, and wondering if we can ever do enough to thank her.

They say when the settlers came to push us out of our homelands and communities, that our ancestors kept a spark of the sacred fires. They carried that spark so we could keep our families, our ceremonies, our communities. Mama Janet—she was our spark, our ember of the sacred fire. We trace our ability to burn, to have light, to rise, resist, reclaim back to her. She is a mother, auntie, grandmother, cousin, connected to so many of us through blood and family. Even for those whose blood she does not share, she has been an elder and community inspiration, becoming family to our people across the diaspora. We are all broken, but because of her, still burn. Mama J was and is and will always be our Ishki isht ikhana—Mother memory/memorial. Like the great mother mound birthplace Nanih Waiya—She has is Holitopa Ishk—Beloved Mother, the home space our movement began. Mési, yakoke, hiweyú, tikahch—thank you.

Chi hullo li. Chi yukpali—Rain

MIMI'S PAPER MAGNOLIAS

For our matriarch, Mama Janet

>Mimi's paper magnolias flit like prayers
>at base of ancient Cane River oaks.
>Chart cartographic maps in familial blood.
>Unlock memories to trace our way home.
>
>At base of ancient Cane River oaks,
>trees deep rooted, wild, contained,
>unlock memories to trace our way home.
>Stories of blood dance to drum of red water.
>
>Trees deep rooted, wild, contained,
>she taught our tongues the trifecta of place.
>Stories of blood dance to drum of red water,
>shell shaking sisters and chain cries blues.
>
>She taught our tongues the trifecta of place,
>we offer chants in tear stained voices,
>shell shaking sisters and chain cries blues.
>Cane River sing our way home till dawn.

We offer chants in tear stained voices,
Cane River sing our way home til dawn.
Mimi's paper magnolias flit like prayers,
Chart cartographic maps in familial blood.

                Rain Prud'homme-Cranford and Carolyn M. Dunn

APPENDIX

Louisiana State Legislature Resolution and Certificate of Special Recognition from the Governor of the State of Louisiana in honor of Janet Ravare-Colson

PROCLAMATION / CERTIFICATE OF HONOR

Whereas in the year 1997, Janet Ravare-Colson began her crucial local, state, national, and international work as the Director of the Louisiana Creole Heritage Center at Northwestern State University in Natchitoches, Louisiana, where over the course of twenty years she worked to revitalize and bring greater visibility to the language, history, and culture of the Louisiana Creole People

Whereas Janet Ravare-Colson did organize hundreds of workshops, seminars, and conferences that brought local, state, national, and international scholars and community leaders from various communities together to highlight the contemporary experiences and realities of Louisiana Creoles and other Creole communities around the world at a time when they were severely neglected or misrepresented

Whereas Janet Ravare-Colson did expand the body of literature, genealogical research, and public visibility of one of the nation's oldest and least documented ethnic and cultural groups for the advancement and educational development of future generations

Whereas Janet Ravare-Colson mentored, taught, and supported the intellectual, cultural, and social development of dozens of Louisiana Creole scholars, musicians, genealogists, and cultural preservationists throughout the course of her lifetime

Whereas Janet Ravare-Colson was a daughter of Louisiana and the Creole Heritage born on March 21 who contributed in multiple ways to the people of the state of Louisiana and to the United States of America

Therefore be it resolved that her birth date of March 21 be recognized as Janet Ravare-Colson, Mother of the Creole Culture and Revitalization Movement Day throughout the state of Louisiana.

CONTRIBUTORS

DARRYL BARTHÉ, PHD, is a husband, father, brother, son, and nephew and a métis Louisiana Creole of Mi'kmaq, Caddo, Chitimacha, Choctaw, Cajun, and African American heritage, born and raised in New Orleans. He earned a PhD in history from the University of Sussex, in Brighton, where he taught American politics and wrote his dissertation, "Becoming American in Creole New Orleans: Family, Community, Labor and Schooling, 1896–1949." In 2016, with colleagues from the University of Leiden, Barthé founded the online (Dutch language) public history journal *Over de Muur*, which was awarded the 2018 valorization award from the Amsterdam School of Historical Studies. He served as a consultant on the Woorden Doen Ertoe / Words Matter project at the Rijksmuseum in Amsterdam, and for the Dutch public broadcasting program *Andere Tijden* while teaching history at the University of Amsterdam. Barthé has previously taught in the department of history at the University of New Orleans, and in Memory studies at the University of Leiden. He has published most recently in the field of critical race theory and historical criminology, and has been a contributor to the Hampton Institute, a "working-class think tank" based in New York. At the end of 2018 he moved to New York City, where he lives with his wife and their children; he is currently a lecturer in the Department of History at Dartmouth.

LEILA K. BLACKBIRD (Apache/Cherokee), née Garcés, is an unenrolled/stolen Two-Spirit activist and writer from Bulbancha. Leila completed both a bachelor's and master's in history at the University of New Orleans and is currently a doctoral fellow in the Department of History at the University of Chicago. Research interests include comparative colonialisms and slaveries, subaltern studies, global

Indigenous histories and perspectives, comparative ethnicity and nationalism, the French and Spanish Atlantic worlds, transnational British imperial-colonialism, borderlands, historical trauma, and state violence.

ROBERT B. CALDWELL JR. (Choctaw-Apache Tribe of Ebarb) has a PhD in transatlantic history from the University of Texas at Arlington, where he focuses on colonialism, imperialism, and cartographic history. He holds bachelor's in anthropology and history from the University of New Orleans, a master's from the University of Massachusetts at Amherst, and a master's in heritage resources from Northwestern State University. He is enrolled in the Choctaw-Apache Tribe of Ebarb and a founder of the Ho Minti Society, a group dedicated to teaching the tribe's traditional culture. He is the author of *Choctaw-Apache Foodways*.

KELLY CLAYTON is a Louisiana Creole native. She is the author of the poetry collection *Mother of Chaos: Queen of the Nines*. Her poetry has been published by, among others, Future Cycle Press, Delacorte Press, China Grove Press, and Random House. She is a VONA/Voices Hedgebrook Alumnae, and recipient of the 2014 Hedgebrook Women Authoring Change Award. She recently completed an artist's residency with the Acadiana Center for the Arts for the production of her original play *Dancing with Aurora Borealis*. Kelly develops and facilitates custom-made creative writing workshops in Louisiana schools, both public and private, for the Lafayette Juvenile Detention Center, and to groups of formerly incarcerated adults. Kelly lives in Lafayette, in a little house, with her husband, Brian, and youngest son, Jackson.

TRACEY COLSON ANTEE is a Louisiana Creole activist, artist, educator, wife, and mother. She has spent her professional and personal life working for community as the former director of the Creole Heritage Center, Natchitoches, working for the American Cancer Society, and as an entrepreneur and founder of GumboLife, a Louisiana Creole educational blog and store. She has been a cultural adviser on a number of projects, and her creative work has appeared in *Yellow Medicine Review: A Journal of Indigenous Literature, Thought, and Art*, among various other publications.

JEFFERY U. DARENSBOURG, PHD, is a Monroe Research Fellow at the New Orleans Center for the Gulf South at Tulane University, an educator, and an activist. He is an enrolled member and tribal councilperson of the Atakapa-Ishak Nation of Southwest Louisiana and Southeast Texas, and is of Louisiana Creole, Ishak, and Choctaw ancestry, with family roots across South Louisiana. Darensbourg is the editor of the zine *Bulbancha Is Still a Place: Indigenous Culture from New Orleans*, and his work has appeared in *Situate Magazine* and is forthcoming in various publications. He is currently working on a monograph addressing Ishak land, culture, and language.

JOHN DEPRIEST, PHD (Choctaw Nation), is an instructor of ESL who specializes in linguistics, with an emphasis on the phonetics, phonology, and syntax of English. He earned a bachelor's degree in psychology and German from Belmont University in Nashville before going on to earn both a master's and doctorate in linguistics from Tulane. His dissertation focused on phrase boundary perception in language and music, utilizing EEG and behavioral results to compare neurotypical and autistic individuals' responses. In the English for Academic and Professional Purposes program, he teaches "Writing for Academic Purposes," "Structure of English for Teaching," and "ESL Speaking Skills" as part of the regular curriculum, and "Intensive English," two writing classes, and two speaking classes as part of the non-credit ESL program. When not teaching, learning, or researching languages, John plays banjo in numerous bands around New Orleans, and is a prolific songwriter.

CAROLYN M. DUNN, PHD, is the Artist in Residence at University of Central Oklahoma. She is of Louisiana Creole, Tunica-Biloxi-Choctaw, and Ishak descent on her mother's side and Cherokee, Muskogee Creek/Seminole Freedmen descent on her father's. Her poetry books include *Outfoxing Coyote*; *Echolocation: Poems Indian Country, LA*; and *Stains of Burden and Dumb Luck*. Coeditor of *Through the Eye of the Deer*; *Hozho: Walking in Beauty*; and *Coyote Speaks*, her academic work has appeared in *The American Indian Culture and Research Journal*, *Belles Lettres*, and the anthologies *American Indian Performing Arts: Critical Directions*; *Reading Native American Women*; and *Cultural Representation and Contestation in Native America*, among others. Her plays *The*

Frybread Queen premiered in Los Angeles in 2011, and *Soledad* at the Oklahoma City Native Playwright Festival in 2017. She is co-Editor-in-Chief, of That Painted Horse Press: A Borderless Indigenous Press of the Americas.

JOSEPH DUNN served for three years as executive director of the Council for the Development of French in Louisiana (CODOFIL), after which he began work as an independent tourism and cultural entrepreneur in 2014. Currently, his primary role is to oversee the communications, public relations, and marketing efforts at Laura: Louisiana's Creole Heritage Site, among other projects and collaborations. He has held positions at the Consulate General of France in New Orleans; the Office of the Lieutenant Governor; the Louisiana Office of Cultural Development; the Louisiana Travel Promotion Association; Laura: A Creole Plantation; and the Louisiana Office of Tourism. He has presented in English and French at conferences, workshops, and political and economic trade missions in the United States, Canada, the Caribbean, and Europe. Joseph is often featured in francophone print and broadcast media and documentaries as a leader in the French and Creole language movements in Louisiana. He is an outspoken advocate for the development of professional and economic opportunities for these heritage language communities.

FRANCES E. HOPSON-CUEVAS is Senior Employee Relations Attorney for the NYC Department of Education. She served as Chairman of the Board of Directors for the American Indian Community House, and is an active Board member. She's a Louisiana Creole descendant of Albert Decuir, one of the first colonists of Louisiana. Hopson-Cuevas is also an enrolled member of the Echota Cherokee Band of Alabama (state-recognized tribe) and a descendant of Chief Louis Tensa of the Taensa.

ANDREW JOLIVÉTTE (Atakapa-Ishak Nation of Louisiana [Tsikip/Opelousa/Heron Clan]), PHD, is professor and chair of the Ethnic Studies Department at the University of California, San Diego, as well as the founding Director of Native American and Indigenous Studies at UC San Diego. A former professor and department chair of American Indian Studies at San Francisco State University, he is the author or editor of nine books in print or forthcoming, including the Lammy

Award-nominated *Indian Blood: HIV and Colonial Trauma in San Francisco's Two-Spirit Community*. His scholarship examines Native American, Indigenous, Creole, Black, Latinx, queer, mixed-race, and comparative critical ethnic studies. Dr. Jolivétte is the 2020-21 Multi-Racial Network Scholar in Residence for the American College Personnel Association and the series editor of Black Indigenous Futures and Speculations at Routledge. His current book project, *Thrivance Circuitry: Queer Afro-Indigenous Futurity and Kinship*, is under contract with the University of Washington Press. He is the Board President of the American Indian Cultural Center of San Francisco and the Institute for Democratic Education and Culture (Speak Out). Dr. Jolivétte was recently appointed to the editorial review boards of the *American Indian Culture and Research Journal* and to the new *Journal of Transdisciplinary Trauma Studies*. A former Indigenous Peoples representative to the United Nations Forum on HIV and the Law, he has spoken to thousands of college students, educators, government employees, private-sector, and nonprofit organizations over the past two decades across the United States, Canada, the Netherlands, and Australia. Dr. Jolivétte is a Louisiana Creole of West African, Ishak, French, Spanish, Italian, and Irish descent.

KENNETH L. JOLIVÉTTE was born in Eunice, Louisiana, and raised in Opelousas and Bayou Mallet until the age of ten when he moved with his family to California, where he studied and worked at the United States Post Office for forty-five years. He is a Creole storyteller, father of eight, and grandfather of fourteen. He has been a surrogate father and grandfather figure to many in the Creole community and to others in the San Francisco Bay Area, where he ran Next Generation Childcare for nearly two decades. Prior to that, he worked with group home and foster care youth. He has dedicated his life to preserving his family's Creole heritage and to supporting youth in the community.

JOHN LAFLEUR II is the author of *Louisiana Creole Peoplehood: Louisiana's Creole-Metis, Euro-Afro, and Caribbean Foodways*. He is a Louisiana Métis-Creole, gourmet, and author of twelve books pertaining to Louisiana food, culture, and identity. His paternal ancestor, Jacques Andre Barza dit LaFleur (Tapske was his Choctaw name) was Governor Bienville's high interpreter for the Choctaw and Creek nations of Fort Toulouse at what is now the present-day state of Alabama before the founding of New Orleans in 1718, when Mobile was the first capital of the lower Louisiana Purchase territory. Mr. LaFleur was born in the upper, northwest center of Louisiana's French-speaking triangle, where the Alabama Creoles settled along with their Choctaw-Creek cousins who joined them in forsaking Alabama after the Seven Years War. Being cattle raisers, the prairielands, or "vâchéries," were ideal in supporting this lucrative Métis-Creole tradition. A former educator of twenty-five years' experience, he taught courses in French, Latin, fine arts, and speech communication. He has been writing about Louisiana Creole culture for the last ten years. He lives and works in New Orleans as a licensed, bilingual tour host. He has led and organized international, bilingual tours (French-English/English-French) to Europe for thirty years now. On weekends, he operates John LaFleur's Louisiana Creole Guesthouse and Kitchen in Washington, Louisiana, near Opelousas.

M. CARMEN LANE is a two-spirit African American and Haudenosaunee (Mohawk/Tuscarora) artist, cultural worker, poet, popular educator, and consultant living in Kahyonhá:ke (Cleveland, Ohio). Carmen attended Earlham College, receiving their bachelor's in women's studies with a focus in feminist art history, theory, and criticism, and later earned their master's in organization development and change from American University. Their work has been published in numerous journals and anthologies, including the Lambda Literary Award–nominated *Sovereign Erotics: A Collection of Two-Spirit Literatures*. Carmen's first collection of poetry is *Calling Out After Slaughter*. They are the founder and director of ATNSC: Center for Healing and Creative Leadership, an urban retreat center and social practice experiment in holistic health, leadership development, and Indigenous arts and culture located in Cleveland's historic Buckeye neighborhood. Carmen is a member of NTL Institute for Applied Behavioral Science and Wordcraft Circle of Native Writers and Storytellers.

DANNY LEE LANDRENEAU-PETRELLA is from Mamou, Louisiana (Pins Clairs, "Clear Pines"), the settlement area of the Mamou Choctaw Band.

OLIVER MAYEUX, PHD, researches and lectures in sociolinguistics at the Faculty of Modern and Medieval Languages, University of Cambridge. Using quantitative and qualitative methods, his research examines the endangerment and revitalization of the Louisiana Creole language, focusing on how specific linguistic changes are shaped by social and political factors. He has been involved in Louisiana Creole language activism for around a decade, acting as a consultant linguist for the *Louisiana Creole Orthography Guide* and coauthoring the *Ti Liv Kréyòl*. He also publishes poetry, in English and Louisiana Creole. Mayeux is half Louisianan, half British, and grew up in Scotland and Nigeria.

TANNER MENARD is a Q2S, nonbinary poet and composer whose work embodies their Creole/Acadian/NDN lineage. Poems are their method of survival, a linguistic medicine of ambiguity which is certain that love prevails. As a composer of experimental music, menard has been published and anthologized internationally on labels such as Full Spectrum Records, Rural Colours, Tokyo Droning, Install, Slow Flow Rec, H.L.M., Archaic Horizon, Kafua Records, and Milieu Music. Their recent album/chapbook collaboration with Andrew Weathers was published on Full Spectrum Records. menard's poetry and essays have been published in *The Squawkback, Rabbit & Rose, Cloudthroat, University of Arizona Poetry Center Blog, Red Ink Magazine, Mockingheart Review, American Indian Culture and Research Journal,* and *Wire Magazine*. Their poem "see eye my memory my" was nominated for a Pushcart Prize by *Cloudthroat*. menard is a member of the Atakapa-Ishak Nation of Southwest Louisiana and Southeast Texas, and resides in Tempe, Arizona.

PIERRE BROOKS METOYER is a Cane River Creole living in the Creole diaspora of Chicago. A father to Angel and Rachal and various stepchildren—known as "PaPierre" and Gran Pere—he works both locally and through social media to connect Cane River decedents in preserving Louisiana Creole culture and family.

ANNALYSSA GYPSY MURPHY, PHD, is a mixed-ethnicity (Cherokee, Blackfeet, Scottish, Jewish, Irish, distantly French and African) woman born in Chicago. Dr. Murphy has an AA Century College bachelor's degree, a master's from Hamline University (Minnesota), and a doctorate from Clark University (Massachusetts). Murphy did master's work in museum studies at Harvard University and Holocaust and genocide studies at Gratz College, and an NEH Fellowship at Oxford University. An adoptee, Dr. Murphy has sought to craft an identity from the varied parts of her narrative. Being the daughter of a white Canadian man and an Indigenous US woman has challenged Dr. Murphy to look at border constructions of ethnicity and Identity from a very early age, crafting a space where her worlds could coexist. She has been a visiting professor of ethnic studies, political science, psychology, women's studies, and sociology at several colleges and universities. She lives in Salem, Massachusetts, with her three fantastic daughters.

THOMAS PARRIE, MFA, is affiliated with the Choctaw-Apache Tribe of Ebarb in West Louisiana. He is from Natchitoches, Louisiana, where he earned a bachelor's and master's in English at Northwestern State University. He is also a graduate of the McNeese State University MFA program and has presented work at numerous conferences, including AWP. He has published fiction and poetry and is a 2014 Pushcart Prize nominee for the poem "Dog Head Park" from *Codex Journal*. He was the School for Advanced Research's Indigenous Writer in Residence Fellow for 2018. Thomas writes and teaches at Southeastern Louisiana University in Hammond. He is the author of the poetry collection, *Toledo Rez and Other Myths*.

RAIN PRUD'HOMME-CRANFORD (formally Goméz), PHD, is a FATtastically queer Creole IndigeNerd who reads too much and drinks too much black tea. She is a writer, musician, visual artist, and an assistant professor of English, Affiliated Faculty, International Indigenous Studies, and Indigenous Student Access Program at the University of Calgary. Rain works primarily within Gulf Creole, Indigenous, and Afro-Indigenous studies (Louisiana Creole, First Nation / Métis / Inuit / Native American / Latinx); BIPOC rhetorics; fat studies; ecocriticism; 2SQ/gender/sexuality; STEM and literary theory; and creative writing. Her monograph *Gumbo Stories: Quantum Relation-Making and Decolonizing the Creole South* is forthcoming. Her collection *Smoked Mullet Cornbread Crawdad Memory* (MEP 2012, published as Rain C. Goméz) won the First Book Award Poetry from Native

Writers' Circle of the Americas; and her second poetry collection, *Miscegenation Round Dance: Poèmes Historiques*, was released in the summer of 2021 by Mongrel Empire Press. She is also coeditor of the anthology *Indians, Oil, and Water: Indigenous Ecologies and Literary Resistance* (TPHP 2021). Prud'homme-Cranford's current critical projects include *Gather at the River: Spiritual Ecologies in Red/Black Literature*; *"Nobody Loves a FAT Girl": Obesity, Obsession, Exile, and Largeness of Literary Resistance*; *"Remember the Red River Valley": Transcontinental Red River Literacies of Métissage/Méstizaje*; and the coedited collection (with Carolyn M. Dunn) *Red/Black Social Justice Beyond #s: Literary Representation and Agency from the Jeremiad to R&B*. Critical and creative work can be found in the *Southern Literary Journal, Louisiana Folklife, Undead Souths: The Gothic and Beyond, Swamp Souths: Tracing Literary Ecologies, Mississippi Quarterly, American Indian Culture and Research Journal, Tidal Basin Review, Yellow Medicine Review, Sing: Indigenous Poetry of the Americas, Sovereign Traces Vol. 2: Relational Constellations, Anomaly: A Journal of Literature and the Arts,* and many others. Rain is the Executive Editor-in-Chief of That Painted Horse Press: A Borderless BIPOC Press of the Americas. Most importantly, she is an Auntie, daughter, sister, cousin, and "adopted/substitute" mom/auntie to a flock of graduate, undergrad, and former students.

T. SHAWNEE, BS/BSED, is a public school educator, wife, and mother. Her work focuses on the intersections of Red/Black Indigeneity and women's health (physical, mental, and emotional). Shawnee is an accomplished artist who works primarily in beadwork, textiles, and mixed media. She and her husband (Bill Shawnee—Loyal Shawnee / Quapaw / Cherokee / Miami / Delaware) own Shawnee Designz: Regalia, Art, and Beadwork. Her ancestry includes Choctaw-Biloxi, Louisiana Creole, Ishak, and Muskogean Freedmen (Choctaw/Chickasaw/Creek) descent paternally and Alberta Métis and Irish ancestry maternally. Much of her work is deeply rooted in her Gulf Coast and Oklahoma homelands.

SUMMER WESLEY, JD/MA, is a citizen of the Choctaw Nation of Oklahoma and a dedicated community advocate, dynamic public speaker, and driven entrepreneur. She spent many years as a social worker and graduated law school from the University of Oklahoma before founding Hopoksia LLC, a company providing educational presentations and diversity and inclusion trainings to organizations; mediation services for parties in civil legal matters; as well as research, writing, editing, and social media management services. Summer has been honored for her dedication to community advocacy and service with the Norman's Human Rights Award, named one of OK Cleveland County's 2017 Women of Influence, and named a member of the 2018 class of "Achievers under 40" by *The Journal Record*. Summer serves on the Board of Directors for three community organizations: Live Indigenous OK, which addresses policy and social justice issues in Indigenous communities; Matriarch, a nonprofit program that focuses on empowering Native women; and the Oklahoma Indigenous Theatre Company, which envisions a thriving, vibrant, and sustainable creative space that gives voice and presence onstage to Indigenous culture. She also donates her time reviewing child welfare cases for compliance with the Indian Child Welfare Act, as part of the ICWA Post Adjudication Review Board. Her passion lies in community-building and empowering others.

INDEX

A

abduction, 127–29, 131, 132, 134
Acadian, 15, 24, 53, 66–68, 70, 72, 77–78, 80–81, 91, 92n6, 107, 116, 123, 145–47, 202, 225, 243, 246, 248, 272, 277; Maritime, 81
Acadien, 145–46
Act 27, State of Louisiana, 68
African American, 8, 27, 32–34, 38, 54, 56, 60, 71, 78, 90, 94, 123, 125–29, 133, 177, 180, 187n1, 188n11, 201, 246, 252, 271, 276
"African American Heritage Site," 89
Africanness, 89
Africans, 4, 7, 31, 35, 51, 54, 66, 76, 88–89, 91, 94, 166, 178, 181, 240–41, 248
Afro-Indigenous, 7, 8, 9, 10, 11, 13–17, 22–23, 25–29, 31, 36–38, 42n44, 45, 47–48, 78, 80, 103, 106, 113n3, 124–27, 135, 173, 175–76, 203, 210–11, 213, 227, 239n13, 240, 253–54, 258–60, 278; Afro-Indigeneity, 8, 9, 49, 176
aging, 199
American Indians and Alaska Natives (AIAN), 127
American Indian studies, 80
Americanism, 55, 70
Americanization, 14, 29, 35–36, 55, 62, 67–68, 70, 72, 74, 76, 145, 153, 254, 257
ANA (antinuclear antibodies), 131
ancestors, 4, 6–7, 9, 21, 31, 35, 46–48, 56, 62, 75–76, 80–81, 81n1, 87–88, 92n5, 109, 112, 118, 122, 127–29, 134, 140, 161, 164–66, 173, 177, 179, 185, 187, 188n10, 224, 226–29, 232–33, 238, 241, 259, 266
ancestral bones, 122
Anglo-American, 40n16, 50–51, 54, 56–57, 145, 155, 253
Annexation of Texas, 95
antebellum, 94, 173, 204, 256
anti-Blackness, 4, 7, 10, 13, 254, 260; prejudice, 4
anti-queerness, 201, 206
Apalachee Massacre, 94, 97n4
Apess, William, 32, 43n48
ascription, 211, 253
Association for Multiethnic Americans, 148
Atakapa Ishak, 5, 15, 23, 27–29, 87, 91, 93, 154, 213, 243, 260n3. *See also* Ishak
Atakapa-Ishak Nation, 25, 116, 118, 165, 273–74, 277. *See also* Ishak
Attakapas, 48, 115
autoimmune diseases, 124–27, 130–31, 135, 138–39, 175, 177

B

Bakken oil fields, 184
Bayogoulas, 97n2
Bayou Bridge pipeline, 96, 167, 183
Beasts of the Southern Wild, 258
BIA recognition, 9
"BIG" bodies, 192
Biloxi-Chitimacha-Choctaw, 25, 257
binolhichi, 255
BIPOC, 10, 17n5, 278–79
bisexual, 203–4, 207, 209–11
Black, 6, 10–15, 23–24, 29, 32–33, 37–38, 39n2, 39n3, 44–48, 67, 71–72,

Black (*continued*)
76–77, 81, 81n1, 90, 94–97, 123, 126, 128–29, 132–33, 146, 173–82, 187n1, 188n10, 197–99, 202, 204, 208, 211, 213, 215, 227, 248, 251–53, 255–56, 275, 279. *See also* Red-Black
Black diaspora, 251
Black Indigeneity, 10, 279
Black-Native, 9, 47, 94
Blackness, 22–24, 71, 181
"Black Wall Street," 238n8, 239n8
Black/white binary, 46
Black-White framework, 14
Black/White paradigm, 48, 253
Blindian, 23, 32, 43n48, 173–76, 178, 233–34
bloodline, 5, 33, 80
blood quantum, 8, 26, 30, 78, 123
blues, 3, 172–74, 177, 178, 187, 192, 197, 201, 266
boarding schools, 128, 134, 167
"boucan," 241
Brooks, Brenda, 24
Brosman, Catherine Savage, 33
Broyard, Anatole, 59
Bulbancha, 14–15, 62, 76, 86–91, 93, 271
Bureau of American Ethnology, 116

C
Caddo, 27–29, 37, 78, 104, 235, 251, 255, 259, 260n3, 271
Cahokia, 93
Cajun, 15, 45–47, 53, 67–68, 70–72, 76–81, 90–91, 103, 105, 118, 144–50, 152–53, 164, 201–2, 227, 234, 241–43, 246, 248, 254, 271
Cajun-Creole binary, 150
"Cajun" French, 144–45
Cajunist movement, 149
Cajun Renaissance, 164
"Cajun-washing," 146
call and response, 9, 12–13, 17, 174, 187, 260
Cancer Alley, 96, 256
Cane River Creole, 23–24, 29, 40n13, 104–5, 107–8, 111–12, 114n4, 263, 277

cardiovascular disease, 125–27, 129, 134
caste, 35, 50–51, 54, 59, 221
Catholic, 52–53, 56, 67, 69, 94, 115, 163, 193–94, 202, 206–7, 211, 222, 224, 233–34, 238n7, 251; Catholicism, 205–6, 221, 233–34
census, 25, 58, 123
Chaouacha, 93–94
Chicano/a Mestizo, 188n11
Chickasaw, 93–94, 179–80, 187, 224, 239n8, 279
Chitimacha, 27–29, 37, 39n2, 78, 87, 89–91, 93–94, 115, 192, 257, 259, 271
Choctaw, 5–6, 23, 25, 27–29, 32, 34–37, 49n7, 50, 78, 86, 90, 93–94, 104–5, 108, 110n9, 122, 136, 180, 187n1, 192, 222, 224, 229, 233, 235, 238n5, 239n8, 241–43, 245, 255, 259, 260n3, 271, 273, 275–76, 279
Choctaw-Apache, 25, 112–13, 222, 272, 278
Choctaw-Biloxi, 23, 25, 28–29, 48, 227, 257, 279
classism, 146
Clifton-Choctaw, 23
closet, 211
colonial economy, 257
colonialism, 13, 16, 23, 28, 35, 42n44, 77, 86–87, 96, 126, 175, 178–81, 183–85, 201, 213, 255, 272
colonial violence, 16, 173, 257
colonization, 3, 54, 78, 96, 117, 124–26, 128–29, 132, 134, 138, 140, 176, 180–82, 255, 259
"colored," 23, 32, 50, 57, 59, 68, 246
color lines, 44, 46, 62, 178
Colson, Janet Ravare, 6, 21, 23, 263–64, 269–70
Colson, John Oswald, 103–4, 106, 111, 113
Columbus, Christopher, 162, 180
Comité créole, 148
concentration camps, 96
Congo Square, 89
cordon bleu, 33

Council for the Development of French in Louisiana (CODOFIL), 71–72, 146–48, 246, 274
coureurs des bois, 53
courtbouillon, 243
Coushatta, 28, 112, 115
COVID, 151, 186, 265
cowan (snapping alligator turtle), 259
Cree, 5, 136, 224, 230, 235
Creole, 3–17, 22–27, 31, 33–39, 39n1, 44–48, 49n7, 50–54, 56–62, 66–72, 76–77, 79–81, 84, 87–90, 103–9, 111, 113n3, 118, 120n19, 123, 133, 135–36, 143–45, 147–55, 161, 163–64, 168, 173–77, 187, 188n6, 192–94, 197–99, 202–13, 225, 232–36, 240–60, 263–65, 269–70, 274–78. *See also* Creole-NDN; Louisiana Creole
Creole Catholics, 193, 202, 234
Creole Crescent, 52–53
Creole diaspora, 14, 36, 80, 113n3, 188n6, 201–2, 211, 213, 225, 254, 277
"Creole E-Naissance," 149
Creole Heritage, 71, 247, 264, 270, 274–75
Creole Heritage Center, 21, 247, 263, 269, 272
CREOLE Inc., 149, 151
Creole Institute at Indiana University, 148
Creole Magazine, 149
Creole-Métis, 245–46
Creole-NDN, 5–6, 15, 124–26, 129, 131–33, 185, 187, 239n13; NDN, 17n1, 166, 277
Creoleness, 24
Creole Peoplehood, 7, 12–13, 16, 143–44, 152, 203–6, 240, 249, 254
Creole Renaissance, 147, 149, 151–53
"Creole Return," 148
Creoles of color, 23, 33, 54, 70–71, 148–49, 153–54, 255
Créolité, 7
creolization, 12, 34, 53, 72, 76, 150, 241
Creolophone, 53, 68, 72, 144, 148, 256
Crescent of the Mississippi, 93
cuisine, 15, 88, 90, 103, 105, 107, 112, 114n4, 240–41, 259
cultural production, 15–16, 72, 257

D

Dakota/Lakota, 5
Daniels v. Canada, 41n28
"dark," 57, 177, 197–98, 202, 208, 234–35
Dawes Act, 82n5
decolonial research, 136
Deepwater Horizon, 256
Depression, 59, 228, 245
diabetes, 124–27, 129, 135–36
diaspora, 3, 5–6, 8, 12, 14, 16, 35–36, 44, 47–48, 80, 113n3, 135, 148, 153, 155, 188n6, 201–5, 207, 210–11, 213, 225, 236, 251, 254–55, 257, 266, 277; Indigenous, 24, 125, 135
diasporic, 46, 74, 77, 81n3, 126, 225, 257, 259
"dirty rice" (Farce), 236, 242
disabled, 172, 185–86
"Disposable Red Woman Project," 179
DNA, 16, 75, 79, 81n1, 81n3, 125, 129, 161, 252
Doctrine of Discovery, 115
Domengeaux, Jimmy, 146
domestic, sexual, and intimate partner violence (DV/SV/IPV), 126, 135
Dunbar-Nelson, Alice, 34–35
Dust Bowl, 227–28

E

eco-colonialism, 173, 180, 183–85, 198, 255, 259
English-Americans, 55–56
English-only, 57, 62, 68
enslavement, 51, 54, 76, 87, 93–95, 166–67
erasure, 13, 15, 33, 44–45, 47, 62, 76–77, 124–25, 132, 144, 147–48, 153–54, 185, 255; Indigenous, 4, 10–11, 14–15, 22, 24, 124, 134, 254, 259–60

ethnic/cultural matrices, 8, 27, 38, 78, 106
ethnic identity, 12, 28, 61, 71, 210–11, 123
ethnicity, 11, 13, 26, 30, 47, 50, 89, 108, 118, 122–23, 143, 145, 174, 188n11, 246, 272, 277
ethnic pride movements, 71
ethnogenesis, 31, 254
"ethnoglossic isomorphism," 145
Europeans, 7, 25, 34, 51, 54, 56, 76, 86–87, 122, 180, 240–41
extractive industries, 183

F

fat, 172–77, 185–97, 189n16, 195, 197–99, 278
federal Indian law, 96, 99n16
filé, 34, 90, 103–9, 111–13, 242, 259, 265; gumbo/gombo, 103, 241
"Filé Man," 103, 111, 113
"first foods," 113n1
First Nation, Métis, and Inuit (FNMI), 179, 182
First Nations, 28, 31, 87, 89–91, 115, 136, 184, 254
Five Civilized Tribes, 24, 26, 187n1, 239n8
fleur-de-lis, 259
Folklife Hall of Fame, 107
food, 13, 15, 27, 45, 90, 103–5, 107–8, 111–13, 113n1, 117, 127, 132, 135, 147, 164, 177, 184–85, 195, 208, 222, 236, 240–43, 245–47, 249, 252–53, 257, 259–60, 275
foodways, 15, 34–35, 103, 106–7, 112, 223, 240–41, 244, 247, 253; Indigenous, 110n9
Forbes, Jack D., 10
forced marches, 128
forced removal, 124, 127
Francophone, 24, 33, 53, 67–69, 71, 72, 88, 103, 147, 256, 274; of color, 147–48
Freedmen, 6–7, 15, 26, 31, 47, 96, 125–27, 131–33, 135–36, 173, 177, 182, 239nn8,13, 273, 279
"Free People of Color," 50, 118, 224. See also *gens de couleur libres*

French, 3, 5, 8, 11, 16, 23–24, 27, 29–30, 32–33, 35, 38, 39n2, 41n26, 45–46, 48, 51–55, 58–59, 66–72, 76–78, 80, 81n1, 87–91, 93–94, 97n1, 103, 105, 107–8, 115, 118, 144–53, 159–62, 165–68, 188n11, 193–94, 197, 206, 224–25, 227, 229–34, 240–45, 248, 251, 260, 272, 274–77
French Canadian, 45, 53, 94, 229, 248
French Caribbean, 94
French Creole, 46, 51, 197, 260
French-Indian, 8, 27, 38, 78, 224

G

gay, 203, 206–7, 209–12
gender performativity, 204
genealogy, 28, 35–36, 41n26, 66, 147, 173, 176; research, 269
genetics, 125, 128, 135
genocide, 42n44, 79, 95–96, 98n10, 125, 132, 134, 159, 174, 179–80, 187, 254, 278
gens de couleur libres (free peoples of color), 11, 32–33, 173
Great Migration, 62, 228
Gulf Coast, 93, 256, 279
Gulf Loop Current, 255
Gulf South, 27, 78, 91, 116, 118, 173, 185, 256, 273
Gulf triangle, 255
gumbo, 34, 57, 103–5, 108, 111, 236, 241–43, 248, 260; "gumbo herbes," 243
"gumbo French," 53
GumboLife, 110, 272

H

half-breed, 52, 215
Hampton Institute, 271
"Han," 116, 122
Harrison, Donald, 3–4
Hattak Apa, 122
health, 12, 15–16, 27, 96, 107, 124–29, 131–39, 175, 178, 199, 212, 253, 276, 279
hegemonic binary, 182
heritage, 3, 8, 21–22, 53, 56, 58, 66–72, 74, 76, 79, 81n1, 87, 89–91,

118, 144, 151, 153–54, 176–79, 181, 192, 196, 245, 247, 251, 269–72, 274–75
heritage language, 66–72, 151, 154, 274
Herriman, George Joseph, 57–58, 63n32
heteronormative, 209
heterosexual, 178, 202–3, 207–10, 212–13
hiraeth, 237
HIV/AIDS, 212
Ho Minti Society, 272
homonationalist, 209
Houma Nation, 25, 89, 96, 185, 257
"hubs," 225
Hurricane Katrina, 88, 257
hybridity, 167
hypodescent, 21, 23, 32, 37

I

identity formation, 12, 49n7, 74, 202, 211
immigrant, 55, 62, 222, 240, 254
immigration, 67, 72, 132, 254
incarceration, 128
indentured servitude, 128
Indian Act of 1850, 95
Indian antiblack racism, 23
Indian Child Welfare Act (ICWA), 82n5, 280
Indian Citizenship Act, 82n5
Indian Civil Rights Act of 1968, 82n5
Indian country, 5, 10, 31, 47, 185, 187n1
Indian Health Service, 140
Indianness, 23, 181–82
Indian Removal Act, 82n5, 180
Indians, 11, 25, 27–28, 31–33, 39n2, 41nn28,34, 50–51, 78, 115, 127, 129, 176, 178–80, 192, 224, 240–41
Indian Territory, 238n8
Indian wars, 95
Indigenes, 32–35
Indigeneity, 6, 8–10, 12–14, 21–22, 26–27, 32, 36, 38, 42n38, 45, 47–49, 80, 163, 176, 188n11, 222–24, 255, 279

Indigenous, 3–17, 22–38, 40nn13,24, 42n44, 44–48, 49n7, 51, 53, 56, 62, 63n22, 66, 72, 74–81, 82n5, 86–91, 93–97, 98n10, 103–7, 111–12, 113nn1,3, 115, 117, 119n7, 120n13, 120n19, 122–27, 133–36, 140, 149–51, 154, 159–62, 168, 173–86, 187n4, 188n11, 189n15, 198, 202–3, 206, 208, 210–13, 227, 230, 234, 236, 240–41, 243, 253–60, 261n3, 272–80
Indigenous-Afro, 23, 29, 38
Indigenous: culture, 23, 72, 76, 90–91, 208, 253, 280; identity, 30, 42n44, 80, 154, 159; epistemological perspective, 5
IndigeQueer, 175, 186, 189n15
interracial marriage, 53, 240
Irving, Washington, 51–52
Ishak, 15, 29, 37, 88, 104, 110n9, 115–18, 121–23, 154, 162–65, 229, 235, 259, 273, 275, 279
Isla Malhado, 122

J

jambalaya, 243, 250
Jim Crow, 4, 15, 21, 23–24, 39n2, 42n44, 44–45, 50, 54, 61–62, 70, 82n5, 128, 145, 173, 204, 235, 254, 257

K

kafi/kaji, 34, 259
"Kill the Indian, Save the Man" policy, 128
kinship, 4–5, 9, 11, 13–14, 21–22, 25–28, 30–31, 35–38, 47, 78, 107, 173, 199, 204, 210, 213, 249, 253
Kouri-Vini, 11, 29, 38, 53, 63n8, 66, 144, 149–51, 232–33, 238n5; movement, 144, 151–54
Kreyolofoni, 149

L

land, 3–16, 21–23, 26–41, 34, 36–38, 41n34, 45–49, 49n7, 51, 66–67, 76–78, 80–81, 87, 93–96, 103–9, 117, 124, 127–28, 132–33, 163, 168, 173–76, 178–87, 187n4,

land (*continued*)
188n10, 193–94, 198, 204, 210, 213, 221, 223, 224–28, 230–31, 233, 236, 238, 241, 248–50, 253–59, 265–66, 272–73, 276, 279
languagehood, 16, 143–44, 152
Lanusse, Armand, 33, 36
Latab Kreyol, 149
Latinidad, 16, 24, 29, 37–38, 174, 188n11, 234
Latinidad-Caribbean, 3, 23, 255
Latinx, 8, 23, 41n33, 49, 125, 129, 174, 187n4, 206, 211, 221, 240, 253–55, 258, 260, 275, 278; studies, 12
La Toussaint (All Saints' Day), 67
LCD (Louisiana Creole diaspora), 201
Leadbelly, 173–74, 188n7
L'eau Est La Vie Camp, 183
Lenape, 10
Les Cenelles, 21, 32–36,
Les Créoles de Pointe Coupée, 149
linguistic erasure, 144
linguistic identity, 50, 53, 62n8, 72, 144, 152, 257
Louisiana Bayou Country, 224
Louisiana Creole, 3, 5–17, 21–23, 25, 27, 29–31, 33–35, 37–38, 39nn1,2, 40n16, 42n44, 44–47, 50, 53, 56, 59–60, 63n8, 66–68, 70, 78, 89–90, 103–4, 103–8, 110n14, 111–12, 116, 118, 133, 143–44, 148–55, 182, 188nn6,10,11, 200–207, 210, 224, 234, 240–43, 247–49, 252, 253–55, 257–60, 269, 271–79; flag, 258–59; revitalization movement, 154
Louisiana Folklife Center, 113
Louisiana Folklife Commission, 113
Louisiana French, 16, 48, 69, 103, 144, 232
Louisiana Purchase, 51, 54, 115, 179, 276
Louisiana regional French, 144
Louisiana Territory, 25, 52, 179, 240
Louisiana Tradition Bearer, 107, 113

M

"man camps," 184
Manifest Destiny, 162
Marinoni, Ulysse, 67

Martin, Gilbert E., Sr., 59
masculinity, 189n15, 197, 201, 208–9, 212; "washboard masculinity," 201–2, 207, 212
memory, 6, 11, 13, 34, 37, 55, 74–75, 89, 104, 108–9, 161–62, 173, 228, 233, 236, 249, 266, 271, 277
mental health, 124, 131–32, 134–35, 139–40
Mercier, Alfred, 67
méstiz@/métis, 11
Métis, 6, 15, 25, 27–29, 31, 38, 41n28, 42nn38,44, 53, 64n22, 76, 78, 91, 106–7, 136, 179, 188n11, 224, 230, 235, 240, 245–46, 259, 271, 275–76, 278–79
métissage/méstizaje, 14, 21, 27–28, 31, 36, 105
Mexican-American War, 95
middens, shell, 117–18
Middle Passage, 35, 234
migration, 62, 67, 72, 113n3, 177, 224–26, 228, 232
Mikinak Nation, 28
Mi'kmaq, 77, 91, 179, 271
miscegenation, 14, 34, 53, 74, 76, 173
mission schools, 166–67
Mississippi Delta, 256
mixed-blood, 7, 258
mixed-ethnicity, 123, 277
mixed-race, 9, 12, 17, 41n34, 46, 48, 67, 74, 81, 81n3, 118, 132–33, 161, 199, 203, 275
mounds, 48, 117
"mulâtre," 63n22
"mulatto," 25, 33, 58, 63n22, 118, 248
Murdered and Missing Indigenous Women and Girls (MMIWG), 95
Muskogean, 255, 260n3, 279

N

Natchez Uprising, 94
Natchitoches-NSU Folk Festival, 113
Natchitoches Tribe, 24–25, 40n13
National Coalition Against Domestic Violence (NCADV), 133–34
nationalism, 12–13, 26, 55, 204, 254, 272

nation-state, 26, 179–80
Native American, 8–12, 16–17, 17n1, 24, 26, 28, 30, 32–35, 38, 45, 47, 68, 72, 93–94, 106, 118, 121, 128, 131, 133, 136, 173, 187n1, 192–96, 202, 243–44, 248, 252–53, 255, 257–58, 263, 274–75, 278
Native American and Indigenous studies, 12, 17, 274
Native American and Indigenous Studies Association, 11
Native American Graves Protection Act (NAGPRA), 82n5
Native Amerindian, 3
Natives, 26, 32, 34–35, 77, 79, 81n1, 88, 90, 94–95, 118, 127–28, 175–76, 187n1, 259
"Negro," 50, 56–57, 118, 146; "Negro blood," 58
New France, 52, 240
New Orleans, 3, 5, 8, 14–15, 21, 33–36, 39n3, 40n16, 46, 50, 54–62, 67, 69, 74, 76, 81, 81n1, 86–87, 90, 93–94, 96, 112, 115–16, 179, 199, 204–5, 241, 243, 259, 264, 271–76
New Orleans Creoles, 33, 39n3, 55
"new speakers," 144, 149–52, 154
"nigger French," 53
1964 Civil Rights Act, 146
"noble savage," 52
noir, 197, 200
normativity, 176
North American racial exceptionalism, 7, 254
Nova Scotia, 25, 28, 74, 76–77, 80, 81n1, 202

O
obesity, 126, 135–36, 176
oil, 96, 162, 167, 183–85, 227, 256–57
Omi, Michael, 47, 75
"one blood" policies, 53
one drop rule, 30, 39n2
Opelousas, 5–6, 8, 23, 28–29, 37, 46, 188n11, 247, 264, 275–76
orthography, 86, 151–52, 154
Otherness, 44, 48, 60
Oubre, Henry, 60–61

P
passe blanc/passing white, 25, 39n2, 48, 197, 235
passing, 25, 34, 39n2, 40n16, 223
patriarchy, 132, 181, 201, 213
Peoplehood, 7, 13, 26, 30, 34, 36–37, 38, 62n8, 79–80, 153, 155, 198, 210, 213, 259; matrix, 9, 17n3, 22, 29, 38, 46, 48, 49n7, 80, 203; model, 26, 30; Indigenous, 26, 79. *See also* Creole Peoplehood
petites nations, 93
petrochemical corridor, 96
phenotype, 11, 25, 45, 126, 204; phenotypic, 32, 173, 176, 181
pidgin, 38
pilet et pilon, 110n14, 259
pilon, 105, 108–9, 110n14, 112
plaçage/concubinage, 176, 181
place-making, 15
plantations, 41n26, 95–96, 256
Plessy v. Ferguson, 54–55, 82n5
"Pocahontas clause," 77
Point Coupee, 5–6, 8, 29, 46, 188n11
post-contact, 8–9, 11–12, 14, 17, 21–22, 25–29, 31–32, 38, 42nn38, 44, 45–49, 78, 103, 106, 210, 254, 255, 259
Powhatan-Renapé, 10
powwow, 222
PTSD, 134, 139

Q
Quapaw, 28–29, 93, 110n9, 279
queer, 16, 164, 172–73, 176, 186, 189n15, 203–13
queerness, 16, 201–3, 205, 207, 210–13

R
race, 9, 11, 23–24, 26, 30, 32, 44, 47–48, 50, 52–53, 58–59, 67, 69, 71, 75, 77–78, 81, 143, 145–46, 153–55, 172–76, 178, 182, 197, 204, 221, 248, 252, 260, 271; as a social construct, 47. *See also* mixed-race
racial binary, 44, 145, 155
racial caste systems, 35
racial formation theory, 75

racial identity, 62, 203, 208
Racial Integrity Act of 1924, 76
racial mixing, 6, 34
rape, 128, 132–33, 167, 177–78, 181–84
recipe, 80, 240–41, 243, 246
recognition, 8–9, 24–25, 32, 40n13, 87, 96, 115, 120n16, 122–23, 204, 213, 246, 260, 269
Red-Black, 7, 10–11, 16, 178
Redbone, 78
Red English, 17n1, 187n2
religion, 7, 9, 13–14, 26, 29, 38, 48, 205–6, 233, 240, 249, 253, 259
relocation, 77, 127–29, 257
rem arbitrium, 7, 14, 17, 22, 254
removal, 77–78, 94–95, 98n10, 125, 127–29, 132, 134, 180, 183
resistance, 23, 28, 35–36, 42n44, 57, 104, 129, 144, 153, 155, 178–79, 183, 185–86, 230, 253, 260
"revitalization myth," 147
rice, 3, 34, 68, 90, 236, 241–43, 256, 259–60
Roosevelt, Theodore, 54–56

S

sacred history, 9, 13, 26, 29–30, 36, 38, 79
Saloy, Mona Lisa, 7, 32, 35–36
same-sex, 202–3, 207–10; marriage, 116, 119n7
sankofa, 32, 36
sassafras, 34, 90, 103–9, 110n9, 111–13, 241–42, 256, 259
"Sassafras Society," 112
settler state, 17, 77, 210; government, 77
settler-colonial, 7, 11–12, 25–26, 30–31, 50, 75, 132, 173, 175–76, 180, 183, 187, 203–4, 256; discourse, 11–12
sexploitation, 133, 174, 180–82
sexual conquest, 180
sexual identity, 178, 208
sexualization, 180, 182
situational passing, 25, 40n16, 48
skin: color, 35, 66, 71, 221; tones, 252

slave-raiding, 93
slave regime, 54
slavery, 35, 76, 93–96, 97n1, 120n16, 124–26, 128–29, 134, 181, 259
slave-trade, 94, 97n1, 255
Southern Food and Beverage Museum, 113
sovereign nations, 25, 31, 123; sovereign Native peoples, 31
Spanish, 3, 5, 11, 23–25, 27, 30, 33, 38, 41n26, 45–46, 51, 54, 64n22, 66–67, 78, 89, 93–95, 105, 107–8, 115, 118, 174, 188n11, 197, 206, 221–25, 240–41, 243–44, 248, 251, 272, 275
St. Augustine Church, 89
St. Francis Xavier Church, 192
stomp music, 173
St. Martin of Tours Catholic Church, 115
stories, 11, 15–17, 37, 57, 60, 68, 74–75, 80, 103–4, 107–9, 125, 205–7, 210, 222–23, 226, 230, 245, 247, 249–51, 260, 266
storymakers, 107
storytellers, 37, 43n48, 107, 276
"sunset towns," 238n8

T

Taensa, 87, 192, 195, 274
Taíno, 33, 41n26, 255, 261n3
Temple, Johnnie "Geechie," 173–74
territory, 29, 34, 37–38, 52, 66–67, 95, 145, 238n8, 253
Tongva, 225, 230
Trail of Tears, 127, 162, 180
transgender, 204, 213
trauma, 127, 132, 134–36, 138–39, 173, 176, 197–99, 275; ancestral, 75; historical, 16, 75, 124–26, 134, 136, 139, 187, 272; intergenerational, 16, 135, 177
treaties, 82n5, 128, 166
Treaty of Guadeloupe Hidalgo, 95
Tremé, 89
tribal identities, 46
tribalography, 36–37, 43n59, 49n7
Tricentennial, 15, 86–87

Tulsa Race Riots, 227
Tunica-Biloxi, 25, 28, 87, 90, 154, 273
Tureaud, A. P., 57–59
Turtle Island, 5, 11, 31, 87, 94, 105, 187n4, 236, 254
two-spirit, 173, 180, 183, 185, 189n15, 271, 275–76

U

United Houma Nation (UHN), 25, 96, 257
United Nations Declaration on the Rights of Indigenous Peoples (UNDRIP), 8, 27, 31, 47
United Nations Definition of Indigenous Peoples, 22
United Nations Working Group on Indigenous Populations (WGIP), 14, 22, 27
US Department of War, 96

V

VAWA (Violence Against Women Act), 132–33
voyageurs, 53

W

Wabanaki Confederacy, 77–78, 91, 224
Watts, 225, 228, 230
White/Black binary, 11, 39n3, 46
"white" identity, 25, 72, 147, 164
whiteness, 11, 22, 24, 35, 57, 59, 77, 79, 201, 254
whitewashing, 144, 154
Winant, Howard, 47, 75
World War II, 59–62, 66, 70

Z

zydeco, 118, 164, 173, 201–2, 210, 212, 236, 247–50

www.ingramcontent.com/pod-product-compliance
Lightning Source LLC
Chambersburg PA
CBHW030526230426
43665CB00010B/779